875 mc
61

Party Democracy:

Politics in an Italian Socialist Federation

Yale University Press, New Haven and London 1967

Party Democracy:

Politics in an

Italian Socialist Federation

SAMUEL H. BARNES

For Anne

Preface

This book is an inquiry into the functioning of democracy in modern society by means of a study of the internal politics of the Arezzo provincial federation of the Italian Socialist Party.

My concern is with democracy; my method is to study it within the manageable confines of a particular party in a particular time and place. As a result, it is difficult to determine with precision the degree of fit between my general concerns and the findings of the field research. The reader must judge for himself the adequacy of the relationship between theory and data.

Readers concerned primarily with the empirical analysis of political behavior will find Chapters 6 through 12 the most interesting. Chapters 1, 13, and 14 deal with my theoretical orientation and the interpretation of my findings. Chapters 2 through 5 serve to place the behavior of the members and leaders of the party within the context of the national and local environments. Readers with considerable knowledge of Italian politics may prefer to skip Chapters 2 and 3.

This study was made possible by the aid and cooperation of a large number of organizations and individuals, and it is my pleasure to acknowledge publicly my gratitude to them. The Horace H. Rackham School of Graduate Studies of The University of Michigan and the Olivetti Foundation supplied most of the support for the expenses of data gathering. A Fulbright visiting professorship at the Cesare Alfieri Faculty of Political Sciences of the University of Florence made it possible for me to spend the academic year 1962–63 in Italy; I am especially grateful for the support and encouragement of Miss Cipriana

Scelba, the director of the American Commission for Cultural Exchanges with Italy. I also wish to thank Joseph LaPalombara for sharing with me his intimate and profound knowledge of the Italian scene.

Those who have done research abroad know the debt visiting scholars owe those who befriend them on the scene. Four people deserve, in particular, principal credit for whatever merit this study has achieved. Professor Alberto Spreafico, *Incaricato* at the University of Florence and currently general secretary of the Comitato per le Scienze Politiche e Sociali, encouraged me to come to Florence for the year and has been very generous with his advice, time, and friendship in the facilitation of this research and in many other ways. I wish to thank him publicly. Professor Giovanni Sartori, *Ordinario* at the University of Florence, permitted me to utilize a seminar we gave jointly as a planning and training device for the design and execution of the project. His strong support of the study and his friendship and many kindnesses are greatly appreciated. Fernando Magi and Marzio Barbagli, both then students at the Cesare Alfieri Faculty, were my initial contacts in the Arezzo federation of the party and have remained friends and collaborators. Without their sustained enthusiasm and effort the project would not have been possible.

Dott. Barbagli assisted me throughout the research; Dott. Sergio DeClericini also worked closely with me during most of the research. The sensitive and often very difficult task of locating and interviewing the members of the party was carried out with high levels of competence and dedication by students of the University of Florence. I wish to thank the following for their interest, collaboration, and comradeship during the execution of the project: Piero Bellini, Paolo Capodivacca, Pucio Cartoni, Mita Ceccarelli, Renzo Cherubini, Lucia Gucciarelli, Marcello Nieri, Giulio Pacetti, Donatella Pannacci (now Mrs. Marzio Barbagli), and Luigi Vanni Vecchi.

My debts during the data-processing, analysis, and writing phases are many. Abraham Miller assisted me in the initial months. Susan Lawther worked with great skill and diligence

20

on all aspects of the project over an extended period of time. Merrill Shanks was a knowledgeable and tactful consultant on data processing and analysis.

I have benefited greatly from criticisms of the manuscript by several colleagues at Michigan and elsewhere. I am especially grateful to Joseph LaPalombara, Antonio Lopez Piña, James Meisel, Kenneth Organski, and Henry Valen for reading the entire manuscript. I also appreciate the gracious and sensitive contributions of Marian Neal Ash of the Yale University Press to the manuscript.

My wife Anne was an enthusiastic collaborator throughout the project. She knows the magnitude of my debt to her; I wish to acknowledge it publicly.

Finally, I want to express my gratitude to the leaders and rank and file of the Arezzo federation of the Italian Socialist Party for their cooperation. They gave freely of their time, knowledge, resources, and goodwill in a completely disinterested manner. Their generosity and kindness made this book possible.

S.H.B.

Ann Arbor, Michigan
March 30, 1967

Contents

Abbreviations

CGIL   Confederazione Generale Italiana del Lavoro (Italian General Confederation of Labor)
CISL   Confederazione Italiana Sindacati Lavoratori (Confederation of Workers' Unions)
DC   Democrazia Cristiana (Christian Democratic Party)
MSI   Movimento Sociale Italiano (Neo Fascist Party)
PCI   Partito Comunista Italiano (Communist Party)
PLI   Partito Liberale Italiano (Liberal Party)
PMP   Partito Monarchico Popolare (Monarchist Party)
PNM   Partito Nazionale Monarchico (Monarchist Party)
PRI   Partito Repubblicano Italiano (Republican Party)
PSDI   Partito Socialista Democratico Italiano (Social Democratic Party)
PSI   Partito Socialista Italiano (Socialist Party)
PSIUP   Partito Socialista Italiano d'Unità Proletaria (Social Proletarian Party)
UIL   Unione Italiana del Lavoro (Union of Labor)

1.

Democracy and the Organization
of Political Parties

The democratic currents of history resemble successive waves. They break ever on the same shoal. They are ever renewed. This enduring spectacle is simultaneously encouraging and depressing . . . It is probable that this cruel game will continue without end.[1]

These are the pessimistic conclusions of Robert Michels. In *Political Parties,* his study of working-class organizations in early twentieth-century Europe, he formulated the "Iron Law" that oligarchy is the "preordained form of the common life of great social aggregates." The Iron Law of Oligarchy has developed into one of the sturdiest propositions in political science, resistant to numerous logical and empirical attacks. Its persistence is undoubtedly due as much to the perennial importance of the subject with which it deals as to its intrinsic merits as a proposition. For concern with democracy in organizations is a recurring and perpetual theme in political theory and research, and all substantial work on political parties must come to grips with the conceptual and empirical problems stemming from that concern.

SOME PROBLEMS OF THE IRON LAW OF OLIGARCHY

This study continues the line of inquiry that was begun by Michels. Like many seminal thinkers such as Marx and Weber, Michels has been subjected to numerous critiques as to "what he really meant." *Political Parties* is full of insights, asides, speculations, anecdotes, and rephrasing of previous formula-

1. Robert Michels, *Political Parties* (New York, Dover, 1959; the original German edition was published in 1911), p. 408.

tions. Consequently one can with diligence discover differing and even contradictory interpretations by Michels of many topics within the same book. Thus John D. May has argued persuasively that Michels was really complaining that organization resulted in the leader's following the wishes of the led rather than their "objective" interests:

> Contrary to prevailing belief, then, Robert Michels actually provided a favorable account of the compatibility of Organization and democracy. While maintaining that Organization is incompatible with pure democracy, and that increments of Organization produce counter-democratic changes in associations which initially are pure democracies, he also suggested (in the case of European Socialism and in broader theoretical terms), that Organization can and frequently does accompany and facilitate a multitude of changes which constitute or facilitate democratization. . . .
> Far from being a pessimistic democrat, Michels was a pessimistic Romantic Revolutionist and a pessimistic Scientific Paternalist.
> He denounced Organization for promoting the amelioration instead of the radical purification of society. He detested Organization for promoting the manifest wishes rather than the 'objective' Interests of the "masses." [2]

In his concluding chapter Michels does take a somewhat modified view of the possibility of democracy. He does not deny its desirability or possibility. He acknowledges that democratic tendencies would increase with wider education, a theme that will recur in the present study; and he anticipates democracy serving as, "if not a cure, at least a palliative, for the disease of oligarchy." [3] He also seems to accept the viewpoint presented in this study—that democracy and oligarchy are questions

2. "Democracy, Organization, Michels," *American Political Science Review,* 59 (1965), 429.
3. Michels, pp. 406–07.

of degree: "Consequently the question we have to discuss is not whether ideal democracy is realizable, but rather to what point and in what degree democracy is desirable, possible, and realizable at a given moment." [4]

However, these views are alien to conventional interpretations of the book, and most commentators have emphasized his more pessimistic conclusions about the inevitability of oligarchy. As this present study is an inquiry into democracy in a political party rather than a critique of Michels' work, it will concentrate on what is considered by most interpreters as the meat of his argument—the relationship between organization and democracy.

The Iron Law of Oligarchy seems to state that in all organizations above a certain (unspecified) size, organizational elites will constitute an oligarchy, that is, a dominant group that rules in its own interest and opposed to the interests of the rank and file.[5] Only large organizations are necessarily oligarchies, because only in these do bureaucratization and specialization give rise to the conditions conducive to oligarchy. The lower limit at which these dynamics become operable varies according to a number of factors. It is clear that mass organizations surpass that limit, and that oligarchy arises from the very nature of organizations. Nowhere does Michels enumerate these causes precisely, but they permeate the entire book. They may be summarized briefly as follows: Effective organization requires leaders and, for mass organizations, bureaucratization. Competent leaders possess the ability to remain in office; they have a near monopoly of skills within the organization; they have a clear superiority of financial and other resources; they benefit from the gratitude and veneration of the masses; they are from a different social stratum than the rank and file, or, if not, they soon come to differentiate themselves from their former comrades. Perhaps the most important ingredient of oligarchy is bureaucracy itself. Bureaucracy involves a division of labor, ex-

4. Ibid., p. 402.
5. For a similar formulation see C. W. Cassinelli, "The Law of Oligarchy," American Political Science Review, 47 (1953), 773–84.

3

pertise, and job security; and these factors in turn give the incumbents a clear superiority over their opposition.

There is no doubt that the rise of the mass party in the twentieth century has profoundly altered the composition of the "political class," especially in countries such as Italy where the bureaucratic party is of great importance. Some observers in fact view these party bureaucratic elites as the new rulers, a governing class that is self-selected and, in the democratic sense, irresponsible. Others have emphasized that political leaders are, in fact, politicians who have the talents and styles of politicians regardless of their career patterns, whether in party bureaucracies or not. Bureaucrats must become politicians before they can be true political leaders: the individuals at the top of a bureaucratic hierarchy cannot be bureaucratic, even if they rose through the bureaucracy.[6]

This argument suggests that Michels' formulation of the problem of organizational oligarchy suffers from a serious weakness: it accepts the appropriateness of the bureaucratic model for the study of political parties. Michels was intimately familiar with the continental Socialist parties of his time, especially the Social Democratic Party of his native Germany. That "most Prussian of all institutions" indeed exhibited certain of the features that he ascribed to working-class organizations in general. The empirical study of political parties and other voluntary associations, dominated by the tradition of Michels and Max Weber, has focused on bureaucracy and authority. Michels and Weber were heavily influenced by the Prussian state as an ideal type. Whether this led them to misinterpret the organizations of Imperial Germany is not a concern of this study; the general appropriateness of the bureaucratic model, however, is highly relevant.

It is easy to be misled by the formal structures of political parties. These usually reflect the organization of the governments with which they deal. If that structure is hierarchical

---

6. This is the thesis of Giovanni Sartori in "Democrazia, burocrazia e oligarchia nei partiti," *Rassegna Italiana di sociologia*, 1 (1960), 119–36; see also Sartori, *Democratic Theory* (New York, Praeger, 1965), pp. 120–28.

and centralized, the party also is under strong compulsion to adopt a similar structure in order to act effectively. But a political party in a free society exhibits characteristics that differentiate it sharply from many other formal organizations. These characteristics will be discussed at various points in the study; at this point it will merely be noted that the bureaucratic model is inappropriate for the study of parties.

In addition to questioning the appropriateness of the bureaucratic model, the relevance of the oligarchical model itself needs to be confronted. Oligarchy can mean many things, and Michels never defined it with any precision. If it means merely that the few rule, then it is true but trivial. If it means that leaders are free from control,[7] then it may seem to have a more precise meaning but one that defies easy operationalization. How should one evaluate elections, which may provide formal control and yet not be very meaningful? And what about control between elections? *How much* control by the nonelite is necessary?

In a general critique of the ruling elite model, designed to deal with community elites rather than organizational oligarchs, Robert Dahl has pinpointed some crucial components of, I believe, both: "A ruling elite, then, is a controlling group less than a majority in size that is not a pure artifact of democratic rules. It is a minority of individuals whose preferences regularly prevail in cases of differences in preference on key political issues. If we are to avoid an infinite regress of explanations the composition of the ruling elite must be more or less definitely specified."[8] While this clarifies the conceptual problem, problems of operationalization remain. How are preferences measured? If both elite and nonelite share a common value system that legitimizes elite rule is there then no possibility of oligarchy? What portion of the nonelite must possess differing preferences for the ruling elite model to be operative? There are numerous examples of autocratic party and trade union leaders who are warmly and enthusiastically endorsed by an overwhelming ma-

7. This is the view of Cassinelli, "The Law of Oligarchy," p. 779.
8. "Critique of the Ruling Elite Model," *American Political Science Review*, 52 (1958), 463–69.

5

jority of their followers. Outside impartial observers might conclude that the rank and file are being manipulated by oligarchs, but this would seem to be true only from the observer's perspective, that is, from his own system of values and views of what should be the preferences of the members. And the intrusion of such normative elements carries us from the realm of scientific analysis into one where one man's oligarch is another man's champion of the masses.[9]

In the light of the above discussion it seems that oligarchy is a possible condition in mass organizations but that for it to be operationally demonstrated one would have to show that the rank and file, on the one hand, preferred one set of policies or behaviors while the leaders, on the other, possessed contrary choices, and that the latter always had their way. This is by no means an inconceivable situation. But is it a familiar pattern in parties within democratic political systems? Probably not. The reason is that in a democratic system there are alternative avenues of political action. Party leaders who habitually act contrary to the wishes of their followers do not have followers for very long. Perhaps the most effective limitation on oligarchy in political parties within democracies is the ability of the membership to vote with its feet, to become inactive or even to leave the party. As will be clarified below, this fact alone sharply differentiates a political party from, for example, the typical American trade union.

As a result, the nature of authority in a political party is an extremely sensitive problem. Max Weber elaborated three ideal types of authority—traditional, charismatic, and rational-legal. These correspond to authority based on tradition, upon the personal characteristics of the leader, and upon the office held by the wielder of authority. Paul H. Harrison has noted that these are inadequate for dealing with voluntary associations and has proposed three additional subtypes—rational-pragmatic,

9. This is indeed the charge that May has leveled against Michels, that the latter criticized party leaders because they sought to "gratify the wishes of those they are hired to serve, regardless of the Interests of the latter" ("Democracy, Organization, Michels," p. 429).

quasi-charismatic, and mimetic-traditional.[10] Certainly Weber's types of authority are inadequate for the study of parties. Traditional authority in the sense of sentiment and remembered shared experiences is undoubtedly present in parties. Charisma is likewise an important ingredient of party leadership, and some parties have had little else as their base. One wonders, however, what the term can mean when applied to the average ward heeler or precinct worker. And party officials do possess the authority of office, but only over the paid clerical help. Thus these Weberian categories of authority are not irrelevant, but they are inconvenient for the study of authority relationships in parties. This is because they do not sufficiently emphasize that authority, like leadership, involves a relationship: in normative organizations the attitudes and expectations of the nonelite are as important to the authority relationships as those of the elite.[11]

Even in bureaucratic organizations the mere issuing of commands is not sufficient to ensure their execution. The capabilities and reactions of participants must be taken into account. Sanctions are available to elites, however, and participants can be commanded and even ousted. The structure of most democratic parties makes it difficult for elites at one level to dismiss those who may be formally subordinate to them. Dependence on the labor and enthusiasm of volunteers likewise impairs control over personnel. Democratic party leaders often must work with colleagues and subordinates not of their own choosing, and they must abide many situations over which they have little control.

The student of political parties consequently needs to concentrate as much on the recipients as on the wielders of authority. He should examine the decision to participate, the expectations and rewards associated with participation, and the nature and limits of authority within the organization. He must stress

10. "Weber's Categories of Authority and Voluntary Associations," *American Sociological Review*, 25 (1960), 232–37.

11. This point has been discussed in Samuel H. Barnes, "Leadership Style and Political Competence," in Lewis Edinger, ed., *Leadership in Industrial Society* (New York, Wiley, 1967), pp. 59–83.

interpersonal dynamics as well as the formal decision-making structure.

As mentioned above, the decision to participate is closely related to the problem of authority in voluntary associations. People participate in voluntary associations because they want to, often for nonmaterial or only remotely material reasons. In order to survive, the association must make participation seem worthwhile, and this is difficult to accomplish without material incentives. Many so-called voluntary associations are voluntary only in a typological sense. This is true of most American trade unions, for example. Members have little real choice about belonging. While they are free to choose their level of participation, inactive members tend to facilitate the dominance of organizational elites. This may also be true of many political parties; it certainly is true of one-party systems where at least nominal membership is often a prerequisite for many kinds of careers. Where one party is the exclusive representative of distinct occupational groups or strata, membership may be only formally voluntary, as there may be no meaningful political participation except in that particular party. This is the situation of many trade unionists in Great Britain, for example, and also of much of the German working class in the decades before the First World War.

But participation is truly voluntary for lower-class Italians. Communists, Socialists, Social Proletarians, Social Democrats, Republicans, Neo Fascists, and Christian Democrats all seek mass support, and several of these parties can realistically claim to be working-class parties. The would-be participant has several alternatives. If he becomes dissatisfied with one party, withdrawal from political activity is not his only option. Thus party elites who are not able to elicit voluntary participation are ineffectual.

Although there are important differences among Italian parties in the role granted the membership, all are nominally based on rank and file participation. The importance of members increases as one moves leftward across the ideological spectrum, with the Communist and Socialist parties paying great attention

8

to the mass membership. This is not to imply rank and file control; rather, it indicates that these parties of the left are more than mere electoral machines. The party provides the involved member a wide range of activities, encourages him to participate in party life, and promises him symbolic and often material rewards for service. But the parties cannot provide immediate material rewards for more than a fraction of their membership, and they can seldom impose sanctions on recalcitrant or contumacious members. Consequently they must rely more on symbolic than material rewards.

Goal conflict, muddled lines of authority, and marginality of participation render the political party, at least the one under study, quite different from the typical American trade union, even one as deviant as the International Typographical Union discussed below. A brief review of some empirical studies of oligarchy and democracy in voluntary organizations will illustrate this point.

SOME EMPIRICAL STUDIES OF OLIGARCHY AND DEMOCRACY IN VOLUNTARY ASSOCIATIONS

Michels combined traditional scholarship with personal knowledge of many of the people and events of the Socialist parties of his day. Few of those who continue his tradition have the personal experience and involvement reflected in his work. Thus much of the work on oligarchy and democracy has been devoted to analyzing the logical consistency and ramifications of his book. Other scholars have researched Michels' questions in a vaguely empirical manner—vague in the sense that they involve neither rigorous operationalization of his hypotheses nor high standards of data gathering—and have generally concluded, often sadly, that he was indeed correct.

The line of inquiry opened by Michels has been advanced in recent years by several scholars who have utilized various techniques developed for systematic research on political and social phenomena. These techniques provide a rough substitute for the intimate knowledge acquired by Michels through direct experience, and in their self-conscious concern for accuracy and precision they are in many respects superior to the necessarily impressionistic, if insightful and often correct, conclusions of Michels. Numerous works on political parties and other voluntary organizations have provided the empirical basis for new insights into the relationships between democracy and oligarchy in organizations. This study lies in this latter tradition of research. Its point of departure is the study of democracy in an American trade union by Seymour Martin Lipset, James Coleman, and Martin Trow.[12]

The International Typographical Union (ITU) is unusual within American trade unionism because it has maintained within it a competitive two-party system over a considerable length of time. The authors of *Union Democracy* sought to isolate the factors that facilitated democracy within the union. They argued—and this is the point of view of the present study also—that the analysis of a single case can be extremely useful in understanding the dynamics of oligarchy and democracy, the factors associated with the existence of both. If a democratic union (or political party) is a deviant case, then one can isolate the factors responsible for that deviance and better understand the requirements for the existence of internal democracy. Lipset, Coleman, and Trow summed up, in a series of propositions, the factors affecting the chances for democracy in trade unions. These propositions are so closely tied to the specific problems of trade unions that they do not, in the form stated, serve as suitable propositions for direct empirical testing in this study. All of them, however, are touched upon at various points, with suitable alterations to deal with political parties. They isolated factors falling into the following categories: "1. Factors relating to the history and structure of the industry and union, and its relations with its environment. 2. Factors relating to the status of the occupation and to the distribution of status within the occupation. 3. Factors affecting membership interest and participation in union affairs. 4. Factors directly affecting the distribution of political resources in the union. 5. Factors relating to law, legitimacy, and value systems in unions. 6. Factors re-

12. *Union Democracy* (Garden City, N.Y., Doubleday, 1962).

lated to the bases of internal cleavage in a union." [13] Many characteristics of the union itself discouraged internal democracy, such as centralization and lack of local autonomy, bureaucratization of union administration, high prestige of union positions compared with the alternatives available to the leaders, and absence of numerous independent channels of communication within the union. Membership characteristics inimical to internal democracy included divergent interests, apathy, lack of contact with one another outside the job, dissatisfaction with work, low political skills, lack of leisure time and money, lack of ideological concerns, and belief systems not supportive of democracy.[14] The authors of *Union Democracy* reached generally pessimistic conclusions concerning the democratic potential of most unions. The high status of printing as an occupation, the relatively high level of skills and opportunities for developing them among the membership, the distinctive history of unions in the printing trades, and the structure of the industry itself facilitated internal democracy in the ITU. But these factors are generally not present in most American unions.

This study of the Italian Socialist Party (PSI), like *Union Democracy*, focuses largely on the organization in a restricted locale; it likewise involves interviews with leaders and with a dense sample of the rank and file, as well as extensive archival and documentary research. Although many of the factors remain the same, there are differences between a trade union and a political party that render precise comparison impossible.

These differences include the central role of goal formulation to the party, the absence of clear-cut lines of authority, and the fragile nature of the "decision to participate" in an organization that is truly voluntary. The objects of many studies of organizational behavior are of a custodial or pragmatic type, in which goals are reasonably well defined and hierarchical relationships are maintained by means of sanctions.[15]

13. Ibid., pp. 465–68.
14. These are summarized from *Union Democracy*.
15. See Amitai Etzioni, *A Comparative Study of Complex Organizations* (New York, Free Press, 1961).

Without maintaining that business firms, armies, and governmental bureaucracies have well-defined goals, it seems that matters of degree are extremely important in this discussion; and the maximization of profits, victory, or the implementation of public policy seem to be reasonably clear goals compared to the confusion that often surrounds the formulation and pursuit of goals in a political party.[16]

While some parties pursue electoral success at all costs, it is by no means a universal goal; in many parties it must compete with the goals of ideological purity or the maintenance of internal subcultural integrity. In short, political parties are normative organizations in which goals themselves are a subject of internal debate and possible conflict.[17]

This is certainly true in the Italian Socialist Party. Conflict over goals and tactics for achieving them provides a basis for internal cleavage different from that found in a party oriented largely toward survival, as the Imperial SPD, or electoral success as American parties. In a normative organization, identification with its goals is an important motivation for participation.[18] Although status and fellowship are admittedly other motivations, these can be achieved in many ways, while the party may be

16. See Joseph A. Schlesinger, "Political Party Organization," in James G. March, ed., *Handbook of Organizations* (Chicago, Rand McNally, 1965), pp. 764–801; and Samuel H. Barnes, "Party Democracy and the Logic of Collective Action," in William J. Crotty, ed., *Approaches to the Study of Party Organization* (Boston, Allyn and Bacon, 1967).

17. It is no accident that the rise of business unionism in the United States has been accompanied by agreement on "more" material benefits as the dominant union goals and simultaneously by a decline in internal democracy and conflict among factions, which were often political in origin. Organization theory suggests that this is a recurring uniformity in organizational behavior: the more strictly goals are defined the less important are internal democracy and membership participation in decision making. See Charles Schutz, "Bureaucratic Party Organization through Professional Political Staffing," *Midwest Journal of Political Science*, 8 (1964), 127–42.

18. "Normative organizations are organizations in which normative power is the major source of control over most lower participants, whose orientation to the organization is characterized by high commitment. Compliance in normative organizations rests principally on internalization of directives accepted as legitimate. Leadership rituals, manipulation of social and prestige symbols, and resocialization are among the more important techniques of control used" (Etzioni, p. 40).

the only vehicle for pursuing some political goals. Just as churches are pragmatic organizations (as Etzioni uses the term) for pastors and priests, parties are pragmatic organizations for their bureaucrats and elected office holders. But for their members parties are normative organizations, and internal democracy thus assumes greater importance for members of mass parties of the Socialist type. The nature of these parties thus renders the bureaucratic model inappropriate.

Several studies of party organization have cast doubt on the general utility of the oligarchical model of the party. The study by Samuel J. Eldersveld of parties in Wayne County, Michigan (part of the Detroit metropolitan area), introduces the notion of a "stratarchy" as a special kind of hierarchy. It is one in which there is "a proliferation of the ruling group and the diffusion of power prerogatives and power exercise." As the name implies, there are several "strata" of leaders who are relatively independent of one another, with the result that relations between them take the form of bargaining and mutual accommodation. Because they accord so closely in general with those of this study, Eldersveld's conclusions merit quoting in detail:

> The political party is thus to be visualized as a "reciprocal deference structure." Contrary to the bureaucratic and authoritarian models of social organization, the party is not a precisely ordered system of authority and influence from the top down, though as a "paper" structure it may give this appearance. The organization does not function through the issuance of directives from the top which are obeyed without question. Rather, there is tolerance of autonomy, local initiative, local inertia. The factors contributing to this property of the party are several: sparsity of activists, voluntary nature of recruitment for party work, limited rewards available to activists and irregularity of their loyalty. But, primarily, this "downward deference" stems from the absence of effective sanctions, the strong drive for votes, the instinctively adaptive tactics of success-minded party leaders, and the need for lower-echelon support. More than any other social organiza-

13

tion, the critical action locus of the party structure is at its base. And since there is high potential for inefficiency, indifference, and displacement of group (leadership) goals with personal goals among activists at the base, leaders defer. In fact, the basis for the authority of the leadership of party organization is one of the most puzzling to understand. It does not seem to be a function of expertise, or of role, or of normative expectations. Rather, the party structure appears to be characterized as a "rapport system." [19]

Eldersveld found the party elite to consist of "pluralized sets of separable 'career classes' or 'career categories,' with considerable differentiation in congruence, communicative interchange, and self-consciousness." He concluded that the Iron Law of Oligarchy did not apply to the party he was studying.

Similar conclusions were reached by Henry Valen and Daniel Katz in their study of *Political Parties in Norway*.[20] They found that lower echelons played an important role in influencing party policy at the next higher level. Democratic control of party structure was real. Although party leaders stayed in office for long periods of time, they remained sensitive to the opinions of the membership as well as the electorate.

Renate Mayntz, in a study of the Christian Democratic Party in Berlin, found no conscious efforts on the part of the party elite to manipulate the party or to co-opt leading positions. Seeming oligarchic tendencies had less dramatic explanations.[21] Eldersveld and Valen and Katz relied primarily on survey research techniques; Mayntz used participant observation over a considerable period of time. All reached substantially the same conclusions.

The one study of democratic parties that reached ambivalent conclusions was Robert T. McKenzie's analysis of leadership in

19. *Political Parties: A Behavioral Analysis* (Chicago, Rand McNally, 1964), pp. 9–10.
20. Oslo, Universitetsforlaget, 1964.
21. "Oligrachic Problems in a German Party District," in Dwaine Marvick, ed., *Political Decisionmakers: Recruitment and Performance* (New York, Free Press, 1961), pp. 138–92.

the British Labor and Conservative parties.[22] He concluded that leaders of both parties exercised overwhelming authority within their respective organizations. Significantly, he was concerned primarily with the top leadership of the parliamentary parties and he did not rely on the empirical techniques of the authors of the studies mentioned previously. And it is equally important that he discovered that over the long run there were substantial limitations on the authority of the leaders of both parties. His study emphasizes the extent to which the structure of government conditions the organization of parties; he concentrated on the area of party organization where the structure of British government almost certainly has its greatest impact. Nevertheless, he too noted that the "Law of Oligarchy" was not an "Iron Law." [23]

THE THEORETICAL FOCUS OF THE RESEARCH

Michels analyzed the impact of factors such as bureaucratization and the leadership's near monopoly of competence and information on the relationship between the leaders and the led, and this gives him his perennial freshness. For even if the Iron Law of Oligarchy has been demonstrated to fit poorly with the empirical data on the organization of political parties the eternal problem of organizational democracy remains. Michels' general law has proved to be inadequate. His middle-range analyses, on the other hand, have stood the test of time remarkably well. The general themes that he introduced are still the important ones, and they will recur in the chapters that follow.

This study of democracy within a provincial federation of the PSI reflects several theoretical interests related to the tradition of Michels. One of these is the study of party organization. Another is political participation. Still another is leadership. All of these interests converge in the study of party democracy.

There are many meanings of democracy. They cannot all be granted equal legitimacy, as this would render "democratic" synonymous with "desirable," and would render operationaliza-

22. *British Political Parties* (New York, St. Martin's, 1955).
23. Ibid., p. 587.

tion of the concept impossible. To give content to the phrase "party democracy" requires a more limited conception of democracy; otherwise the term has no operational meaning. This admittedly means that conceptions of democracy that are shared by large numbers of people are rejected in this study. The reader is not obligated to agree with the conception of democracy used here, but it is important that the usage be made explicit: as operationalized in this study, democracy at any level of analysis involves extensive and widespread influence on decision making by those who are affected. This can be through direct participation in the making of decisions or choice between alternatives. This latter formulation is Joseph Schumpeter's restatement of democracy for a complex society. The level of analysis is important, for an organization that is not internally democratic may facilitate democracy at a higher level by permitting wider influence to be exercised on decisions.

Democracy is in principle a quantifiable variable. The extent to which any unit is democratic can be expressed in terms of the portion of individuals within that unit who do in fact influence decisions. In complex units the existence of democracy becomes a matter of competence and organization as well as of desires and wills. The strategic factor in democracy is thus the existence of multiple autonomous channels of communication that tie together the diverse parts of a unit and permit the extensive exercise of influence.

If democracy is operationalized in this manner, certain general hypotheses can be suggested. The first is that democracy is facilitated by the inability of unit elites to control all communications channels affecting the unit, especially those that provide information and those that serve as a structural basis for an opposition. The second general proposition is that democracy necessitates high levels of political competence, which facilitate communication and the construction and maintenance of channels. Low levels of competence render the existence of democracy precarious regardless of the personal intentions of leaders and followers.

The following chapters examine the variables that facilitate or hinder the establishment and maintenance of multiple autonomous communications channels. These include such general factors as the Italian political culture and the structure of politics, especially the structure of the PSI both nationally and locally. Personal characteristics of leaders and followers also greatly affect the maintenance of multiple autonomous communications channels; these in particular include characteristics relating to political competence (knowledge, sense of efficacy, social stratification, participation, and others), motivation, ideology, and attitudes. Finally, the channels of communication affecting the party also require special attention. These include not only the channels deriving from the formal structure of the party but also extraparty channels at the local level as well as the conventional channels of a free society such as the mass media and the general political structure of the country.

2.

Italian Politics and Parties:
An Overview

Every political situation contains aspects of both the universal and the particular. In laboratory experiments idiosyncratic factors can be carefully controlled; in field research on political parties this is not possible. Although careful analysis can detect and isolate much of the impact of the particular, the mixture remains. This study seeks patterns of interaction that promise to have a general significance rather than those peculiar to this particular situation. It is a study of relationships between leaders and followers in a party of a particular type, not a study of Italian socialism. But it is also a study of relationships in a particular party at a particular time, and some attention to Italian national and local politics should prove useful in fixing the party in its social and political context.

THE STRUCTURE OF POLITICS

Political parties everywhere seem to be strongly affected in their organization and functioning by the political structures with which they deal. Italian parties are no exception. Parties and government are both characterized by a high degree of formal centralization combined with a wide assortment of patterns of accommodation to local, regional, religious, economic, and other interests. Both are widely considered to suffer from excessive bureaucratization. The government and the party system both reflect the legacy of fascism, two world wars, imperfect national unification, and religious, regional, and ideological divisions. The formal structure of government was consciously designed to frustrate and overcome these divisions; but it often seems that the Italian political tradition was consciously designed to frustrate and overcome governments. The interaction of formal norms and traditional practices is a recurring theme in the analysis that follows.

Having created Italy, the leaders of the Risorgimento faced the task of creating Italians. They began with some advantages and some handicaps. Except for small areas where it today borders France, Austria, and Yugoslavia, Italy was a cultural, linguistic, and geographical unit, at least in the sense that it contained no hard core elements that did not exhibit a great potential for eventual unity. It possessed a common literary language, a common religion, and a unified high culture; that is, educated Italians possessed the same cultural tradition, one that they shared with other educated Europeans. At the level of mass culture, however, Italy exhibited considerable internal variation; these local habits and traditions often diverged markedly from the normal range of local variations expected in, for example, northern Europe. Local dialects were often incomprehensible to people from other areas and local allegiances were very strong. Poverty and backwardness bred ignorance of the world beyond the sound of the village bell (*campanilismo*); ignorance in turn encouraged the cycle of poverty and backwardness.

The Italian masses have largely been the objects, not the subjects, of history. The movement for national unity was an elite movement; for the masses, the concept of Italy had no meaning. In this century the Italian masses have come to play the role of voters in their political system, if little more. In the nineteenth century only a few hundred people at most played any significant role in the politics of any particular electoral constituency. Deputies were brokers between their local clientele and the cabinet. The latter provided local improvements and rewards for the representative in return for his votes; he in turn used these local improvements and other rewards to solidify his influence among the voters. Since only those few citizens with property or education could vote, the representative had little incentive to cultivate mass publics; and these latter, with few positive feelings toward government, had little reason to identify with the system.

These were the largely unplanned consequences of the system. The architects of unification intended that a unified nation would emerge from a unified, centralized state. At a time when the masses were not highly mobilized politically anywhere in the world it is understandable that unification would be viewed as a problem of elite mobilization. But the political settlement following unification guaranteed that local patterns would be changed as little as possible, for local elites had a strong bargaining position vis-à-vis the cabinet and they could hardly be expected to use this power to favor programs that would undermine their positions. The chief revolutionary force in the latter part of the nineteenth century in Italy turned out to be economic development, and its impact was limited in scope and intensity. The role of the government in economic development was restricted mainly to protecting and promoting several industries deemed essential to national power. Catholics were forbidden by the Church to participate in politics; anarchists and Marxists as yet had little influence; local notables were suppliants rather than co-conspirators. It was the liberal era and a liberal system, and the advocates of progress settled for government-assisted laissez faire.

The principal components of this governmental structure need to be mentioned briefly, for the behavioral patterns exhibited within them have shown a remarkable tenacity down to the present time. This is not to suggest that the liberal system established these patterns: they are very old and deeply rooted. The liberal founders of Italy established a governmental structure patterned after those of northern Europe, but it was heavily influenced by the behavioral patterns of Mediterranean Italy. Their effort at forced political development was frustrated; the excolonial areas of Italy have been exacting their revenge ever since.

The governmental structure that emerged from unification did not reflect the historic regions of Italy. The Napoleonic-Piemontese system of departments and prefects was extended to all of Italy. Demands for local autonomy, which were especially strong in the south and the islands, were refused. The entire country was divided into provinces (the equivalent of departments), each containing one of the principal cities of the country plus its hinterland. The provinces were in turn divided into communes, each with a chief village and the countryside extending up to the boundaries of the neighboring communes. Thus every inch of Italy was within a commune and a province. This is the territorial organization of Italy today, except that regions, grouping in most cases several provinces, were authorized by the constitution that went into effect in 1948. Four (Sicily, Sardegna, Valle d'Aosta, Trentino-Alto Adige) had already been created before 1948. Friuli-Venezia Giulia was the only additional region established by 1966, though the implementation of the rest ranked high on the program of the center-left government. The regions, provinces, and communes all have elected representative bodies; only the regional bodies have much initiative.

The most important figure in local government is the prefect, a career official representing the central government. He is appointed by and responsible to the Minister of the Interior. Under the liberal regime he was, among other things, the agent of the cabinet in local politics, performing intelligence functions, organizing elections, and disbursing favors in collaboration with the government's supporters in his area. Under the Fascist regime he continued this role, though surpassed in importance by the local party organization. Under the republic his role is more restrained, limited by local political configurations and competing hierarchies. He is one of the devices through which local and national politics are integrated. All national governmental activities in the province are his responsibility, though recently the field administrations of other governmental ministries have acquired considerable autonomy. He is also responsible for ensuring that communal and provincial governmental affairs are conducted properly.

The parties competing on the local level are the national ones. The fragmentation of the party system often results in the absence of a majority for any *giunta* in the larger communes, which employ proportional representation. The unacceptable alternative of a prefectoral administration has encouraged the formation of local coalitions that would appear strange at the national level, and these experiments at coalition building have often had national ramifications. The center-left government, for example, reflected the precedents of several years of cooperation between these parties in large communes of northern and central Italy. The prefectoral system and the lack of autonomy of local from national politics have served to prolong the image of government as an alien force reflecting distant interests, no different for being Italian from previous occupying powers.

The central government that extended throughout Italy following unification was based on the constitution of Piedmont. It provided for a constitutional monarchy, an elected Chamber of Deputies, and an appointed Senate. The Cabinet, headed by a prime minister, was the executive. Relationships among these bodies were never completely clarified. The Cabinet needed a majority in the Chamber, but in practice it dominated the Chamber not through party organization but by means of *trasformismo*. This is the label given the system of forming cabinets on the basis of patronage and favors to individual deputies in return for their votes. The basis of political divisions consequently was personal advantage rather than party or program. The system as a whole could not adapt to the age of mass-disciplined parties and universal suffrage, but many of its components preceded and survived the decline of the liberal era. Just as democracy under the monarchy was undermined by these habits so was the harshness of fascism softened and humanized by general involvement in mutual favoritism.

The monarchy was severely compromised by fascism and the lack of political skill of Victor Emmanuel III; a bare majority of voters chose a republic in 1946. This election reflected and sharpened the divisions of the country, as the South overwhelmingly favored the monarchy and the North the republic.

The monarch was replaced by a president, who is elected for

a seven-year term by the two houses of parliament in joint session. Members of the Chamber of Deputies are elected by proportional representation in thirty-two constituencies. Senators are elected within regional constituencies, with the result that the two houses are quite similar in composition. Although they are also similar in their formal powers, the lower house is in fact the predominant one. Universal suffrage was achieved in 1945, with the minimum age for voting being twenty-one for the Chamber and twenty-five for the Senate. In elections for the Chamber, seats are assigned to parties on the basis of proportional representation, but the party's candidates are declared elected on the basis of preference votes rather than position on the list. Although the Senate and Chamber originally had staggered terms, in practice the Senate was dissolved with the Chamber, thus contributing further to the absence of great differences between them; the amended constitution gives the Senate a five-year term also, with the consequence that the Senate is largely redundant.

The Italian president is more than a mere figurehead but far less than the president of the United States or of the French Fifth Republic. The chief executive is the head of the government, or President of the Council of Ministers. He is appointed by the President of the Republic but cannot be removed by him. He must secure a vote of confidence in both houses soon after his election and must resign if he loses a vote of confidence or a vote of censure. In practice most prime ministers resign because their legislative proposals are defeated.

Although all prime ministers since December 1945 have been Christian Democrats, they have represented several different substantive programs and wings of that party. The Christian Democratic Party no longer has an absolute majority by itself and must govern in coalition; even if it had a majority, however, a prime minister of that party would not be guaranteed a majority of parliamentary votes, for he must build a coalition not only with other parties but also within his own party. It has generally been the withdrawal of support by a faction of his own party on an important legislative act that has caused the resignation of the prime minister. In forming a Cabinet the would-be prime minister must pay careful attention to the balance of forces within his own party and ensure that his program and the distribution of Cabinet positions reflect the distribution of influence within his party. The shift to the left in the electorate has meant that the party has had to seek coalition allies on the left rather than the right, and this has increased the influence of those elements of the party that are able to collaborate with the center-left parties such as the Socialists and Social Democrats.

It has just been pointed out that almost every government is a coalition. The only exceptions have been all-Christian Democratic—*monocolore*—governments composed completely of members of that party but supported by other parties. These have been temporary arrangements resorted to when efforts at a coalition failed. As these coalitions are composed not only of competing and antagonistic parties but also of warring factions within the Christian Democratic Party, they are fragile creations incapable of giving strong direction to the formulation of policy. The general lines of policy are determined by the coalition agreement. Within this framework each minister tends to go his own way. There is little incentive for cooperation. Primary loyalties are to the party or faction, and to one's own career. Individual ministries may pursue contradictory policies. The weakness of the coalition makes it vulnerable to the appeals of special interests. This has been particularly true of the Christian Democratic Party, whose dependence on the Church and its auxiliary organizations has given rise to complicated patterns of consultation and accommodation. And the practice of secret ballots on important legislation enables recalcitrant members even of the coalition parties to "snipe" at the government by withholding their support; several cabinets have resigned for this reason.

The role of the state bureaucracy is an important one. Originally patterned after the French administration, it has not undergone the transformations effected after the Second World War to modernize that bureaucracy. Each ministry does its own recruiting and examining. Lateral transfer is rare. Pay is low and promotions give excessive weight to seniority. The preparation of higher civil servants is poor; most have law degrees and receive little pre- or postentry training. Higher civil servants are increasingly drawn from the South, where the oversupply of lawyers combines with the prestige and security of government employment and the absence of alternative careers to render such posts attractive. Its morale sapped by the long years of Fascist and Christian Democratic interference at all levels and in all spheres, the civil service is not an independent force in Italian politics. It is low in morale and efficiency. Especially at lower levels, the civil service has been used for welfare purposes, providing posts for the needy, lame, and unemployed. It has not contributed greatly to the effectiveness of government or to the process of national integration.

Italy has a strong tradition of vitality in local affairs. The city-states held the primary political loyalty of their citizens, and even today Italians are likely to think of themselves as citizens of their city first and Italians second. There are marked variations in the caliber of local government in different parts of Italy. Some larger cities have remarkably effective administrations, and some parties have provided efficient, honest local administration. The Communist Party, for example, benefits from such a reputation. Centralization, however, severely limits the independence of local government. Expenditures are closely controlled by law. The prefect and agencies of the national government intrude in many aspects of local affairs, and their intervention is not free of partisanship in favor of the party or parties dominant at the national level. Thus one possible reason for the probity of Communist local administrations is that they are closely scrutinized by national authorities.

Despite the close legal controls exercised over local government there is a multitude of ways in which political considerations can enter. There are many possibilities for patronage and corruption, and the latter probably flourishes most precisely in those areas that most need the example of a strong, honest administration to offset the alienative local political patterns. This

25

is certainly the case in Sicily, for example, and probably in other areas as well. Special interests often continue to exercise dominant local influence despite the seeming power of outside authority; thus in many areas the network of local industrial, agricultural, and religious interests working through the Christian Democratic Party continues to exercise a virtual veto on local policies and personnel despite the lack of a local electoral majority. They can do this because of the importance of the prefect and the national administration, which are sensitive to claims from these interests.

This general discussion of local government and politics has of necessity been vague. Little research has been carried out on this level of Italian politics and still less of a rigorous kind typified by the community power literature on American politics. In a later chapter on the province of Arezzo it will be possible to be more specific about the locale of the study.

POLITICAL PARTIES

The Italian party system is a complex one, reflecting the historical discontinuities as well as the regional, religious, ideological, and interest fragmentation of the Italian polity. The system defies simple analysis, as the differences between parties encompass several dimensions of conflict. And the differences are often not what they seem to be.

Contemporary parties have their origins in the organizations and conflicts of earlier days. The Liberal Party is the survivor of the party that dominated Italian politics before the First World War. The Christian Democratic Party is a revival and expansion of the Popular Party that emerged at the end of the First World War when the ban on Catholic participation in politics was rescinded in the face of the growth of socialism. The Communist, Socialist, Social Democratic, and Social Proletarian parties are the result of various schisms within Italian socialism. The Communists split off in 1921, the Social Democrats in 1946–47, and the Social Proletarians in 1964. The Republican Party has kept alive the tradition of Mazzini for almost one hundred years. The Monarchists survive on the money of southern notables plus some nostalgia for the monarchy in many parts of Italy. The neo-Fascist Italian Social Movement espouses the more idealistic and nationalistic aspects of fascism. These parties are often viewed as representing separate competing subcultures. Although the point can be overemphasized, in one sense they do: Italian political divisions cut deeply into the Italian consciousness and social structure, and some parties come close to encompassing the entire existence of many of their adherents. But the fit is not a perfect one, for not all practicing Catholics vote Christian Democratic, not all industrialists vote Liberal, not all workers vote Communist.

The electorate divides among the parties in the manner outlined roughly below. (For the results of postwar elections see Table 2-1.) The Christian Democratic Party is the only one to attract substantial numbers of voters from all social classes.[1] It receives the votes of a strong minority of the working class, most independent farmers, and much of the middle class. It gets more than its share of the women's votes, thanks to its religious ties; and of course it is the party favored by most fervent Catholics. The Communist vote is strongly concentrated in the lower working class, though in some areas its rural vote is very high; and it has a substantial middle-class, especially lower middle-class, following. The Socialist Party appeals to the same groups, but the party is more attractive to the upper working class of skilled laborers and to the middle class than the

1. Due to the refusal of many respondents to divulge their party identification or vote to interviewers, knowledge about who votes for whom in Italy is limited and should be used with caution. For indications see Mattei Dogan, "La Stratificazione sociale dei suffragi," in Alberto Spreafico and Joseph LaPalombara, eds., *Elezioni e comportamento politico in Italia* (Ivrea, Comunità, 1963), pp. 407–74; Dogan, "Les Bases sociales des partis politiques en France et en Italie," paper presented at the Fifth World Congress of Sociology, Washington, D.C., September 2–8, 1962; Gabriel A. Almond and Sidney Verba, *The Civic Culture* (Princeton, Princeton University Press, 1963); Pierpaolo Luzzatto Fegiz, *Il Volto sconosciuto dell'Italia: dieci anni di sondaggi DOXA* (Milan, Giuffre, 1956); Spreafico, "Orientamento politico e identificazione partitica," pp. 689–732, and Paolo Ammassari, "Opinione politica et scelta elettorale," pp. 733–84, both in Spreafico and LaPalombara, eds., *Elezioni*.

27

Table 2-1. Elections to Chamber of Deputies

	Constituent Assembly		1948		1953		1958		1963	
	%	Seats	%	Seats	%	Seats	%	Seats	%	Seats
Communists	18.9	104	31.0	183	22.6	143	22.7	140	25.3	166
Socialists	20.7	115			12.7	75	14.2	84	13.8	87
Social Democrats	—		7.1	33	4.5	19	4.5	22	6.1	33
Republicans	4.4	23	2.5	9	1.6	5	1.4	6	1.4	6
Christian Democrats	35.1	207	48.4	304	40.0	262	42.3	273	38.3	260
Liberals	2.8	16	3.8	19	3.0	13	3.5	17	7.0	39
Monarchists	—		2.8	14	6.9	40	PMP 2.6	14	1.7	8
							PNM 2.2	11		
Neo-Fascists	—		2.0	6	5.8	29	4.8	24	5.1	27
Other parties	18.1	90	2.4	5	2.9	3	1.8	4	1.3	4
TOTAL	100.0	555	100.0	573	100.0	589	100.0	595	100.0	630

Percentage is of total popular vote.

Source: Giovanni Schepis, "Analisi statistica dei risultati," in Alberto Spreafico and Joseph LaPalombara, eds., Elezioni e comportamento politico in Italia (Ivrea, Comunità, 1963), pp. 354–55, through 1958; for 1963 results, Tempi Moderni, 13 (1963), 75.

28

Communist Party. This is likewise true of the Social Democratic Party, though its class appeal is even more toward the skilled worker and middle class than is the Socialist. There are no hard data as to the source of support for the Social Proletarians. The Republican Party has a clientele not unlike that of the Social Democrats except that it is extremely limited geographically to a few regions and cities. The Liberals are an upper middle- and upper-class party in electoral appeal. The Monarchist voters are either upper-class, or lower-class voters attracted on a clientelistic basis. The Neo-Fascists attract voters across a wide social spectrum.

Examining the leadership of the parties in terms of class origin, a surprising pattern emerges: all the parties except the Communist are predominantly middle-class led.[2] Only the Communists have a substantial portion of deputies of lower-class origin, and the Chamber contains most of the national leaders of all the parties. The other parties are similar except that the median class level rises from a predominance of the lower middle class on the left to the upper middle on the right of the ideological spectrum. This aspect of party leadership undoubtedly reflects the more general elitism of Italian culture and is a theme that recurs in the chapters that follow.

The middle-class background of the leaders of most parties assumes greater significance because of the importance within most parties of the party bureaucracy. Italian parties are roughly similar in formal structure. Most have a national congress as the supreme body, with a large central committee elected by that congress as the sovereign body in the interim between congresses, which are held sporadically in most of the parties. National activities are coordinated by a smaller executive committee selected by and from within the larger committee. There is in turn a central direction or staff or bureaucracy headed by a secretary responsible to the executive committee. This staff is divided into sections dealing, for example, with organization, press, auxiliary groups (unions, women, students, etc.), and

---

2. See Giovanni Sartori et al., *Il Parlamento Italiano* (Napoli, Edizioni Scientifiche Italiane, 1963), pp. 168–72.

29

finance. This central staff controls the party press (in most of the parties), oversees local activities, serves as a financial clearing house, runs electoral campaigns, serves as the research and drafting service for the parliamentary delegation, and performs many other crucial services.

Local party organization focuses on the province. Most parties have at least a skeletal organization in most provinces of Italy; these are invariably called the Provincial Federation of the —— Party of ——. These federations may be subdivided into sections, cells, or local units with other names. Typically, the federation has an embryonic bureaucracy with an impressive—on paper—table of organization. It repeats the national structure of a provincial congress, large directing committee, and smaller executive committee; and like the national organization, the local federation is headed by a secretary, who is generally the dominant figure in the local party.

This general organizational structure describes the PSI, PCI, and PSDI quite accurately. In these parties the organization of the party on paper reflects, at least generally, the actual structure of influence in the parties. These are all membership parties; they have fleshed out this structure with varying degrees of success; and the important figures in these parties are usually the ones who hold the important formal positions. The PCI has been most successful organizationally. Although it has lost much of its membership since its peak years immediately following the Second World War, it still has an impressive membership organization, in addition to a large bureaucracy in Rome and also, at least in central and northern Italy, large provincial bureaucracies. There are many indications that its cell organization has undergone a long period of decay but its presence is felt throughout the working-class milieu. It has a capable cadre, and it is still an impressive organizational weapon.

The structure of the PSI will be analyzed in detail in a later chapter; this discussion is to place it in context. In most parts of Italy it is smaller than the PCI. It cannot equal its rival in number of members or of paid party workers. But it has been able to maintain its presence as a working-class party almost everywhere that the PCI is active. It is likely that its members and local leaders derive from slightly more prosperous levels within the working class than those of the PCI, though both are of essentially the same stratum. It is probable that the two parties veer apart as one goes up the party hierarchy, with the leaders differing far more from one another than the rank and file. The PSI is much more dependent than the PCI on unpaid workers at the local level. Both parties undoubtedly deviate markedly from the table of organization in various ways and regions but the Communist Party is more highly articulated than the Socialist.

The PSDI is less highly articulated than the above two parties, mainly because of its size. While its paper structure is similar to the PSI and PCI, it does not have as much meat on the organizational bones. Moreover, it is much more middle-class than the above parties, and its lower-class supporters include a higher proportion of highly skilled workers. The table of organization of the PSIUP (PSI of Proletarian Unity) is similar to that of the other three parties of the left. Because of its small size it is certainly not as highly articulated as these parties, but no firm generalizations are possible at this time.

It is difficult to generalize about the Republican Party. Never very large, its support has dwindled steadily since its goal of the establishment of the republic was achieved; nevertheless, it has retained a nucleus of loyal members and voters. Although it is a membership party like the above four, it is probable that formal membership plays less of a role in party affairs. In the Romagna, however, it is, in fact, a small mass party. Despite its size it possesses the same general structure and internal divisions of the above parties.

It is even more difficult to generalize about the Christian Democratic Party. It is a mass membership party with a highly articulated structure, formal members, and the complete set of bodies described above. But it is far more than that. The formal organization of the party is only one element, albeit an important one, in its overall structure. The most important nonparty element is the Catholic Church. Given the realities of Italian politics, the ties between the party and the Church are of necessity close. The party could not exist over the opposition of the Church, which in the past has intervened directly in Italian politics in a manner equaled in few other countries. The relationship can be generalized as follows: The Church establishes the outer limits on the programmatic and doctrinal positions the party can take. It often insists on certain particular policies. It provides immense organizational and electoral support for the party. It claims a privileged position vis-à-vis the party and the state bureaucracy for its agents and those of its associated organizations.

Nor is the Church the only agency outside the party that greatly influences its policies. Several of the top leaders of the party are notables whose influence derives not so much from their support within the party structure as from their personal electoral machines based on clientelistic and other relationships. These ties, especially in the South, are likely to involve local alliances having little to do with the formal party organization. These leaders are only in part under the authority of the formal structure of the party, which is thus only one of several influences within the party. It was largely a paper organization in the early postwar years, and the party was dependent on Church-related agencies, especially the Civic Committees of Catholic Action, for electoral assistance. One of the more important developments of the decade preceding the PSI study was the rise of the party organization. The growth in its influence was associated with a number of factors, including the partial retreat of the Vatican from many exposed positions in Italian politics, the leftward drift of the Italian electorate, and the political ambitions of such Christian Democratic leaders as Amintore Fanfani and Aldo Moro. These two were the principal agents in the strengthening of the party structure. The party continued to be divided into several factions representing conservative or traditional interests, trade unionists, the Catholic left, and personal ambitions. The opening to the left, which involved cooperation between Socialists and Christian Democrats, was rendered possible by the shift of internal factional

32

strength; a slight shift could also reverse the process of accommodation.

The Liberal Party is the heir of the liberal tradition in Italy. It did not adapt easily to the era of mass parties and remains restricted in its appeal and skeletal in organization. Its central organs reflect the patterns described above, but local organization is not highly articulated.

The disintegrating Monarchist Party likewise possesses no mass organization. Its table of organization hardly masks the reality of a party dominated by a few individuals whose personal feuds fix the terms of internal debate and competition.

Of the parties on the right only the Italian Social Movement has any pretensions to a disciplined mass organization. A party of the very old and very young, its structure is similar to that of the leftist parties, though the nomenclature is original; but its size prevents it from achieving the degree of organization of the parties of the left. Nevertheless, it is capable of rapid mobilization of its activists and can generate considerable enthusiasm for protests and demonstrations.

It would be easy to exaggerate the importance of the ideological differences between the parties. They exist, and undoubtedly they are of considerable importance. However, the structure of the party system reflects ideological differences only in part. The parties can be viewed as "parties of integration"; the two largest parties, the DC and the PCI, approximate this type in several respects. They demand—though they do not necessarily receive—the total allegiance of their members, they possess a full range of affiliated organizations serving virtually all the associational needs of their members and supporters, and they reflect total world views. But even in these parties it is not possible to understand the belief systems of members solely by reference to official ideologies.

Catholicism is compatible with several political and social ideologies, and most of them are to be found in Italy. Many Italian Catholics are integralists, who prefer a "Catholic" society that reflects religious values in all aspects of its life. Others are not so much Catholic as traditionalist; they simply would

33

like to avoid changing the known and familiar. Others are conservatives of several varieties—conservatism in Italy can be differentiated from traditionalism—some reflecting the values of the industrial middle class and others the rural gentry. Still other Catholics are far to the left in their social and political outlooks, advocating programs that differ little from those of the various Socialist parties. It is thus a mistake to view Italian Catholicism as an ideological monolith. It is capable of acting as a political monolith in the sense that the hierarchy can and does often intervene forcefully on behalf of particular policies and individuals. But this action represents no ideological unity. Usually, in fact, it reflects the absence of agreement and the necessity of the Church to enter directly to preserve unity and resolve conflicts.

Italian communism has long exhibited numerous idiosyncrasies and one of the most important has been its ideological individuality. It has one of the saints of communism in Antonio Gramsci, an unorthodox thinker who died in a Fascist prison. The PCI was a leader in the advocacy of polycentrism within the international Communist movement. While still following the principle of democratic centralism the PCI has tolerated considerable internal debate and in the mid-1960s seemed headed toward even greater internal freedom. Furthermore, there is considerable evidence, admittedly fragmentary and inconclusive, that suggests that the appeal of the party to the Italian masses is not primarily ideological. It is doubtful that mass publics anywhere are highly ideological; given the low levels of education and knowledge of Italian Communist members and voters it is even more doubtful that the party attracts them in this manner.

Class differences are basic in Italian politics and the significant thing about ideological differences is that no ideology dominates the outlook of a class. Communism has great appeal for the lower classes, but so does socialism and Catholicism. And the middle and upper classes embrace both Catholicism and liberalism. Communism and socialism are primarily lower-class

34

ideologies, liberalism upper and middle, and Catholicism spreads across all classes. Ideological dimensions such as the liberal-conservative (in the American sense) continuum on socioeconomic issues are more useful in analyzing the Italian party system. One can, for example, array parties and voters from left to right on this continuum. Analysis along a continuum of egalitarianism would result in a similar array. On the other hand, the clerical-anticlerical dimension is of immense importance in Italy and the lineup on this dimension would be somewhat different. The liberal-conservative dimension is thus a highly important one, but there are other ideological divisions that are of great importance, too. And these do not crisscross the parties in the same manner as the liberal-conservative one.

Ignorance about politics is widespread in Italy. In *The Civic Culture* study, Italians scored dramatically lower than citizens of the United States, Great Britain, and Germany, and substantially lower than Mexicans on a political information test.[3] The importance of education is revealed in Table 2-2. Differences remain when very gross controls are introduced for educational level, but they are much smaller; and they are further reduced, for example, among university graduates. The portion attending a university is normal for a European country, but mass education is quite low. For many, five years is the maximum. Many of those with less than five years of formal education are functionally illiterate. Few people in the lower categories pay much attention to politics; this is especially true of women. In short, Italians are in general extremely poorly informed about the operation of their political system.

Consequently, considering the low levels of education and knowledge, it is likely that relatively few Italians possess an ideological perspective toward politics. On the other hand, elites tend to interpret events in an ideological frame of reference, and much of the public debate is couched in highly abstract terms. Thus, ideological divisions are important, but are mediated through organizational and other ties before making an

3. Almond and Verba, *The Civic Culture*, p. 393.

Table 2-2. Percent High Scorers[a] in Political Information Test, by Sex and Nation

Nation	Total				Primary or Less				Secondary or More			
	Male		Female		Male		Female		Male		Female	
	%	N[b]	%	N	%	N	%	N	%	N	%	N
United States	59	455	40	515	45	248	25	269	77	207	61	246
Great Britain	60	459	36	503	54	277	30	340	70	182	52	163
Germany	71	442	51	499	66	352	38	440	90	90	88	59
Italy	32	471	14	524	27	293	4	403	66	178	46	121
Mexico	43	355	15	652	32	285	9	592	77	67	52	60

[a] High scorers on information can name at least two party leaders and two ministries or cabinet positions.
[b] Numbers refer to the bases upon which percentages are calculated.
Table is taken from Almond and Verba, *The Civic Culture*, p. 393.

impact on mass publics.[4] The impact of ideology on the members of the local federation is discussed in detail in later chapters.

Although ideology alone may be overrated as a source of division between Italian parties, the effects of several lines of division are cumulative. The result is a fragmented political culture in which many people find their party preferences reinforced by their social class, socioeconomic interest, ideological preferences, religious allegiances, and associational ties. Thus there is a leftist Socialist-Communist subculture, a Catholic subculture, a Liberal subculture, and so on. In this situation, multiple associational memberships reinforce subcultural identification rather than subject the individual to cross-pressures.[5] This kind of pluralism in the structure of politics does not result in an open group struggle as suggested by proponents of the group theory of politics. Rather, the political subculture that controls a governmental or nongovernmental structure seeks to exclude representatives of other subcultures from benefits.[6] The results are intense partisanship and alienation.

The great political partisanship of Italians is evident from any superficial acquaintance with the system; several dimensions of it were documented empirically in the five-nation study of Almond and Verba. Italians viewed supporters of parties other than their own much more negatively than did respondents in the other four countries.[7] And Italians were much less willing to have their son or daughter marry a supporter of another party. These attitudes reflect far more than just political partisanship: they reflect social, religious, and other divisions as well, and consequently should not be viewed as simply political. But the fact that the divisions are cumulative for so many people has great political significance. However, as

4. For a discussion of this point in greater detail, see Samuel H. Barnes, "Ideology and the Organization of Conflict: On the Relationship Between Political Thought and Behavior," *Journal of Politics*, 28 (1966), 513–30.
5. See Sidney Verba, "Organizational Membership and Democratic Consensus," *Journal of Politics*, 27 (1965), 467–97.
6. These are the findings of Joseph LaPalombara in *Interest Groups in Italian Politics* (Princeton, Princeton University Press, 1964).
7. *The Civic Culture*, pp. 130–37.

pointed out above, the fit between divisions and subcultures is not a perfect one.

The above comments on the functioning of interest groups suggest that supporters of the left are alienated from the system. This is perhaps true in a strictly political sense, but the fact is that a sense of alienation permeates the entire political system. The authors of *The Civic Culture* document the extent of this disaffection and evaluate it in the perspective of other countries.[8] They point out that paradoxically many leftists possessed attitudes toward others and the environment that made them potential supporters of a democratic system while the Christian Democrats have many supporters who are not democratic or even political.[9] These latter support the system as little as do the leftists, but they strongly support their subculture and its political arm, the Christian Democratic Party.

The significance of alienation should not be overstated. Alienation has a negative connotation that perhaps is inappropriate in this context. The Italian attitude is much more one of lack of national integration or support, a concentration on the immediate and familiar. It is an aspect of national style not limited to politics. Some observers view this as pathological, but in the light of modern Italian history it can also be viewed as realistic and healthy. There is no reason why an Italian should view his political system in as positive a light as, for example, an American or Englishman might. A middle-aged Italian has lived under several regimes, one of which gave its name to a major form of modern dictatorship and lost a disastrous and unnecessary war. Another regime won a disastrous and unnecessary war and did little better than the other. The present regime has brought about the highest standard of living in the history of the peninsula but has not satisfied the accumulated grievances of centuries. Nor has it served to integrate the many subgroups of Italy into the national polity. The kind of national integration achieved in some other countries is probably not immediately achievable in Italy. The major and most enduring

8. Ibid., pp. 402–14.
9. Ibid., p. 160.

obstacles are regional differences and political differences based upon conflicting fundamental beliefs about the nature of man. Regional differences will probably slowly diminish in significance. The improving relations between communism and the Vatican will perhaps slowly erode some other antagonisms. However, some differences are so fundamental that they can be overcome, if at all, only through a concerted effort over time to seek mutual accommodation. The emerging polity in Italy is thus likely to follow its own logic of development. The Anglo-American model of the civic culture is probably not immediately relevant to the Italian context.

3.

Italian Socialism:
A Review

There has been recurring conflict in the Italian Socialist movement between those who hope for the revolutionary reconstruction of Italian society and others who favor the reform of the existing order. These tendencies have been present from the beginning. This chapter will review these divisions and indicate their importance within the party at the time of the field work in 1963.

UNTIL THE END OF THE SECOND WORLD WAR

Several factors combined to retard the development of a unified and disciplined Socialist movement in Italy.[1] The delayed industrialization of the country was a major factor; its effects were compounded by the small size and paternalistic structure of most of Italian industry. The late achievement of national unity and the political inequalities of the Liberal era were likewise contributing factors. During the latter part of the nineteenth century the Italian left was divided between the Marxists and the anarchist followers of Michael Bakunin. Of special significance was the romantic streak that is still discernible; the absence of political power and organizational vitality encouraged irresponsibility.

The national party was founded at Genoa in 1892, and it was symbolic that this congress was unable to agree on a pro-

1. The literature on the development of the Italian Socialist and labor movements is very large. Useful overviews in English include W. Hilton-Young, *The Italian Left: A Short History of Political Socialism in Italy* (New York, Longmans, Green and Co., 1949); Daniel Horowitz, *The Italian Labor Movement* (Cambridge, Harvard University Press, 1963); and Maurice Neufeld, *Italy: School for Awakening Countries* (Ithaca, School of Industrial and Labor Relations, 1961).

gram of action. Eventually two formulations of a Socialist program were adopted at a later congress, a minimum and a maximum program. The minimum program called for immediate reforms in the electoral laws and in capitalist society itself; the maximum program accepted the wider aim of the revitalization of Italian society through social, economic, and political reforms of a revolutionary nature. These minimalist and maximalist tendencies have persisted down to the present.

Schism, expulsion, and reunification have been endemic in the party. In the first decade of the century the syndicalists—who advocated industrial activity rather than parliamentary action—were expelled from the party. The conciliatory policy of Giovanni Giolitti during a period of economic growth and political stability that is now sometimes viewed as the Golden Age of Italian Democracy encouraged moderation in the party during the early years of the century. But this reformist period was followed by the triumph of the radical maximalists at the 1912 party congress. Mussolini was one of the most vehement spokesmen for the latter and became editor of the party paper, *Avanti!*, following the congress. Some of the reformists were expelled from the party; other moderates, placing party unity ahead of their personal convictions, remained in the party but had little influence among members. It was a period of demagoguery, irresponsibility, and uncertainty for Italian socialism, as well as for the rest of Italy.

Giolitti accepted the desirability of incorporating the Socialists into the parliamentary system. His scheme for accomplishing this involved the introduction of quasi-universal suffrage for the elections of 1913. This innovation, which was strongly desired by the Socialists, was to be offset by the cultivation of the Catholic masses, who would also be enfranchised by the reforms. One result of the continuing feud between the Vatican and secular Italy was that Catholics were forbidden by the Church to hold office or vote in elections. Alarmed by the growing strength of the Socialist Party, the Church relented and permitted Catholics to vote and serve, though the formation of a Catholic Party was not permitted until 1919. Catholics voted heavily in 1913 for those Liberal candidates who agreed to oppose divorce and favor religious schools and orders.

Like other continental Socialist parties in 1914, the PSI was pacifist and international in its outlook. It was consequently badly divided at the outbreak of the First World War over the issue of Italian participation. Mussolini supported the war effort, for which he was deprived of his editorship of *Avanti!* and expelled from the party. He started another paper and began the long road that led him to the leadership of the Fascist Party. The PSI suffered from nationalist and governmental attacks because of its stand on the war, and the resulting bitterness deepened the gulf between the left and right in Italy.

The PSI was again badly divided by the October revolution in Russia. Most Socialist leaders supported Lenin and favored cooperating with the newly formed Communist International. Many wished to duplicate Lenin's achievement in Italy. Discontent was widespread at the end of the war and reached its peak in 1919. Strikes swept the country, and it seemed that an Italian revolution was beginning. The Socialist leaders vacillated, talking about revolution yet stopping short of committing themselves to it. The mass fury spent itself in futility, and the opportunity passed.

The Socialists won a resounding victory at the elections of 1919, the first in which proportional representation was used. They won 156 seats and the Popular Party 100; these two parties together had an absolute majority. The Popular Party was a completely new structure representing largely the Catholic rank and file. Its formation was rendered possible by changes in the Vatican's attitude. While it reflected conservative interests in part, the Popular Party was also committed to reform. The Socialists and Populists together could have inaugurated the many reforms upon which they were agreed. But cooperation was rejected by both parties. With the Socialists in opposition, a series of weak governments dealt ineffectually with the mounting crisis of parliamentary democracy.

Conservative forces in Italy were deeply frightened by the strikes and violence of 1919, and the electoral results demonstrated the potential power of the masses at the polls. As the leftist wave subsided, Fascist attacks on the left—often carried out with the acquiescence of the police—became more violent and disruptive. The Fascists used force and intimidation to damage and finally destroy the Socialist organization. The Socialist Party, which had recently threatened to overthrow the government and which was the largest party in parliament, was forced to turn to an unsympathetic government for protection.

The Socialist movement was in fact in disarray. The Socialists themselves were divided into the Maximalist Socialist Party and the reformist Workers' Socialist Party. The former was badly split over the issue of joining the Comintern. While a clear majority of the Italian leaders favored joining, they would not accept the conditions imposed by the Russian leaders. The issue was resolved when a dissident group withdrew and formed the Italian Communist Party in 1921. Thus during the crucial months leading up to the formation of Mussolini's first government in 1922 and also between then and the destruction of the opposition parties, which was largely accomplished by 1925, the Socialist movement was split into three major parties.

The division undoubtedly contributed greatly to the triumph of fascism, and many Socialist leaders went into exile believing that the fragmentation of the left made possible Mussolini's seizure of power. Cooperation among the left parties improved in exile. Nenni emerged as leader of the left Socialists and Saragat the reformists, and the two wings reunited. In 1934 the PSI and the PCI reached agreement on a Unity of Action Pact under which they undertook to cooperate while maintaining separate identities. The Communists built up the best clandestine organization in Italy; they excelled in the underground and in some regions dominated the Resistance at the end of the war.

THE POSTWAR ERA

In 1946 the PSI (or PSIUP, as it was then called) emerged as the larger of the two parties in voting for the Constituent Assembly; but this was deceptive, for PCI members were more

43

militant and the Communists were stronger in local governments, unions, and cooperatives.[2]

In these elections to the Constituent Assembly in June 1946 the PSIUP received 21 percent of the vote to 19 percent for the PCI and 35 percent for the Christian Democrats. The dominance of the PSIUP ended at the end of 1946 when Saragat led most of the moderate Socialists out of the PSIUP and, after several fusions and changes of name, formed the Italian Social Democratic Party (PSDI). The secession reflected the old dualism between revolutionaries and reformists within the Socialist movement, exacerbated by the intensification of the Cold War and the prospects of a Communist or leftist seizure of power in Italy. The PSIUP took the name PSI and cemented its close relations with the PCI in an agreement for the two parties to present joint lists in the 1948 elections. Shortly after the Saragat secession, Nenni was replaced as party secretary by Lelio Basso, a theoretician of the radical wing of the party. An impressive intellectual with little organizational experience, Basso was quickly discredited by the gains of the PCI in the 1948 elections. Through greater discipline and a betrayal of the spirit if not the letter of the electoral agreement, the PCI was able to concentrate preference votes on the Communist candidates, with the result that they far outnumbered Socialists elected on the joint list.

A reformist group under Giuseppe Romita combined with a centrist group under Alberto Jacometti and Riccardo Lombardi (who had recently entered the PSI from the disintegrating Action Party) to oust Basso and install Jacometti as PSI national secretary. The new direction did not survive for long, for the times were not opportune for the moderates. The bitterness of Italian anticommunism, the entrance of the PSDI into the government with the Christian Democrats, and the administrative

---

2. Two useful introductions to postwar Italian politics are Giuseppe Mammarella, *Italy after Fascism* (Notre Dame, Notre Dame University Press, 1966), and Norman Kogan, *A Political History of Postwar Italy* (New York, Praeger, 1966).

inadequacies of the centrist leaders enabled the PSI left to return to power at the 1949 congress. The left was led by a triumvirate of Nenni, Basso, and Rodolfo Morandi, with Nenni as party secretary. Morandi, serving as director of organization, attempted to convert the party apparatus into an effective instrument of the leadership based on Leninist principles of democratic centralism and professionalism. By 1951 all opposition had been silenced or had left the party. Romita's group, for example, joined the PSDI. Basso, too, though of the left, declined in influence and the effective leader of the party appeared to be Morandi, with Nenni as a figurehead secretary.

In retrospect, it is obvious that the pro-Communist victory of Morandi and the party apparatus was not as complete as it had seemed. Nenni's long concern with party unity reasserted itself. He soon began to move cautiously away from unity of action with the Communists. Using the slogan of "A Socialist Alternative" the PSI ran a separate list of candidates in the election of 1953. The victory of the party apparatus remained incomplete also because the organization itself never became as highly structured and competent as was needed. Nevertheless, a legacy of Morandi was the most influential bureaucracy in the history of the party. If it did not become the omnipotent machine that the Communists seemed to possess, the apparatus did become a force in its own right in intraparty disputes.

Following the Twentieth Congress of the Soviet Communist Party and Soviet intervention in Hungary in 1956, the PSI began to exhibit the pattern of internal divisions apparent at the time of the field research in 1963. The changes in the party were facilitated by a number of factors. The shifting Italian political situation was of considerable importance. The PSDI reasserted its independence of the Christian Democrats, and Nenni and Saragat even held a "summit" conference in France that many hoped would lead to the reunification of the two parties. Some Christian Democrats also began to work for a new parliamentary majority based on the support of the PSI, the "opening to the left." Italian economic growth during this pe-

45

riod was remarkable, and the possibility of revolution receded. Events exterior to the party thus encouraged and reinforced the steps taken in an autonomist direction by Nenni.

Nenni moved very slowly. Aware of the fate of past PSI reformists who lost contact with the rank and file, he always stopped short of measures that would endanger his position. He did not allow the appeal of reunion with the Social Democrats or the lure of governmental position to interfere with what he deemed to be his prime task, that of bringing the party along with him. As a consequence, he retained his post and influence even during an especially delicate period when his faction did not always have a clear majority on the party's central committee and directorate.

Following the elections of 1958, in which the PSI gained some 750,000 votes over 1953, Nenni sought to differentiate the PSI even further from the Communists. He charged that the U.S.S.R. shared some of the blame for the failure of the summit conference, and the PSI began to compete openly with the PCI for members and to enroll ex-Communists. In August 1960 the PSI abstained from the vote of confidence on the Fanfani cabinet, thereby giving it a majority; and in 1961 the PSI supported several center-left (DC, PRI, PSDI, PSI) coalitions in communal administrations where the local situation was opportune, especially in some of the larger Italian cities. By 1963 Nenni was speaking of the possibility and desirability of Socialist participation in a center-left government dedicated to specific social and economic reforms. At the time of this field research, policy conflict in the party focused on that question, the "opening to the left" in Italian politics.

The opening to the left was required by parliamentary arithmetic. Table 2-1 indicates the increasing difficulty of putting together a coalition. Erosion of electoral support for the center parties that had governed Italy from 1948 through the end of the 1950s led to increasing governmental instability. The crisis atmosphere generated by fear of a leftist seizure of power provided the tension that led to the Christian Democratic Party's electoral strength and also encouraged collaboration among the center parties. As this coalition included the Social Democratic, Republican, and Liberal parties along with the Christian Democrats, the relaxation of tension and fear also led to a diminution in the enthusiasm for cooperation.

The laissez faire orientation of the Liberals and the interventionism of the Social Democratic and Republican parties in particular rendered a coalition virtually impossible. Yet a parliamentary majority was necessary for the support of the government. Although single-party governments supported on an ad hoc basis were able to survive from month to month, a long-term shift in the basis of the governing parties was needed.

One alternative was a government of the center-right, but this was not practicable. The Social Democrats and Republicans, and perhaps some Christian Democrats, would not accept it. Also, the right itself was somewhat in decline, especially the Monarchist groups, and such a coalition would thus run counter to electoral trends. Trends in the Vatican were also moving in opposite directions, toward increasing understanding and perhaps even accommodation with the forces of secularism and revolution. This meant that in practice the barrier between Christian Democratic and Socialist collaboration was lowered, though doctrinal accommodation was still far from achievable.

The personal ambitions of several Christian Democratic politicians, Amintore Fanfani and Aldo Moro in particular, were also tied closely to the opening to the left. The attempt consequently began under Fanfani, who had to court the PSI and the right wing of his own party simultaneously.

Those members of the PSI who favored autonomy from the PCI were known as autonomists; most of them also favored the opening to the left, though with varying degrees of enthusiasm. Those favoring close ties with the Communists were known as leftists. These were the labels given the minimalists and maximalists in 1963.

INTERNAL FACTIONS IN 1963

Factionalism in the PSI has a number of bases: personal differences among national leaders, historical memories and attach-

47

ments, ideological preferences, local issues and personalities, interests, and clientelistic relationships. Any short analysis inevitably distorts by oversimplification, and the following undoubtedly suggests greater rigidity and permanence than alignments in fact possess.[3]

In the spring of 1963 the major factional division within the PSI was between the autonomists and the leftists. The autonomists were the supporters of Nenni in his efforts toward accommodation with the center parties. They were not of a single mind or background. On the national level, many of the leaders were devoted personally and politically to Nenni and had been at his side in all the intraparty disputes since 1945. This was the case, for example, of Mauro Ferri, who in 1963 was the provincial secretary in Arezzo, a PSI deputy, and a member of the Central Committee of the party.

Riccardo Lombardi, on the other hand, led a subgroup of autonomists who supported Nenni, but from an independent position. In 1963 they favored the center-left experiment, but demanded far more concessions and guarantees than the Nenni supporters. They were also much more solicitous of the feelings and opinions of the left within the PSI. Emphasizing party unity and the need for a truly radical departure by the center-left government, this group of autonomists formed a bridge between the supporters of Nenni and the adherents of the left. Both of these subgroups contained individuals who had recently switched to the autonomist position and who maintained contacts with their former colleagues in other factions. The process of conversion to the autonomist position involved individuals as well as subgroups, and one tactic of the autonomists was to make it easy and rewarding for middle-echelon leftists to come over to the

3. For a short review of the divisions in the postwar Socialist movement see Raphael Zariski, "The Italian Socialist Party: A Case Study in Factional Conflict," *American Political Science Review*, 56 (1962), 372–90. Representative Italian interpretations include Giorgio Galli, *La Sinistra Italiana nel dopoguerra* (Bologna, Il Mulino, 1959); Antonio Landolfi, *Il Partito socialista oggi e domani* (Milano, Azione Comune, 1963); Rodolfo Morandi, *Il Partito e le classi, 1948–55* (Torino, Einaudi, 1961); Giuseppe Romita, *Panorama socialista* (Roma, Opere Nuove, 1956); Leo Valiani, *Gli Sviluppi ideologici del socialismo democratico in Italia* (Roma, Opere Nuove, 1962).

majority. This tactic was especially useful for leaders with a strong local following based either on an efficient organization, as in central or northern Italy, or on clientelistic arrangements, as is sometimes the case even among leftist parties in southern Italy.

The left faction in the party in 1963 was united under the leadership of Tullio Vecchietti. It included most of the former followers of Morandi, especially the party bureaucrats (but note that these bureaucrats were especially susceptible to the appeals of the majority with its offer of jobs, etc.). Another overlapping group was the *carristi* (a name given them because of their support of the Russian intervention in Hungary with tanks—*carri* in Italian) who were often pro-Communist out of sentiment as well as or in spite of personal interest. Finally, Basso and his followers had united with the left. An independent position was assumed by Sandro Pertini in the Central Committee. At the Milan Congress of March 1961, the last held before the 1963 elections, the autonomists received 55 percent of the votes, the left 35, Basso 7, and Pertini 1. When Basso united with the left it thus had 42 percent of the votes and the autonomists 55. Seats on the Central Committee were divided accordingly, with the autonomists receiving 45, the left 35, and Pertini 1. Seats on the party Directorate were likewise assigned proportionately, with 13 supporting Nenni and 8 the left.[4]

The significance of internal factions has varied greatly over the past twenty years. The *Statuto* of the party guarantees internal democracy but forbids organized factions. Despite this prohibition, the factions in 1963 in fact formed parties within the party. The autonomists, being the majority, controlled the official organs of the party, including the newspaper *Avanti!* and the theoretical review *Mondo Operaio;* the left issued the review *Mondo Nuovo,* published irregular newsheets, and had its own press agency in Rome. At all levels of the party organizational structure, the members of the two factions met

4. Partito Socialista Italiano, 34° *Congresso nazionale* (Milano, Biblioteca Socialista, 1961), pp. 264–70.

49

separately to decide policy and tactics prior to general meetings. Thus the leftist members of the PSI Directorate served as the leftist Directorate and the autonomists the autonomist Directorate, the leftist members of the Central Committee the Central Committee for the left, and so on. It was necessary for the minority faction at the local level to establish separate communications channels. Factions became so rigid that transfer from one to another was sometimes accompanied by a formal letter of resignation addressed to the national leader of the former faction.

The inflexibility of the factions in 1963 was recognized by both leaders and militants in the province of Arezzo. They complained that the factions had hardened into separate political parties cohabiting a single organization; as such, they inhibited rather than facilitated internal discussion and exchange of ideas. This was true on the national level as well. Factional leaders negotiated with one another more like chieftains of separate parties than colleagues in a common cause. The issues selected by top factional leaders became the focus of discussion at lower levels; local problems became subordinated to national considerations. Paradoxically, factions thus encouraged centralization despite the relative independence of strata within the party.

A POSTSCRIPT

This was the situation of the national party at the time of the field work in 1963. A postscript can add the wisdom and knowledge of hindsight to the reader's understanding of what was happening to the PSI at that time.

The party entered the electoral campaign of April 1963 badly divided over its future course. The autonomist majority campaigned for the center-left government, soft-pedaled differences between the PSI and the center parties, and in general defended the achievements of the center coalition that the PSI had supported by abstaining on votes of confidence. The left, on the other hand, opposed these policies but stopped short of open rebellion. The election was widely interpreted as a victory for the PCI, for its share of the vote rose from 22.7 to 25.3 percent of the total. The PSI dropped very slightly, from 14.2 to 13.8, and the Christian Democratic share fell sharply from 42.3 to 38.3 percent. (See Table 2-1)

It is probable that the internal unity of the PSI would have been threatened by its participation in the government regardless of the outcome of the election. However, these results strengthened the hand as well as the will of the PSI left; the autonomists retained control at the party congress of 1963 by a slender margin. In January 1964 Nenni accepted the post of vice-premier in the DC-PSDI-PSI coalition headed by former Christian Democratic party secretary Aldo Moro, and other Socialists accepted ministerial portfolios. Mauro Ferri of the Arezzo federation became PSI leader in the Chamber. Many PSI leftist deputies would not support the coalition, and party discipline was invoked. Twenty-five deputies and thirteen senators then resigned from the PSI, and most joined the new PSI-*Unità Popolare*, PSIUP. Vecchietti became its secretary-general and most leftist leaders followed him into the new party. The old autonomist majority then divided into less well-organized tendencies around Nenni and Lombardi.

Purged of its old left wing the PSI moved toward unity with the PSDI. Unity was facilitated when Saragat was elected president of the republic following the resignation of Segni for reasons of health. Saragat's elevation to the presidency made it easier to choose Nenni as leader of the unified party. Unity was achieved in October 1966.

Factions, however, remained; the old divisions re-established themselves. These factions seemed to lie along the right and center dimensions, with the historic left not in evidence. Whether the old maximalist-minimalist division was permanently overcome could not be determined. At the time of the field work in 1962–63 these events were still in the future.

4.

The Provincial Party, 1944–1963:
The Persistence of Factions

Italian socialism has suffered repeated divisions involving ideology, strategy, tactics, and personalities. We have just sketched these disputes on the national scene, paying particular attention to the period between 1944 and 1963. Here we will examine their reflection on a smaller stage, that of the provincial party, during the same period. Of particular importance are the local impact of national events and the transformation of national factions into competition between individuals and groups within the narrow and life-size dimensions of personal struggle for local party supremacy.

THE PROVINCIAL SETTING

In 1961 the province of Arezzo was forty-fifth among the Italian provinces in population but twenty-first in total area. Its population of 308,000 represented a decline of 25,000 (8 percent) from 1951.[1] The commune of Arezzo, however, grew by 7,000 to 75,000 while the thirty-eight other communes in the province declined by 32,000. Emigration has been heavy from mountainous regions where poor soil and a declining sharecropping system have greatly increased the attraction of the cities; the majority of emigrants have bypassed the urban centers of the province in favor of better opportunities in Florence and northern Italy. Although there has been little emigration from the plains, there has been a shift from agricultural to industrial employment. Between 1951 and 1961, for example, the number of people employed in industry in the commune of Arezzo (fig-

1. Data in this paragraph were provided by the communal administration from unpublished results of the 1961 census.

ures for the province were not available) increased by 146 percent. This was the largest percentage increase for any commune in Tuscany, the region in which Arezzo is located, or Umbria, the contiguous region; and in these two regions only the commune of Florence, with seven times the population of Arezzo, had a larger absolute increase.

The shift to industrial employment is not always accompanied by a change of residence. Many workers remain in their rural dwellings, commuting to work by public transportation, bicycles, scooters, and, increasingly, car pools. Several families often live together in rural compounds. Some members of each family, usually the older ones, cultivate the land while others work for wages in the urban centers of the commune. Most of the small farms do not require more than a part of an individual's or family's time; they provide inexpensive living quarters and insurance against unemployment. Actual removal to the city is expensive. Much of the improvement in area living standards stems not from increases in individual wage levels but from an increasing number of members of the family who are employed. With expenditures attuned to rural peasant standards and income derived from both agricultural and industrial sources, the average family has an income that is far more adequate than it would be in a strictly urban economy.

Thus many industrial workers in the province still live in rural areas and spend much of their time commuting. They probably retain more of a traditional outlook than those who have actually moved from familiar surroundings and relocated in a new and strange environment. The resulting survival of face-to-face relationships in an increasingly urban and industrial environment magnifies the importance of personal contacts and loyalties within the federation.

The pattern just described is related to another one that has been important to the party. This is the traditional socialism of much of the agricultural population. On the border of the former Papal States, an area of Italy with strong anticlerical traditions, the province is one in which political divisions correspond remarkably closely with socioeconomic ones. Until recently, its economy was dominated by large land holdings and the *mezzadria* (a sharecropping system), and many urban Aretini come from rural peasant backgrounds.[2] Whether a man is considered a *colono* (farmer or tenant farmer), *contadino* (peasant), or *mezzadro* (sharecropper), his reality is the same, and the social ascent from these to *piccolo proprietario* (small landowner) and *proprietario terriero* (large landowner) implies a similar progression from left to center to right in politics. Although few data are available, the relationship between social class and vote in the province, as in the rest of Italy, seems to be remarkably strong.

For the peasant, a vote for the left is simultaneously a vote for its program, a protest against the rural landholding system, and an affirmation of solidarity with his fellow contadini. Secretaries of PSI sections in small communities, for example, know how everyone in the community votes and are considerably upset when the electoral results deviate even slightly from those anticipated. The contadini are overwhelmingly of the left and continue this tradition when they become workers. For most, this is not a matter of ideology; it stems from tradition, the conventions of voting with one's group and against the powerful. Nonleftist parties simply are not viewed as parties of the lower classes. It is less clear why some voters prefer the PSI and others the PCI. Although no firm evidence is available, it is probable that tradition, education, and the politics of friends and relatives all enter into the choice. Federation leaders suggest that the PSI members are slightly better educated and well-to-do than PCI members. Both parties appeal to the lower classes; more than 80 percent of the PSI membership sample, for instance, were from the lower class.

The similarity of the clientele of the PCI and PSI, the emotional appeal of working-class unity, and the actual alternative alignments available in the province combine to encourage a PCI-PSI alliance in local politics. The center and right-wing parties are

2. Now being reformed out of existence, the traditional Italian *mezzadria* involved a legally sanctioned set of mutual rights and responsibilities for tenant and landlord. It was more than simply an economic arrangement, though far less than feudalism.

54

discounted as potential local allies and Social Democracy (i.e. the PSDI, or Saragat Socialists) was a dirty word in 1963. Hence discord between the PCI and PSI is viewed as divisive of working-class unity, no matter what one may think of communism in the abstract, the Soviet Union, or the opening to the left in national politics. A large arsenal of prejudices, rational arguments, and personal loyalties can be called into play against any reversal of the existing system of local alliances.

These sentiments seem to be held by the Communists as well. Although the PCI is the largest party in the province, it would not have an absolute majority without the PSI; indeed, if the PSI were to switch sides the PCI would be as isolated on the provincial level as it is on the national level. The PSI has consequently received greater consideration and rewards than is warranted by its membership or electoral strength alone. The Socialist Party has several able and attractive local leaders who can in some respects function more effectively than their Communist counterparts; but it is doubtful that PSI leaders would have been secretary of the Provincial Chamber of Labor and mayors of Arezzo and numerous other communes in 1963 if the PCI were unwilling to pay a considerable price for local PSI cooperation. The PSI leadership believes that its rank and file would oppose disruption of the cooperation between the two parties in local government and unions, and there was overwhelming agreement on this among the members interviewed. Of those who held an opinion on the statement "The PSI must maintain its friendship with the Communists in local administration regardless of what happens," some 70 percent agreed with it; and more than 80 percent agreed that "The PSI must maintain its friendship with the Communists in trade unions regardless of what happens."

There is consequently little opposition to continued cooperation between the PCI and PSI on the local level. Following the Second World War the two parties informally apportioned the province between them. The Communists received primary jurisdiction over the provincial administration, and the communal administrations were divided between them with the

55

PSI receiving primacy in the commune of Arezzo itself. Although these agreements were not always honored elsewhere in the province, the administration of the commune of Arezzo has remained Socialist-dominated and the provincial administration Communist.

Members of the PSI do not view cooperation between the two parties on the local level as incompatible with PSI collaboration with the Christian Democrats, Social Democrats, and Republicans in a national center-left coalition. This conflict between national and local politics is a source of friction within the PSI, with the left emphasizing closeness to the PCI in the unions and local government while the autonomists seek to reconcile national and local demands. Thus the study of the politics of the local PSI federation must take account of the historical ties between the PSI and the PCI in the province and the resulting constraints on the freedom of maneuver of PSI leaders.

THE FEDERATION IN HISTORICAL PERSPECTIVE

Reorganization, 1944–1946

A recurring theme in the immediate postwar politics of Tuscany, as in much of the rest of Italy, was the legacy of the Resistance. In the last year of war large numbers of citizens took part in the national opposition to the German occupation. Their motives undoubtedly varied greatly. Many of them technically were deserters from the Italian army, soldiers who had simply faded away when their units dissolved after the armistice. Others were young men seeking to escape forced labor in Germany. Others were political leaders, especially of the leftist parties, who in the confusion of the liberation saw a great opportunity for the reform of Italian society or for personal gain or for both. Many other Italians who were not directly involved in the Resistance as combatants supported it through either direct aid or moral encouragement. The actual Resistance, in short, was a mosaic of men, motives, and political ideologies.

The mountainous region around Arezzo sheltered several partisan bands, and the cities contained groups of anti-Fascists who were remarkably well organized and open in their activities in the final months of the war. The most important of these were Communist, Socialist, and Action Party sympathizers. In this traditionally leftist area these three parties had a great initial advantage and dominated provincial politics in the early postwar months. Distinctions between the three parties were rather vague below the elite level. Tradition as well as ideology dictated which of the parties an individual would support, and some informal division of the province seems to have been made by the Communists and Socialists to restrain or eliminate competition between the two working-class parties. In some areas of traditionally strong Socialist sympathies the Communists did not attempt to organize; despite their general strength in the province, even today they still lack sections in some local communities. The Socialists likewise did not immediately attempt to operate throughout the province. The Action Party suffered from the very beginning from a fatal malady—an absence of support from the rank and file. A highly intellectual party, it created no local sections. Although the first postwar mayor of Arezzo was from the Action Party, its influence seems not to have extended beyond the walls of the city itself. As a result, several small-town leftist intellectuals who might have chosen the Action Party were attracted to the PSI and PCI almost by default. Consequently, it was early apparent that the principal parties were to be the PCI, the PSI, and the DC, and these first two together had a clear majority in the province.

Relations between the PSI and PCI were excellent in the early postwar period; however, the PSI does not seem to have benefited greatly in any material way from these ties. Minutes of the early PSI executive committee meetings suggest a continual shortage of resources, with the party secretary virtually running the party on his personal energy alone. Debts went unpaid, salaries for organizers were nonexistent, even small expenditures had to be forgone for lack of funds. The party was reborn in a poor region among predominantly low-income groups, and the importance of the meager outside assistance that later materialized from the PCI can be understood in this light; possession of a typewriter and a regular income, no matter how small, assumed considerable importance.

The provincial party (federation) was reorganized in 1944 by a nucleus of pre-Fascist Socialists. Membership expanded quickly. In the shadow of what seemed a great social revolution in the making, large numbers of middle-class members were taken in. While many of these were to leave, especially following the split between the PSI and the PSDI, others remained to occupy important leadership positions. As the enthusiasm of the local population found an organizational outlet and as ex-Socialists drifted back from exile, military service, and prison, local sections sprang up throughout the province.

Much of the energy of the party was devoted to the absorption of the numerous new members who flooded the party. The delicate problem of ex-Fascists arose early. Having been a member of the Fascist Party during the twenty years of the Mussolini regime was not itself a bar to membership, because for many people at least nominal membership was necessary in order to hold a job or attend school. Only peasants and sharecroppers were generally able to avoid all compromise. The more important question concerned what kind of Fascist one had been. A special committee, which seems to have taken its job quite seriously, was established to screen new members. The application for membership forms are still in the party archives and provide valuable data on the characteristics of members of the period. For most potential members it was sufficient to have the backing of an active member. But any member could challenge the new ones; the party itself retains Fascist Party membership lists that were "liberated" along with the office furniture of the party headquarters, and the local Committee of National Liberation kept files on the major Fascist collaborators.

Party archives contain numerous case histories of applicants and members charged with various pro-Fascist activities and the hearings on their cases. The special committee seems to have done its job well. The records show a careful attention to evidence and to due process in providing opportunities for the individual charged to defend himself. The great efforts necessary to screen and absorb new members, to expand the organizational structure into the outlying regions of the province, and to organize the local and national electoral campaigns during 1944-46 seem to have absorbed the energies of the party. Neither internal policy debates nor competition for leadership positions during these early years is reflected in materials available in the party archives.

The first secretary of the federation after the war was Enzo Verdelli, a social reformer of middle-class origins. He had received considerable publicity as an anti-Fascist as a result of an incident in which he lodged a vigorous personal protest against the refusal of Fascist authorities to permit a proper burial service for a relative of his. A dedicated and selfless organizer who took on great responsibilities, Verdelli devoted himself to the PSI with little material reward. It was consequently a great shock to the party when he resigned as PSI secretary in December 1946 to become the local leader of the groups that were to form the PSDI. Six of the fourteen other members of the executive committee of the PSI resigned with him, four of them joining the dissident PSDI. Having served as adult adviser to the Socialist Youth Federation of the province, Verdelli was also able to induce that organization to follow him out of the party. His departure hurt the PSI greatly.

As no other members of the executive committee of the party were both qualified and willing to succeed him, a young lawyer of middle-class background, Socialist mayor of a small commune in the province, was brought into the provincial capital as provisional secretary. This was Mauro Ferri. He has remained, whether in office or in opposition, the most important single individual in the federation since that time. Ferri became acting secretary in December 1946 and was made regular secretary the following month.

Factional Struggle, 1947-1949

The eighteen months that followed Ferri's appointment as secretary were very important ones, for they included the de facto emergence of factions within the party and that rare thing in well-run organizations, the overthrow of the leadership. These months also illustrate the importance of the dual cultural environment of a political party, the fact that it must operate simultaneously within the context of the local political culture, within which its recruiting and other activities are carried out, and also within the limits set by the national party organization.

While local issues may or may not always reflect national disputes, the structure of local conflict in the PSI in the postwar period has replicated national lines of cleavages. Local considerations and leaders were surrogates for the national ones. This will be seen in the succession of factions at the local level. The internal dynamics of a tightly organized party seem to force divisions at all levels into a framework in which issues are defined at the top. On examination, however, these divisions turn out to reflect far more than the ideological and policy differences of national leaders: they also involve the personalities and ambitions of local politicians. National and local considerations intertwine, with now the one, now the other, assuming greater importance as the basis of local party divisions. Hence factionalism is a recurring problem in the PSI, and it is faced with a recurring dilemma: How can such a party maintain sufficient unity to present a coherent face to the public and opposition parties without repressing and stifling internal democracy? The first crisis of this type within the PSI arose in 1947 following the schism of the future members of the PSDI.

As was recounted in the previous chapter, the departure in 1946 of the more moderate elements of the PSI left the organization largely in the hands of those who favored a closer working relationship with the PCI. It also provided the psychological impetus for a pact of common action between the PSI and PCI to avoid the isolation portended by the increasingly anti-Communist stance assumed by the center parties. This led on the national level to a hastily formulated electoral agreement between the two leftist parties that provided for a single list of candidates and a unified campaign. The local PSI leadership under Ferri supported the national Nenni-Basso line and cooperated with the PCI on the local level in the elections of April 18, 1948.

Paradoxically, the Saragat schism had led to the enrollment of many members of the Action Party in the PSI. Although many of these were moderates closer in policy preferences to Saragat than to Basso and Nenni, some chose the PSI in preference to the Saragat group out of fear that the latter would be ineffectual. The Action Party had from the beginning suffered from the absence of a mass base, and its leaders feared the same fate for the Saragat group. They therefore entered the PSI in order to seek to influence it in a more moderate direction. Most former Action Party adherents in the PSI consequently found themselves out of sympathy with the electoral alliance with the PCI. But as new members in a party that had recently and justifiably become quite concerned about internal unity, they accepted the alliance, but without enthusiasm and with reservations uttered aloud at party meetings. The provincial PSI has suffered from the low average level of political skills of its predominantly lower-class membership and these weaknesses were accentuated by the departure of many middle-class members with the Ver-delli (Saragat) group. The infusion of skills by the ex-Action Party members was therefore greatly welcomed and the new members were well treated. Several of them were quickly named to important positions within the party; the former secretary of the provincial Action Party, Aldo Ducci, became a member of the PSI provincial executive committee.

When the electoral agreement with the PCI resulted in that party's surpassing the PSI in parliamentary representation, there was a strong rank and file reaction against the PSI leadership. On the national level, Basso was replaced as secretary and a former leader of the Action Party, Riccardo Lombardi, was almost elected in his place. On the provincial level, the post-election convention held in June 1948 replaced Ferri as provincial secretary with Ducci. The new secretary had been a member of the PSI for only a little more than a year. He was not well known to the rank and file and had no experience in running a mass party. His background as secretary of the elite Action Party had not prepared him for this task and, by his own admission, he tried to accomplish too much too quickly. Aided largely by ex-Action Party members, he set out systematically to eliminate the old leadership from all positions of importance in the party. Ferri and others were excluded from the new executive committee, which henceforth was to represent only the PSI right wing; the opposition was included only on the larger directing committee. But Ducci was never able to gain the loyalty of the rank and file, and his efforts at reform were repeatedly undercut by the opposition, which had found new bases of influence.

An examination of these bases is instructive of the ways in which alternative channels of communication not under the control of the formal leadership are useful to an opposition. Ferri was an extremely resourceful leader and used varied weapons in his struggle with Ducci. One of the most important of these was the support of the local Communist Party. Having been leader of the PSI in its alliance with the PCI, Ferri was able to call on his former collaborators for aid in his struggle to regain control of the PSI. It is difficult to assess the importance of this aid, for evaluations vary greatly. Thus in interviews Ferri emphasized that there was little direct aid, though he acknowledged that the indirect assistance was considerable. As present leader of the autonomist wing of the party he undoubtedly finds memories of dependence on the Communists distasteful. Ducci, on the other hand, would not be expected to underestimate the role of the PCI in his overthrow and indeed did not in interviews. The following brief analysis will concentrate on those aspects of the struggle about which there was little disagreement in the interviews and party records.

When Ducci took over as secretary, he removed all opposition leaders from positions over which he had control. These included the party bureaucracy and some positions in other organizations to which the party had the right of appointment. The trade unions, for example, especially the Chamber of Labor, were controlled jointly by the PSI and PCI. Unlike in 1963,

Communists and Socialists in 1948 were involved in a struggle for dominance in the local Chamber of Labor. A Socialist holding an important position in the Chamber in 1963 needed to be able to work well with the Communists, hence at the time of this research the Chamber of Labor was an excellent place for leaders of the PSI left. In 1948, however, this was not the case, due to the antagonism between Socialists and Communists in the Chamber and also due to the unwillingness of Ducci and the right to support the former Socialist leaders in any organization. The Chamber thus did not provide a refuge for the opposition in 1948.

Instead, other organizations close to the PCI were more important. Ferri had been a mayor before becoming party secretary; he also held a law degree. Consequently, he was an obvious choice to head the League of Communes, an organization established to aid the inexperienced leftists who took over many of the communal administrations in the province in the immediate postwar period. This position enabled Ferri to travel throughout the province, maintaining ties with Socialist leaders, rank and file, and governmental officials; and, most importantly, it provided him with an income while devoting himself full-time to political activity. Had it been necessary to earn a living as a lawyer, he would have had much less time to devote to his counterattack. Other Communist, or Communist-dominated, organizations such as the Peace Partisans and the cooperative societies provided employment, support, and communication channels for other provincial leaders of the PSI left. The PCI also aided the PSI opposition with access to printing presses and automobiles.

The PSI minority thus was able to reach the same milieu as the majority by means of structures independent of the PSI. These structures also provided jobs, and earning a living is a crucial problem for party officials. In the province of Arezzo, being a party functionary even at an extremely low salary may be a desirable position for an ambitious worker, and it sometimes also has appeal for middle-class teachers and professional men. But in such an area of strong political prejudices and low labor mobility a party bureaucrat who loses his position has difficulties in finding another. Job security consequently becomes an important consideration in internal factional struggles; the support the Communists were able to provide in 1948 in the League of Communes and cooperatives and in 1963 in the Chamber of Labor strengthens the left within the PSI while it increases its dependence on the PCI. Further chapters will indicate the importance to the PSI left of closeness to the Communists.

The Morandi Era

The combination of the mistakes of Ducci, the astuteness of Ferri, and the radical temper of the times enabled Ferri's faction to recapture control of the local party at the provincial congress of late 1949. This congress was preliminary to the national congress that inaugurated the era of "democratic centralism" in the PSI under the organizational leadership of Morandi. Ducci and several of his associates were to be the first victims of the new line in the party: in July 1950 he and several others were expelled from the party for "indiscipline." These exmembers of the Action Party then joined the Popular Unity Party composed of ex-Socialists plus some Action Party members who had not entered the PSI. Although they had several well-known figures on the national level this group never achieved any significant electoral success. Ducci and his local associates returned to the PSI at the end of 1957; many ex-Action Party members, however, remained in the PSI continuously from 1947 until 1963. Bitter memories of the earlier period do not seem to affect personal relations today, for the lineup of factions has altered considerably.

Ferri was provincial secretary during the early years of the Morandi era. During this period the principle of internal democracy was replaced by that of democratic centralism, which permits free discussion until a decision is reached, after which everyone is obligated to fall into line with the official policy. In practice this meant that delegates to conventions at all levels were presented with only the resolutions and electoral lists approved by the leadership. Under the democratic system each national faction presented a resolution and list of candidates at each level of the party and the delegates chose between them. As before, under Morandi the basic policy line of the party was decided at the national level, but only one set of resolutions was sent down to be voted on at the level of the section and federation. Similarly, a single list of candidates for party offices was drawn up by the party leadership and accepted by the members. Competition remained, of course, but it took the form of personal maneuvering and bargaining for choice party positions among the leadership, with the role of the rank and file being limited to approving their decisions. In short, during the Morandi era personal factions replaced the organized factions of previous and later periods.

Under Morandi the bureaucracy of the party was considerably strengthened. While this accentuated the politicization of the staff, it did not originate it. The employees of the party were traditionally among the most active policy makers and were expected to take an active part in internal party political struggles as lieutenants of the majority leader. Although it was sometimes suggested in interviews that the bureaucrats should be neutral vis-à-vis internal factions, or at least that the minority be represented among them, these views were not widely shared in the party and were not held by any of the local party functionaries.

What was new under the Morandi system was the increased size and status of the bureaucracy. From being merely one of the better placed contestants in the internal party struggle, the full-time worker became a cog in a well-entrenched machine. For the very things that made him more effective made him also more difficult to displace: these included his greater political skill, his increased employment security, and, especially, his ability to devote full time to the exercise of power. Coupled with a sheer increase in the number of paid workers, these advantages greatly enhanced the influence of the national party, especially in the better organized federations; and as long as the party elite maintained its outward unity it was difficult for an opposition to make headway, whether at the national or provincial levels. The breakdown of democratic centralism on the local level came only with its shattering at the top.

The immediate effects of the strengthening of the bureaucracy seem to have been salutary for the local PSI. The party archives reveal increased activity on the part of the party staff in the the 1950s. Reports increased in length and attention to detail, membership drives were carefully organized and executed, and statistical services were given great attention. An effort was made to emulate not only the centralization and discipline of the PCI but also its success in involving the membership in party activities. PSI functionaries attended local section meetings, organized rallies in cooperation with the PCI, began a local party newspaper (which failed for financial reasons), and sought ways of increasing party revenues and putting them on a more regular and dependable basis.

One of these financial arrangements involved a common program with the PCI and—strangely—the Christian Democrats under which individuals who were required to pay large sums to the local authorities in a turnover tax based upon goods brought into and sold in the province would instead pay a percentage of this tax into the party coffers. This widespread practice became a public scandal in the 1950's; numerous important people in all three of the parties were involved, but only one from each party was convicted and sentenced to several months in jail. It was ironic that a dedicated and idealistic PSI leader of humble origins should have been the one to take the blame for what Senator Plunkett of Tammany Hall would undoubtedly have considered "honest graft" which, furthermore, was collected for the party and not for personal gain.

Morandi and his followers are sometimes credited with giving the PSI a Stalinist discipline, of suppressing the least display of internal opposition, and of blindly following the lead of their Communist allies. The truth undoubtedly is that the PSI never achieved anything like the monolithic structure attributed to the PCI, either in the province under discussion or elsewhere. But compared with the informality and organizational languor traditional in Italian socialism, the bureaucratic leaders' ambition was revolutionary indeed. They tried to establish an organizational structure capable of providing professionally competent bureaucratic leaders for the mobilization of the membership for the achievement of party aims. That they were never able to match the Communists in this does not detract from their achievement in improving the organizational effectiveness of the PSI.

It is less certain that the improved organization was worth the cost to the party. The membership largely remained stable during most of the period. Enthusiasm was no longer essential to keep the party functioning and the PSI lost much of the dynamism that internal tension had provided. A tolerable level of internal tension is useful in maintaining interest. Where the leaders make all the decisions without an outward show of dissension, the rank and file are soon conscious of their own lack of influence; when the leaders must court the votes of the rank and file, participation has an increased significance, even if the alternatives are still posed from above.

Following the return of Ferri to the position of provincial secretary, the full-time staff of the party was enlarged (in 1963 there were the full-time equivalents of four party functionaries at federation headquarters, compared with a reputed fifteen doing comparable work in the local PCI, but there were also several Socialists in local government who devoted much of their time to PSI affairs), and responsibilities were divided among them. Rossi was brought in from the Chamber of Labor as Ferri's chief assistant. A young ex-Christian Democrat, Olinto Dini, was brought in to head the Youth Movement, which was deprived of its autonomy and made an administrative subdivision of the federation.

The party was confronted with problems of the bureaucratization of leadership. As one of the local leaders put it: "For a long time we lived and worked for the Socialist revolution—nothing else mattered. Then we began to raise our families and to face serious personal financial problems. It became obvious that the revolution might not come this year or next year, or

the following year. Meanwhile we had to live." The bureaucratization of the party under Morandi consequently cor-
responded with the need to provide some measure of financial
security for party workers, and it was during this period that
salaries were regularized and several benefits provided for functionaries. Henceforth even on the local level party work began
to take on the characteristics of a career, where formerly most
of the work was done by volunteers or part-time workers.

Having enjoyed a secure base in the federation of Arezzo,
Ferri was able to secure election to the Chamber of Deputies
in 1953. This was an important year for the party, as the center
parties enacted an electoral law that would have given any
coalition of parties two-thirds of the seats if it received more
than 50 percent of the vote. This provision greatly upset the
left, and it encouraged renewed enthusiasm within the party
and a vast increase in membership and militancy.

The party *statuto* rendered holding the position of deputy
incompatible with other party positions, and Ferri was forced
to step down as provincial secretary. He was replaced by his
associate, Rossi, who had come to the headquarters of the
federation as a functionary with Ferri in 1947, had gone into
opposition with him, and had returned to office at the Chamber
of Labor as secretary of the Sharecroppers' Federation in 1949.
He became Ferri's assistant in the federation the following year,
and his successor in 1953. An idealistic "man of the masses," son
of a Socialist skilled worker, Rossi possessed a strong emotional
attachment to the working class and the ideal of social revolution.
He had always been on the left of the party, and becoming
provincial secretary at the time of intense emotional dissatisfaction within the left reinforced his maximalist tendencies. Personal conviction and trade union experiences left him strongly
committed to working-class unity, and it is not surprising that
he remained on the left of the party when factions re-emerged
in 1957, despite his close ties with Ferri, the autonomist leader.

Rossi remained secretary until placed in the minority in 1958
except for a short period when he was temporarily replaced by
Cornelio Vinay. A former leader of the Action Party in the

Valle d'Aosta who had joined the PSI in 1947, Vinay came to Arezzo in 1950 as a school teacher and immediately became active in the local PSI, quickly acquiring a leadership position. He was elected mayor of the commune in 1956 and was re-elected in 1961. Because of his personal qualities and doctrinal position, Vinay played an important role in the federation. Although he was a former member of the Action Party, he did not always take the more conservative position in party disputes. He supported Lombardi in 1949, Basso in 1956, and Nenni after that. But he felt himself closer to the position of Lombardi, and hence was one of those who supported Nenni while remaining fearful of the effects on the party of too close contacts with the Social Democrats.

The Re-emergence of Factions

The divisions of the national party that emerged at the end of 1956 were gradually duplicated in the federation. Ferri became the leader of the majority autonomist faction and a strong supporter of Nenni. Ducci, the exsecretary who had rejoined the party in 1957, was a supporter of Ferri and in general favored even closer ties with the center parties. Vinay was also a supporter of Ferri, but as mayor he was able to use his appointive powers and other influence to build up an independent personal clientelistic following within the PSI. It was also of considerable utility for him as mayor to remain on good terms with the left in the province, both within and without the PSI. Consequently, Vinay served as a personal and doctrinal bridge between the two factions.

The revival of factions gave rise to the problem of what to do with party functionaries who were no longer in sympathy with the policies favored by a majority within the party. This is a dilemma in any organization, but it assumes more significant dimensions within a political party for several reasons. In the first place, party work requires a measure of commitment and involvement greater than that in many voluntary organizations. A party worker cannot function effectively at higher levels as merely an impartial bureaucrat; issues and personal relations are too sensitive to permit it. In addition, the staff is too small to permit extensive manipulation of positions with each change of administration as can sometimes be done in governmental or other large organizations. Furthermore, in a factional situation, the party secretary is almost certain to be a factional leader as well, and cannot function effectively if some of his principal collaborators are also his chief competitors for party leadership. The alternative that all factions be represented in the bureaucracy thus does not seem workable.

On the other hand, there are few party bureaucrats and they are highly visible. Bureaucrats holding minority viewpoints undoubtedly have a substantial following in the party, and the party can dismiss them only at the risk of alienating their supporters. In the case of the left opposition in the PSI in 1963 this might have meant giving up an unknown portion of the membership to the PCI, as Rossi was thought to have a large following among union members and, more generally, among those who had joined the party during his years as party secretary. Furthermore, the party in general and the majority leadership in particular were indebted to Rossi for his years of sacrifice and service to the party.

A solution was worked out at the provincial level that worked well for a period of four years. In 1958, Ferri replaced Rossi as provincial secretary. The explanation given by Ferri was that the party generally wanted to alleviate the expected disruption resulting from the revival of factions by having a well-known figure as party secretary during troubled times. Concomitantly, the prohibition on a deputy's being a provincial secretary was rescinded. Rossi returned to the Chamber of Labor as head of the Sharecroppers' Federation and member of the Chamber's executive board. The other principal leader of the left was Dini, who had been youth leader a decade before. He was secretary of the provincial Chamber of Labor, one of the few Socialists to hold this position in all of Italy. The provincial Sharecroppers' Federation had generally been more Socialist than Communist, but industrialization and the decline of traditional landholding practices had contributed to a severe diminution of

70

the ranks of sharecroppers and a radicalization of those who remained. The two leaders of the left, consequently, were given positions where their factional allegiances would make their work easier, and also where they would not be involved in the daily administration of the party itself. In this exchange, Ghelli, who had been director of the Sharecroppers' Federation and an autonomist, came to the PSI federation headquarters in 1958 as vice-secretary; and Borri, another autonomist organizer for the Sharecroppers' Federation, came to the PSI headquarters as a functionary in 1961.

This arrangement seems to have permitted continued cooperation between the two factions in a satisfactory manner until the 1963 elections. At that time Dini, who had been placed on the list for the Chamber as the prearranged candidate of the left, resigned from the left faction and joined the autonomists. His defection resulted in increased bitterness, and personal relations between him and his leftist colleagues deteriorated badly. He was said to have been slated to become provincial secretary in place of Ferri, who anticipated that the forthcoming national party congress would reinstate the regulation against a deputy holding a federation position; but the timing of Dini's switch (immediately after having been named to the left's spot on the electoral list) and the bad feelings it caused made such a move impolitic, at least immediately.

Dini's quandary illustrates the plight of the professional bureaucrat-politician. Unlike middle-class intellectuals with other professions to which they can turn, he had only his party career. His future seemed to lie in the long run with the party majority. If relations continued to deteriorate between the PSI and the PCI, he could be deprived of his position at the Chamber of Labor. As a member of the minority faction, his own party could not utilize him in a leadership position; as a part of the majority, on the other hand, he was offered a key position. But because of the passions raised by the factional divisions within the federation, his usefulness to both sides was temporarily destroyed.

5.

The Provincial Party:
Organization

According to the party Statuto, the basic units of organization are the NAS (Nuclei Aziendali Socialiste—Socialist Plant Cells), which are similar to the plant cells of the Communist Party, and the *sezioni* (sections), which are the basic territorial units. The sections are the basic organizational units possessing genuine autonomy, but they may in turn be broken up into *nuclei territoriali* (area subdivisions) when the membership is large or widely dispersed.

The sections, the basic units dealing directly with the membership, elect delegates to the provincial congress. It selects a *comitato direttivo* (directing committee) representative of all the factions and geographical areas within the federation. This body in turn chooses a *comitato esecutivo* (executive committee) to supervise day-to-day operations. The functionaries of the party, who are also members of the executive committee, handle administrative matters under the direction of the provincial secretary, the single most important federation official.

The federation is the provincial organization. A coordinating committee composed of all the secretaries of section within the commune serves as coordinating body for the commune; sometimes the executive committees of all sections in a commune meet together. However, the federation itself assumes this role for the commune of Arezzo. These coordinating committees are especially concerned with budgets and communal political problems.

There are several other organizations that must be included in any analysis of the PSI. Two of these deal with special groups —the Federazione giovanile socialista (Socialist Youth Federation) and the Movimento femminile socialista (Women's Socialist Movement). In addition, the relations between the party and related organizations such as trade unions and cooperatives are important to an understanding of the internal life of the local Socialist federation. Each of these organizational units will be discussed in turn.

THE LOCAL SECTION

The most important local unit in the PSI is the section. Based primarily on place of residence, it groups men and women of all social classes and occupational groups. There were ninety-nine sections of the PSI in the province in 1963. There is usually at least one section for each commune, and larger communes may have several. The chief commune of the province of Arezzo is unusually large, containing sparsely populated mountainous regions and several densely populated *frazioni,* or villages.

It contained sixteen local sections; one was in the city of Arezzo itself, thirteen were in the scattered villages of the fertile valleys that meet at the city, and two were in remote mountainous regions. These sections varied greatly in size, as Table 5-1 indicates. The single large section in the provincial capital

Table 5-1. Sections in the Commune of Arezzo

Section	*Size*	*Section*	*Size*
Arezzo	497	Pratantico	54
Ceciliano	30	Ponte Buriano	52
Chiassa Superiore	62	Palazzo del Pero	32
Frassineto	42	Quarata	29
Giovi	44	Rassinata	40
Matto	85	Rigutino	118
Olmo	23	Ruscello	45
Patrignone	29	S. Firmina	112

was the original and for a long time the only section in the commune, and it remains the only one in the city of Arezzo. It is in fact run directly by the provincial leadership with its secretary usually being a member of the inner circle, the only

73

secretary of section included among the top leaders. Despite its size, federation leaders have resisted its division into several sections.

Although this study includes interviews with leaders from throughout the province, the rank and file interviews are all from these sixteen sections in the chief commune of the province. These sections contain all the social categories found in the federation as a whole—workers, peasants, middle-class professionals, housewives, students, retired persons, etc.—but no claim is made that the proportions reflect the composition of the provincial party.

Before beginning the discussion of the section, the role of the NAS should be clarified. When an individual joins the PSI he is enrolled in a territorial section *and* in the appropriate NAS. There are NAS for employees of particular plants or firms, communal and provincial employees, railway workers, several categories of state employees, and even party employees. Independent farmers, sharecroppers, self-employed, students, housewives, etc. would not belong to an NAS. Designed to compete with the cells of the Communist Party, the NAS never became the basic organizational unit of the PSI. While they performed a useful role in strengthening the PSI in industry by encouraging Socialists to unite, the NAS are of decreasing importance within the PSI today (as are the plant cells in the PCI too). In the sample of members in the commune of Arezzo, only 101 were eligible for membership in any NAS, and of these only 23 were aware that there was an NAS organized where they worked.

Socialist Party activity centers on the section. In 1963 the 99 sections of the province of Arezzo had a total membership of 5,887. While the average membership per section was thus 60, the range was from 7 to 497. The largest section was that of Arezzo itself, with 497 members. Except where special considerations prevail, the birth and death of a section depend both upon the number of members and potential members available *and* on the availability of adequate leadership. Only a few sections have existed without interruption since 1946; they contain today, however, the bulk of the total membership. As a general

74

rule, more rather than fewer sections are desirable, and new sections are formed wherever and whenever there are people and leaders for them. An existing section may dissolve due to lack of interest, internal wrangling (either over party issues or personalities), the relocation of a key individual, or general emigration from the area. This latter has been of considerable importance in several communities of the province; it is often the more energetic and ambitious, the ones most likely to take an interest in party affairs, who desert declining agricultural areas for the growing manufacturing towns of the province and elsewhere.

Although the number of members with cars and motor scooters is increasing rapidly, communications remain poor. Many outlying regions have bad roads and no public transportation. Moreover, many members work long hours and spend considerable time commuting from rural homes to industrial employment. It is consequently difficult to get members to travel any distance for section meetings, and wherever possible separate sections are established. The availability of a convenient section makes recruitment easier. The pattern seems to be that a few militants from an existing section establish a new one, which then grows steadily until most of the Socialist sympathizers in the area are enrolled. The affairs of the section, however, are likely to remain in the hands of the original members, perhaps with a few new young militants. But if the young members are both able and militant they will find wider opportunities elsewhere and hence are unlikely to remain active there for long. The affairs of the smaller sections, consequently, are likely to remain in the hands of a few key people; if they lose interest or move, marginal members will fade away and the section will disintegrate.

One method of achieving the aims of the small, intimate section without excessive organizational problems is the establishment of territorial nuclei. If a larger section contains a number of members in several different communities (these communities may consist only of a concentration of houses along a road, the tenants of a single estate, or the self-identification that has grown up around a rural church), these may be given explicit recognition in the organization of the section by having separate meetings there for local members and designating a neighbor to recruit and raise money. The secretary of the section retains responsibility for the nucleus, attends its meetings, and handles its records; he is its sole link with the larger section. Whether to organize a new section or a territorial nucleus is decided on an ad hoc basis depending on the personnel and leadership available. If members are numerous, *and* a competent (or even merely reliable) leader can be found among them, a separate section is preferred.

The importance of the secretary of the section is apparent. It is he who either does the work of the party himself or recruits others to do it. Among groups of limited education and few political skills, the ability to keep simple records adequately is rare; the initiative and drive necessary to organize meetings and rallies, conduct membership campaigns, and squeeze dues and contributions out of an impoverished membership are likewise uncommon. But instrumental abilities alone are insufficient: the secretary of the section is the single individual who best symbolizes the party in the community and it is important that his image be a good one. In a setting as intimate as most Italian villages, it is essential that the secretary be known as a man of integrity. He is usually a local man, a worker (sharecroppers seem to lack the time, desire, or skills to act as secretaries), dedicated, and not too mobile. This position seldom leads to higher office; the virtues of a good secretary of section are a good reputation, the respect of comrades, reliability, and at least a minimum amount of organizational ability. Maturity is more important than promise and steadiness than brilliance.

Party life at the local level is only in part associated with formal meetings. Informal conversation in the early evening or on Sunday morning probably is more important as a means of communication than section meetings, and the membership can be reached quickly by word of mouth when the occasion arises. Consequently, the statutory requirement that monthly section meetings be held is universally evaded. Most secretaries stated that "three or four" section meetings per year were held, and it is likely that the actual average would be considerably fewer.

Only 56 percent of the members in the sample had attended even one meeting during the previous year. This figure reflects section activity only in part. Some sections have a record of high attendance and more frequent section meetings; in others, party matters are dealt with by the secretary and other activists on an informal basis, with the rank and file being consulted informally. Each section elects a directing committee and a smaller executive committee that includes the more active members (and sometimes others who the leaders would like to encourage to be more active), and these bodies meet as the occasion demands. Most of the executive committee meetings are open to other members of the section, and attendance at these *esecutivi allargati* (enlarged executive committee meetings) was used as a measure of interest in party matters.

The life of the section follows a well-established and predictable rhythm. Like much of Italian organizational life, it slows almost to a standstill in the summer, with sharecroppers busy in the fields and others on vacation or pretending to be. There are bursts of activity in the fall and spring, interrupted by holidays and special occasions during which politics is largely ignored.

Activity reaches its peak at two times—during public elections and just prior to party congresses. During elections party workers are busy with the campaign. Activity is also intense prior to party congresses, for it is ultimately the local sections that determine factional strength in the federation and hence in the national party. The PSI internal electoral sequence is as follows: There is a series of meetings, precongressional assemblies, beginning with the local section, at which representatives to higher organs are elected. Before the local assemblies are held, the national factional leaders meet and issue resolutions concerning party policies. These resolutions set the terms of the debate for all of the other meetings.

The local section debates the resolutions of the national leaders and each member present votes for the resolution of his choice. In practice there is little debate between members of the local section, for the meeting is largely taken up with the presentations of the factional viewpoints by representatives of the federation. Party leaders spend much of their time visiting local section meetings, and precongressional assemblies are especially important. At these meetings Ferri and Rossi or their substitutes present their respective motions and discuss them. In the rare case that no one from outside is available to present a resolution, it is read by the secretary of the section or someone else. For no one to appear to present the resolution in person, however, makes a bad impression on the rank and file; and in most cases there is a personal confrontation between experienced leaders representing opposing viewpoints. As the two leaders deliver roughly the same address to all the sections, and as they are close party colleagues, the debate is seldom very profound or stimulating.

Nevertheless, the membership is usually treated to a competent presentation of alternative orientations in a small meeting at which they can ask questions. The voting that follows is therefore not completely uninformed. But the nature and terms of the debate are established at the national level. The factions consequently function as parties within the party to unite various levels and give coherence to internal debate. Yet, like other Italian political parties, the factions are highly centralized. Innovation and creativity from below are not ruled out, but this system hardly encourages local initiative in policy making and the formulation of alternatives.

The members present then vote for local delegates who represent one or the other factional viewpoint. These delegates are in practice selected by the federation leaders, another device to ensure that debate at the congress stays within the limits established by the national faction's leaders. The voting power of the section at the federation's congress is determined by its number of card-holding members, and section delegates are divided among the factions according to the proportion of votes received. It is consequently to the advantage of a section to have as many members as possible, whether they attend or not; and a section leader who can deliver votes acquires a claim on his factional leader, whether it be for a party or governmental job or merely his personal esteem. The importance of neither of these forms of reward should be underestimated. While several secretaries hold jobs that probably required some political influence, others seemingly have never benefited from their position beyond the personal satisfaction of serving a worthwhile cause.

The most important activities of the section are those connected with party and public elections. Other meetings consider a wide variety of matters, especially in sections outside of the commune of Arezzo. One type that is well attended deals with strictly local political questions such as, for example, a new village pump, road, public facilities for washing clothes, or, in more advanced communities, the construction, staffing, and curriculum of a new technical school. These issues, unrelated to larger questions of policy, are often the major component of the party's local image; and passions can become as inflamed over the location of the parish pump as over the nationalization of the means of production. Party meetings dealing with these questions often attract nonmembers, and, especially if accompanied by a rally or demonstration, they are viewed as excellent recruiting devices.

A second type of meeting that attracts considerable attention is one at which an important party figure speaks. In the smaller sections this is nearly always someone from federation headquarters. An appearance by Ferri, Mayor Vinay, or other party leaders is an important local event. The visiting of section meetings is an important ingredient of leadership in the province; it is in this way that an individual acquires visibility and a wide circle of acquaintances; and even such well-established leaders as Ferri spend several evenings a week visiting sections. It is not unusual for the section in Arezzo itself to have distinguished visitors from parliament or the national office of the party. As Arezzo's section is also the personal vehicle of the majority leadership, meetings can be timed to take advantage of visitors and events. It is the ordinary section meeting at which no one important speaks, no exciting local issues are raised, and no elections are involved that is poorly attended. These are the meetings that are supposed to be devoted to matters of internal party

79

organization and education. These matters seem to be boring to all but the militants: the function of education seems most effectively performed by visiting dignitaries who both have something to say and the ability to hold an audience.

The housekeeping functions are largely left to the enlarged executive committee—that is, to the executive committee plus whoever else wishes to attend. In this way the bother of a large meeting is avoided, yet no one is denied the privilege of participation. Since few of the sections have regular meeting halls, facilities for a full meeting are difficult to arrange. Contacts are excellent even without frequent meetings, due to the daily interaction of what is still a society of face-to-face relationships. The restricted number of section meetings should consequently not be viewed as indicative of total party activity. Meetings are held when there is a reason to hold them, and not otherwise.

It is difficult to evaluate the effectiveness of the local sections in the province. Measured against the formal party norm, the level of achievement is not very high. Although local party leaders all stated that the PCI was not nearly as successful organizationally as it once had been, most felt that the PSI did not measure up to its Communist rival. The PSI undoubtedly does not achieve the full potential of the local section as an educational and agitational tool. But the PSI membership probably differs from that of the PCI in its resistance to overly onerous discipline. As a party the PSI is more complaisant and casual than the PCI; at least this seems to be the case of the militants: the average member probably differs little from his PCI counterpart. Despite attempts at democratic centralism, the PSI is less authoritarian, more easy going than its rival. The pace of section life in the province under study is well attuned to the environment in which the party operates.

THE FEDERATION ORGANS

The federation organs are several bodies that decrease in actual influence as they increase in size and formal authority. Most important is the provincial secretary, followed by the functionaries (they are not recognized as a special category by the Statuto), the executive committee, the directing committee, and the party congress.

The party secretary is, in the formal sense, the most important individual in the provincial party. Whether he does in fact dominate the party depends largely on his relationships with the members of the executive committee. The size of this body is not fixed; it had thirteen members in 1963, all of whom resided in the commune of Arezzo. It meets at least weekly to discuss issues and problems facing the party. Most committee members are in even closer contact with one another, for the party secretary and functionaries are members, and the other members drop by the federation headquarters several times a week to keep informed.

It was surprising that in 1963 all members of the executive committee resided in the commune of Arezzo, though several originally were from other communes or even from other provinces. As conflict within organizations frequently results from tensions between the center and periphery, the possibility that the concentration of the inner circle in Arezzo itself might result from, or lead to, conflicts of that nature was investigated carefully. Extensive probing of leader respondents from both categories suggested that center-periphery tensions within the party are not of great importance. The most important party conflict is between factions. The concentration of the members of the executive committee in Arezzo arose out of chance and convenience, for it is difficult for leaders from other communes to find the time necessary to attend all its meetings. This is not to say that leaders from the periphery had no opportunity for advancement within the party; several leading figures, including both Ferri and Rossi, were from other communes. But the time-consuming nature of party activity and the concentration of political life in the provincial capital make residence there advisable.

The executive committee at the time of the study consisted of the secretary and the three party functionaries; the two leaders of the left minority, Rossi and Dini; the mayor of the commune, Vinay; the former secretary and the future mayor,

Ducci; the latter's chief collaborator and secretary of the section of Arezzo, Gnocchi; and four "promising" younger people. It included all five persons who had served as provincial secretary between 1946 and 1963, a national deputy, and four current communal or provincial *assessori* (elected members of the respective representative councils). As will be analyzed in a later chapter, it was also a well-educated and largely middle-class body.

The executive committee generally operated in a collegial manner. The two chief factions within the party were represented; some matters were decided along factional lines, with the majority of course always formally getting its way. Ferri dominated the executive committee, as he could rely on the votes of the party functionaries and, usually, the support also of other majority leaders. Vinay, however, had a certain independence stemming from his position as mayor and his extensive clientele within the party. Ducci and Gnocchi likewise exercised considerable independence of judgment. The four leftists on the committee were not always in agreement; Rossi, as the acknowledged spokesman for the minority, probably had more influence than votes in the committee.

Against this background of personalities and cliques, Ferri was the skillful organizer, the center of activity—planning, arguing, wheeling, dealing, and healing. He had a remarkable ability to be all things to all people, to work with individuals with whom he competed, to inspire personal affection and loyalty among the rank and file, to accept what he could not change. As provincial leader, he relied upon a combination of instrumental ability, skill in maneuvering his collaborators, and a pragmatic flexibility that some of his detractors called opportunism. It was probably his pragmatism that contributed most to his success. He was an agnostic among true believers, an organizer among ideologues. As party secretary he was more influential than others had been in the post, for when Rossi and Vinay were secretaries, Ferri was still, as deputy, the leading figure in the local party. The post of secretary is what one can make of it, and in the hands of someone like Ferri it is indeed a key position. But the core of decision makers in the party is still to be found in the executive committee, whether acting as a collegial body or dominated by a single strong personality.

The directing committee is selected by the congress to serve as the interim representative body of the provincial party between congresses. In 1963 it consisted of forty-three members chosen, in reality, by the top factional leaders. Each faction is allotted roughly the same proportion of members as votes received in the precongressional assemblies. Thus the actual lists are determined by the factional leaders and the number of seats by the precongressional assemblies of the sections. The provincial congress merely registers the decisions made by the leadership. Although the majority could, if it chose, exclude the minority from the executive committee, the directing committee must represent all viewpoints. The directing committee is thus more representative of the structure of the party; 37 percent of its members live outside the commune and 33 percent of them represent the minority. It is also more representative in terms of social class and education, though it too is an elite body. Members of the executive committee are selected from the directing committee; most other members of the latter are local barons in outlying communes who are also likely to be assessors or mayors. Moreover, they are possessed of considerable independence as a result of their local ascendency, so the relationship between the inner core and the rest of the elite has a bargaining aspect that cannot be overlooked.

The provincial party is indeed a stratarchy, with federation leaders closely controlling the sections in the commune of Arezzo but working largely through local satraps in dealing with the sections of the other communes of the province. There are sharp discontinuities in the hierarchical structure, and larger communes can achieve a great deal of independence of the federation. If the federation leaders in Arezzo are largely free from close control by lower-echelon leaders, it is equally true that these latter are likewise subject to little supervision.

Although the formal autonomy of the local section serves to protect the local potentate, perhaps of more importance is the party's dependence on local leaders for its existence. The PSI does not have a large bureaucracy under the direct orders of the party leaders, nor does it possess a communications network equal to that of the PCI. Instead, it must rely on its militants to keep the wheels turning, and it has little to offer them apart from gratitude. The party benefits as much from having a member serve as mayor or assessor as the member does from his party affiliation. The local image of the party rests on those members who are highly visible. These men are crucial, and members of the directing committee who hold public office are not easily intimidated by threats from federation headquarters. It is true that they can be ousted from the party for violating party doctrine, but this is a last resort. Despite the formal disciplinary powers of the party, expulsion for heresy or malfeasance is rare.

At the level of local office holding the model of the disciplined membership party is inadequate. While the party controls nominations at all levels it is often quite restricted in its. actual alternatives. An incumbent is difficult to dump without loss of face for the party as a whole. And lacking numerous paid officials the party is forced to rely upon volunteers for all its activities in most communes of the province. These volunteers are able to maintain almost as much independence as they wish vis-à-vis the provincial leadership. They must be convinced and pacified; they cannot be commanded. As long as they avoid open heresy and can maintain the support of a majority in their sections they are relatively independent.

The necessity of a majority, however, results in a curious paradox: internal democracy reduces local independence by increasing the importance of factions. These factions link together the various levels that are formally largely autonomous, for the internal factional struggle permits dissidents to appeal to factional leaders at the higher level. Federation leaders thus enter into sectional politics. This need not be the case, however, and it is rare in smaller sections, which tend to vote one way or the other with little real competition. But the larger and more important sections, the ones that provide a strong basis for party influence, are much more likely to have an organized opposition.

84

The organizational structure is still stratarchical, but most units of the party exhibit a similar basic internal cleavage along factional lines.

The provincial congress is held shortly before the national congress. As has been pointed out above, the national leaders of the factions meet several weeks before the national congress and compose the resolutions that they will present to the congress. These resolutions then become the basis of discussion at all the congresses held preparatory to the national one. Even at the level of the section, factional leaders present the alternative motions and members choose between them. The delegates from the section to the provincial congress have the confidence of their faction leaders and are in fact selected by them. The congress is organized by faction, which means that the majority on the executive committee make the major decisions in consultation with the minority. Each presents its resolution, speeches are made, and the delegates vote; however, the outcome is predetermined by the voting at precongressional assemblies. This is indeed a form of democratic centralism, but a two-party democratic centralism. For the national factional leaders must recognize the provincial ones, and these in turn dominate everything that occurs on the provincial level. Ultimate choice remains with the membership: the dominant faction must still secure a majority of the delegates to the provincial congress, which means a majority of the votes at the section level. There is little indication that these local elections are anything but genuine. The only case of serious irregularities in a party election that was uncovered in the research occurred at the height of the struggle between the left and right in 1948, when the left packed a precongressional assembly in one of the large sections, prevented the representative of the right from presenting his motion, and declared the left motion accepted by acclamation. The report to the executive committee on the incident was found in the archives. There was no indication that this was anything but a rare and isolated incident.

That is not to say that there are no significant techniques for reinforcing the position of the majority at the precongressional assemblies. One factor in its favor is its advantage in manpower. As has been pointed out, the party bureaucrats are not impartial; they represent the majority and work to further the interests of that majority in party elections. The majority thus has more leaders to send to section meetings. It is difficult for minority resolutions to be presented at all the precongressional assemblies throughout the province because of the sheer effort involved for a small group of people in a short space of time. It is in this connection that the left benefits greatly from its strength in the Chamber of Labor, for these paid personnel can serve the left in much the same way that the party functionaries serve the autonomist majority.

Party democracy in the provincial PSI is thus an imperfect democracy when measured against models that emphasize the vigorous involvement of the rank and file in the formulation and execution of policy. Decisions as to alternatives are largely formulated at the national level, and local factional leaders present and defend these alternative policies. The member has in reality only the choice between the alternatives thus formulated. But there is a choice and it is usually a meaningful one. If this is less than most Socialists would desire, it is more than could be expected were not the alternatives greatly simplified in this fashion. For considering the level of interest, education, knowledge, and sense of efficacy of the rank and file within the party, such a system probably involves the optimal amount of membership participation compatible with organizational survival.

AUXILIARY AND ASSOCIATED ORGANIZATIONS

There are several organizations that are connected with the PSI in one way or another. In order to round out this panorama of the organization of the party, several of the more relevant ones require brief mention.

The Socialist Youth Federation is the party's structure for youth from fourteen to twenty-five. The PSI has had repeated difficulties with its youth organization. In the immediate postwar period the organization was independent of the party and it caused the elder body great embarrassment by joining the dissidents. In the days of democratic centralism within the PSI, the youth movement was denied any independent status and was administered as a department of the parent hierarchy. Its return to an independent status was a result of the growing concern for democracy within the PSI. It is housed in the federation office in Arezzo with its own secretary (who is also one of the paid functionaries of the PSI federation), news bulletin, organizational structure, sections, and congress. Its principal value to the federation at the time of the study was as a recruiting ground of potential leaders. It did not play an autonomous role in the power structure of the party; rather, it functioned effectively if not spectacularly as an auxiliary of the party.

The same could not be said of the Socialist Women's Movement. While not even on paper granted the autonomy and importance of the youth organization, the women's organization was nonexistent in the province. With thirty-nine women forming 13 percent of the sample, only two of the militants were women, while seventeen of the women were nominal members only. Except for several outstanding individuals (including one of the two women secretaries of sections in all the PSI), women play a very small role in either the activities or the concerns of the party. The woman secretary of the section referred to above was also the nominal head of the provincial women's organization. But she was opposed to treating women separately from men in the party and in a familiar fashion killed the women's movement through inactivity.

The organizations for youth and for women are the only auxiliary bodies directly connected with the party. Of those outside the party that deserve mention, the most important today are the unions and the cooperatives.

The PSI supports the Confederazione Generale Italiana del Lavoro (CGIL), in which it plays a decidedly secondary role to the PCI. PSI members are required to belong to the CGIL if they are in employment covered by the union. In practice this means that PSI members cannot properly belong to any union not affiliated with the CGIL. Although no respondents admitted it, a few were thought by PSI leaders to support the Unione Italiana del Lavoro (UIL). In the sample of members in the commune, only 48 percent claimed membership in the CGIL, though even a conservative estimate would suggest that at least 70 percent of the members were eligible for one or another CGIL affiliate. The connection with the CGIL is important for the PSI in the province, for it enables Socialist leaders to penetrate into the working-class milieu that would otherwise be abandoned to the Communists. While the portion of CGIL members who are Socialists is undeniably small, the party can make and sustain a claim to be a truly working-class party in a way in which other non-Communist parties cannot. Relations with the CGIL are consequently very important to the party.

In the province of Arezzo there are two particular labor bodies that receive most of the party's attention, the Chamber of Labor and the Sharecroppers' Federation. This latter body has traditionally been a Socialist preserve. No membership figures are available; Socialists are not necessarily in a majority, but Socialist leaders have been active in the Sharecroppers' Federation since the early postwar years. The organization is said to have been much more strongly Socialist in the past than at present. As previously noted, this is attributed to the general decline in the number of sharecroppers in the province due to industrialization and the growing radicalization of the remainder. Nevertheless, the federation remains an important base for the PSI left.

The Chamber of Labor is likewise an important base for the left. There is one principal Chamber in each province, with branches in the most important communes. Although most Chambers in Italy have a Communist secretary, in this province the PSI provided the secretary in 1963. A Socialist leader thus presides over the most important labor center that services all of the affiliates of the CGIL. The communications network that this provides throughout the province gives the PSI left a secure base and an excellent source of contacts with most of its supporters among the membership. The Chamber was thus an important body in the structure of the PSI in the province.

88

The cooperatives in the past were an important source of influence for the PSI. In cooperation with the PCI, and sometimes with other parties, the Socialists helped to establish and expand cooperatives in the province; but the cooperatives no longer play an important role within the PSI. The same is true of several other organizations, especially those in which there was a joint effort with the PCI, as in the Peace Partisans and the local People's Centers (Case del Popolo) and other recreation activities. Cooperation between the PSI and the PCI in these organizations ended before 1962.

The final structure to be mentioned fits somewhat uneasily among the others as an associated organization of the PSI: that is local government. But the communal and provincial governments perform roles similar to the unions and other nonpublic bodies. For governmental position is a source of influence within the party, and the communications network it provides makes its wielders independent of the party in several important respects. As noted, the mayor of the commune was a Socialist who used this position to build up a clientelistic following within the party by the use of patronage. As mayor and an acknowledged vote-getter, moreover, his counsel carried increased weight within the party. The same is true of those who were communal or provincial assessors. These positions provided them with additional income (part of which was returned to the party), increased visibility, and greater prestige. All these factors could be converted into influence within the party.

From the above sketch of party-related structures, it is clear that any study of influence and communications that ignores the informal or nonparty networks and sources of influence within the party would miss an important dimension. The benefits of these other channels of power are only potential, however; they still must be converted into *party* influence.

The provincial level of the party structure consists of the secretary of the federation, the party functionaries, the executive committee, the directing committee, and the party congress. The day-to-day management of party affairs is in the hands of the first three of these. The most important element of party structure for the rank and file member is the local section. The secretary of the section provides the link between the local and provincial levels. The majority faction dominates the official party structure, though the minority is represented on the executive and directing committees. Nonparty structures, especially the Chamber of Labor, provide the principal communications channel for the minority.

6.

The Provincial Party:
An Introduction to the Actors

The PSI is a classic Socialist mass party. The formal conception of membership permits little ambiguity: a member is one who buys a party card, is entered on the party rolls, and hence enjoys the full rights of membership. A sharp distinction is made between members and nonmembers, and all members are formally equal in having the right and duty to participate:

> Every party member has the right and duty of participating in the meetings of the organization of which he is a member, of expressing his own opinion on subjects discussed, of making up his own mind, of taking part in all decisions and elections that take place. Every party member participates at the meetings and activities of the party wherever he might be.
> All comrades may be elected to all party organs, and may be named to positions and assignments outside the party. The only limitation is that in order to be elected to the Central Committee it is necessary to have been a member for at least five years, to the Directing Committee of the Federation at least two years; to the Directing Committee of the Section, except for those newly established, at least one year.[1]

Membership is open to men and women who have reached the age of eighteen and who accept the duties deriving from party membership. Inscription is individual; a written application stating the occupation and the present and past political

1. PSI, *Statuto*, 1957 text, article 2.

orientation of the applicant must be submitted to the directing committee of the section where the applicant lives. If the applicant has been an official in other parties, is a former PSI member who has been expelled, or has left the PSI and joined other parties, the application must be cleared through the directing committee of the federation. Most applicants are known personally by the section leaders, and approval is usually a formality. However, the party archives contain dozens of cases of individuals who were denied admission largely because of past political activities, or who were expelled because of fraudulent applications.

Many of these stem from the immediate postwar period. While mere membership in the Fascist Party was no bar to joining the PSI, enthusiastic supporters of the regime were not admitted. Many of the early postwar members admitted Fascist Party membership. The party devoted great efforts to being fair, and the archives contain numerous dossiers on the more contentious, and often pathetic, cases. Special reports, available in the archives, that covered their activities in the Fascist period as well as their instrumental abilities were prepared by party agencies on leaders and potential leaders. In recent years few people seem to be denied membership; however, the screening is more than nominal and some "undesirables" have been rejected or expelled. There is no hint of restrictiveness being applied for reasons of internal party partisanship.

Membership is further restricted to those willing to accept the *Statuto* of the party, which states that the "PSI, founded on the theory of scientific socialism and on the experiences of the class struggle in Italy and in all the countries of the world, guides the struggle for the emancipation of the worker and the construction of a Socialist society." [2] Members must accept its aims and its methods; their "philosophical and religious conceptions" are irrelevant. Rejection or expulsion for violating party principles seem to be rare, though frequently discussed. More important has been expulsion for disciplinary reasons, often deriving from internal factional disputes and the necessity of im-

2. Ibid., article 1.

posing majority decisions on a recalcitrant minority. However, expulsion of the representatives of a large minority is difficult; and this power, though real, is exercised with prudence.

The above discussion has served to demonstrate that in a formal sense membership is not open to all. Some minimal doctrinal affinities with the aims and methods of the party are required of all applicants. While the PSI is by no means an elite party, membership can be and sometimes is denied to applicants with questionable political pasts or personal integrity. All members included in the sample had at least taken the trouble, or someone had taken the trouble for them, to apply for admission and to buy a card for at least the year 1962.[3] Unlike American parties, where "membership" is in most cases a matter of identification, or British parties, with indirect membership and associated organizations, objective PSI membership is well defined. As demonstrated below, however, the subjective significance of membership is not as clear; some members approach the "ideal" Socialist in activity on behalf of the party while others have done nothing beyond the initial gesture of taking (or receiving) a party card.

THE MEASUREMENT OF PARTY PARTICIPATION

In devising a measure of participation in the party, two considerations were foremost: the measure should leave as little to the discretion of the coder as possible (should be mechanical) and should reflect conventional notions of levels of participation. The interview schedules contained questions concerning attendance at section meetings, precongressional assemblies, open section executive committee meetings, and rallies; questions about activities performed for the party, such as recruiting voters and members, distributing party literature, serving as a collection

3. Interviews were taken in March and April of 1963. Although there are special membership drives, applications are accepted throughout the year, and the final lists are not compiled until the end of the year. When the sampling process started in February the authoritative 1962 party lists were still being submitted to the federation. The 1962 party lists consequently include those who were members at the beginning of 1963, that is, who had bought a 1962 card. For details on the sampling see Appendix I.

93

agent, driver, poll watcher, or party representative; and questions about formal positions held in the party. To be classified as a *militant* the respondent must have attended at least one section meeting or precongressional assembly plus two other activities. A *participant* must have attended at least one section meeting or the precongressional assembly plus one other activity, or have attended both a meeting and the assembly. A *marginal* member is one who exhibited at least some interest in the party as evidenced by having attended a rally or meeting, or by having performed one of the activities on behalf of the party. The *nominal* member is a member in name only: he had done nothing more than take out a party card. The 301 membership interviews divided as shown in Table 6-1.

Table 6-1. Members: Level of Participation

	N	%
Nominal members	43	14
Marginal members	102	34
Participant members	79	26
Militant members	74	25
Unable to participate	3	1
	301	100

These categories combine ease of measurement with conventional usage. The militants, for example, are militants in the party's understanding of the term; the participants are likewise a familiar party category. In evaluating the data that follow it should be remembered that the "membership" sample includes only the rank and file. All members who at the time of the field work held posts at the federation level or who served as secretaries of sections were considered leaders.

All but one of these fifty-nine leaders were interviewed. These interviews were unstructured and are not comparable with the membership interviews on many variables, especially those of a scalar nature. They will be referred to where appropriate to facilitate a comparison between members and leaders. The single leader not interviewed was a member of the directing committee who resided outside the commune and was no longer active in the provincial party. The leadership census, then, consisted of the secretaries of all the sections from which the membership sample was drawn and all the members of the directing committee (which included the executive committee).

SOME GENERAL CORRELATES OF PARTICIPATION

Social Stratification

Perhaps the most striking characteristic of the party is its working-class nature. The membership is 83 percent working-class and only 17 percent middle-class. And of these middle-class members 82 percent are lower middle-class, while only 18 percent are what Italians refer to as middle-class (mainly business and professional people) and none are upper middle-class (very well to do but without titles of nobility or great inherited wealth).[4] By contrast 36 percent of the leaders are from the middle class. (See Table 6-2.)

Table 6-2. Social Class of Members and Leaders (in percent)

	Members	Leaders
Lower-lower	55	43
Upper-lower	28	21
Lower-middle	14	31
Middle	3	5
	100	100
N	298	58

There are important class differences in levels of membership participation, also, as is shown by Table 6-3. Differences in so-

4. This usage reflects the common Italian classification of upper, upper-middle, middle, lower-middle, and lower, with the lower class being divided into upper-lower (skilled workers) and lower-lower (unskilled workers). See the usage of Sartori, et al., *Il Parlamento Italiano*, pp. 168ff. Social class was determined by the coder on the basis of education and occupation. Because of the greater rigidity of the Italian class system, this method is less subject to error than it would be, for example, in the United States. A question probing self-defined social class produced an interesting assortment of answers that, unfortunately, are not useful in the context of this chapter.

Table 6-3. Members: Levels of Participation, by Social Class (in percent)

	Lower-lower	Upper-lower	Lower-middle	Middle
Nominal	20	9	7	—
Marginal	31	42	29	25
Participant	26	24	29	50
Militant	23	25	35	25
	100	100	100	100
N	161	79	42	8

cial class are even more striking within the leadership. The two higher leadership groups include most of the middle-class members. (See Table 6-4.) Section leaders are very similar to the

Table 6-4. Leadership and Social Class (in percent)

	Executive Committee and Higher	Directing Committee Only	Secretary of Section Only
Lower-lower	35	39	62
Upper-lower	18	18	31
Lower-middle	35	36	7
Middle	12	7	0
	100	100	100
(N = 56)	13	29	14

rank and file in social class. The directing committee and executive committee, on the other hand, contain many middle-class members. The lower-class members of the executive committee are party or union functionaries who now perhaps merit inclusion at least in the lower middle class. Party activity has led to upward mobility for several of the leaders. If education alone had been chosen as a measure of social class the advantages of the middle-class leaders would have been even clearer, for those with higher education are clearly favored in the top party positions. (See Table 6-5.)

Table 6-5. Leadership and Education (in percent)

	Executive Committee and Higher	Directing Committee Only	Secretary of Section Only
Less than five years	0	0	14
Five years	23	34	57
Six to twelve years	23	55	29
Some university	54	11	0
	100	100	100
(N = 56)	13	29	14

Sex Differences

Some 13 percent of the members are women. While several individual women play important roles in the party, most women are courtesy members enrolled by their husbands or fathers. They devote almost no time to party affairs. The striking difference in the levels of participation of men and women is indicated by Table 6-6. Women are heavily concentrated in

Table 6-6. Participation, by Sex (in percent)

	Men	Women
Nominal	10	44
Marginal	33	41
Participant	29	10
Militant	28	5
	100	100
(N = 298)	259	39

the lower two categories. Few women in this province take an interest in public life and party affairs. Party leaders are aware of the situation but make little effort to interest women in politics. On the other hand, there is no outward opposition to women participating and achieving leadership positions in the party. But few have done so.

97

Occupation and Residence

It is physically easier for some people to participate than others. Proximity to population centers, time spent commuting, active neighbors—all of these factors help account for the heavier participation rates of the more urban members. Table 6-7 shows these differences. The three residence categories employed are (1) within the walls of the old town, (2) in the urban periphery, and (3) outside this urban area. Unlike American cities, there are no "city limits"; the commune is the administrative unit and it includes the countryside as well as built-up areas. The city walls no longer separate the urban from nonurban areas because the city spilled over these walls generations ago and is still expanding. Members who live outside the major urban center do not necessarily live in rural areas. Most in fact live in settlements ranging from a few houses up to a small town with several thousand inhabitants. These settlements, called *frazioni,* have no separate administrative existence; however, as pointed out in an earlier chapter, they form an important basis of party organization, and some have a well-developed communal sense of identity. Many of their inhabitants work elsewhere, especially in the chief urban center of the commune, hence frazioni cannot all be viewed as agricultural settlements; indeed, several of the larger frazioni have some industrial activity. Consequently, the strict antithesis of town and country suggested by Table 6-7 is misleading. Very few people

Table 6-7. Participation, by Place of Residence (in percent)

	Urban	Urban-Periphery	Frazioni
Nominal	7	3	19
Marginal	32	37	33
Participant	36	31	25
Militant	25	29	23
	100	100	100
(N = 295)	28	62	205

live in isolated houses anywhere in the commune. Only those in mountainous regions find it extremely difficult to participate because of transportation. For these, attendance at meetings sometimes means a walk of several miles on a dark and rocky trail. For most, however, it is not physically difficult to attend section meetings or rallies, and factors other than urban versus rural residence must be introduced to account for differences. Much of the difference in participation levels by residence can be accounted for by occupational differences. Members with agricultural occupations are much less likely to participate than those with industrial jobs. The dynamics of political competence will be explored more fully in the next chapter. At present I will merely note the difficulty that people in isolated occupations and of low intellectual skills have in articulating political demands and engaging in sustained cooperative effort. As a consequence, there are significant differences in the participation levels of those in agricultural and industrial employment. (See Table 6-8.)

Table 6-8. Participation, by Occupation (in percent)

	Agri. Worker	Nonagri. Worker	White- Collar	Bus. & Prof.	Other
Nominal	18	14	8	6	17
Marginal	38	32	20	38	42
Participant	28	26	24	31	22
Militant	16	28	48	25	19
	100	100	100	100	100
N	61	132	25	16	58

Similar dynamics seem to be at work among the party elite. There are few agricultural workers among the leaders; only two are presently primarily engaged in farming. Several have worked as farmers, some for many years, others only for a short time in their youth; but few have remained on the land when other opportunities presented themselves. For many, these opportunities were connected with party work, and the party is obviously a means of rapid upward mobility. For others, rewards came only after long service for the party. For still others, party work has seemingly not facilitated mobility. But what is of most in-

terest is the large portion of the elite that was never involved
with the land or with industrial employment; for whom party
work brings no social benefits; and, especially in such a status-
conscious society, for whom party work may involve considerable social losses. These business and professional middle-class
leaders are indeed a crucial group. (See Table 6-9.) Thus levels

Table 6-9. Leaders' Principal Nonpublic Occupations, by
Level of Highest Current Position Held (in
percent)

	Exe. Comm.	Directing Comm.	Sec'y. of Section
Professional	27	12	0
Business	0	19	0
Nonagricultural worker	27	38	77
Agricultural workers	13	4	8
No principal nonpolitical occupation	33	27	15
	100	100	100

of participation of the membership and levels of leadership positions reflect the social stratification of the province. As will be
seen later, this seems to be more closely associated with the educational system and levels of political competence than with any
conscious effort to restrict the advancement of those of lower
status.

Age and Seniority

There are important differences in the participation rates
of various age groups in the party, with members above age
thirty participating more than the others. A few young members
are very active, and these provide some of the present and potential leaders of the party. But despite encouragement of
youth in the party, many young people are preoccupied with
nonpolitical activities. They do not form a coherent and articulate group within the local party. The youth organization is
headed by competent and committed leaders, but they function

as a subgroup of the official elite without a sharply delineated identity. (See Table 6-10.) It is difficult to know whether this

Table 6-10.   Age and Participation (in percent)

	20–29	30–39	40–49	50–59	60+
Nominal	28	15	12	10	8
Marginal	40	32	31	34	36
Participant	15	24	34	31	27
Militant	17	29	23	25	29
	100	100	100	100	100
N	53	74	68	55	48

age differential in participation is due to age alone or to the political environment that was characteristic of the province when the present members reached maturity, for the most active group is of the generation that grew up under fascism and reached maturity during the Second World War. Many took part in the Resistance and helped reorganize the party in 1944; they have been very active throughout the party's history. As Table 6-11 demonstrates, this forty to forty-nine age group has

Table 6-11.   Age of Leadership (in percent)

Age	Position Held in Party in 1963		
	Exec. Comm.	Directing Comm.	Sec'y. of Section
20–29	15	20	7
30–39	15	27	26
40–49	62	43	47
50–59	8	3	13
60+	0	7	7
	100	100	100
N	13	30	15

provided a remarkable portion of the party elite, especially at the highest level.

The relationship between length of party membership and level of participation is striking. (See Table 6-12.) Considering

Table 6-12. Participation and Length of Membership (in percent)

	Pre-1950	1950–59	1960–62
Nominal	7	10	27
Marginal	30	38	41
Participant	23	35	24
Militant	40	17	8
	100	100	100
N	115	92	74

the connection in conventional wisdom between the fresh spirit of the new member and the waning enthusiasm of the old, the seniority of the militants is especially surprising; members of long standing comprise a high portion of the militants and participants. The more senior members have had more time to perform the activities that add up to militancy, but this still doesn't account for the high percentage of recent members who have done *nothing*.

It is possible that the intense politicization of the period when the respondent joined the party is largely responsible for his greater militancy. Highly politicized periods serve to excite and motivate potential members; people are attracted to the party who might not have become involved in more normal times. Although many of these drop away, the personal or public issues that served to activate the political interests of some members may also serve to motivate them to participate more fully than those who join in less dramatic times. Thus those who joined in the immediate postliberation era who remained in the party are still very active; more recent recruits tend to rank lower on the participation scale. There is no present way to determine whether this intensity hypothesis is valid or not. The higher rate of participation of those who joined in 1953, the year of a bitterly contested election, tends to support it, but the number of cases is too small to permit statistical testing.

There is also considerable evidence for the "proportion of the individual's life spent as a member" hypothesis.[5] Those who have been members longer are more dedicated and more active. Finally there is a third hypothesis that requires examination: over time the less active members drop out of the party, leaving only the more committed among the senior members. In a truly voluntary organization such as this party it is certainly true that the less involved tend to drop out. However, many members of long standing seem never to have become deeply involved, yet they remain in the party. Why? There is no ready explanation, apart from the psychological characteristics of the individual. Those who remain members and do not participate highly tend to possess the characteristics of low participants in general—low knowledge and sense of competence combined with low-status occupations.

Unfortunately, I do not have interviews with exmembers of the party and know little about their characteristics. I therefore cannot choose among the several hypotheses. I can merely note that the proportion of high participants increases among those of longer membership in the party.

Even more striking is the proportion of the leaders who have long service in the party. The federation is dominated by people who joined the PSI before 1948. If those who were under twenty-one in 1948 and those who came to the PSI through the merger of other parties are eliminated, the percentage that joined before 1948 is even higher. (See Table 6-13.) The PSI

Table 6-13. Length of Service of Leaders (in percent)

	All Leaders	Restricted Group
Before 1948	51	68
During and after 1948	49	32
	100	100

in the province is dominated by the generation that came of age during the Second World War.

5. See Angus Campbell, Philip E. Converse, Warren E. Miller, and Donald E. Stokes, *The American Voter* (New York, Wiley, 1960), pp. 327–31.

It has been demonstrated that there are great differences among the members and leaders in level of participation by education, sex, residence, occupation, age, and length of membership. These differences are not randomly distributed; instead they tend to be cumulative. Those who rank high on one measure tend also to rank high on others. Now the relationship between several of these variables and the factional divisions within the party will be examined.

FACTIONALISM AND THE ACTORS

Previous chapters have pointed out the persistence of well-defined internal divisions within the PSI. In 1963 these factions were the leftists and the autonomists. The analysis that follows will examine some important differences between those who identified with these factions, as well as between these and those who identified with neither. Wherever possible, the breakdowns for the leaders are given. The analysis, however, relies mainly on the rank and file, as leadership interviews did not secure comparable measures on many of the variables discussed. This section is intended only as an introduction to differences between the factions; succeeding chapters will analyze them in greater detail.

The data indicate that the organized factions had virtually no meaning at all for more than 60 percent of the membership. Respondents were asked if they knew the names of the factions and the identity of their leaders at various levels. Some 25 percent of the respondents exhibited a thorough knowledge of the factions' names and leaders, 13 percent a partial knowledge, and 62 percent no knowledge at all. Respondents were also asked to which faction they belonged and slightly more (43 percent) could indicate this than exhibited any knowledge of the faction (38 percent). For this analysis the respondents have been accordingly divided into three groups: the autonomists, the leftists, and the independents. (See Table 6-14.) In reality, the "independents" were uninvolved rather than independent. In certain characteristics (especially those having to do with politicization and political knowledge and skills), the autono-

Table 6-14. Members: Factional Identification (in percent)

Autonomists	28
Leftists	15
Independents	57
	100
N	296

mists and leftists (collectively referred to as "identifiers") re-
sembled one another more than they did the independents.
Those who were most involved and active (militants and participants) were also most strongly partisan (as were autonomists
and leftists).[6] Almost half of the autonomists and 40 percent
of the leftists were militants, while only 9 percent of the independents were in this highest category. (See Table 6-15.) Or,

Table 6-15. Members: Level of Participation, by Faction (in
percent)

	Auton.	Left.	Ind.	Totals
Nominal	4	2	23	14
Marginal	17	30	43	34
Participants	31	26	24	26
Militants	48	40	9	25
Not ascertained	0	2	1	1
	100	100	100	100
N	84	43	169	301

viewed from another perspective, only 21 percent of the autonomists and 32 percent of the leftists were in the lower two
categories, compared with 66 percent of the independents.

Factional identifiers were also more similar in social class to

6. For American findings concerning the relationship between partisanship
and participation see *The American Voter*, pp. 142–45; Bernard Berelson,
Paul F. Lazarsfeld, and William N. McPhee, *Voting* (Chicago, University
of Chicago Press, 1954); Robert Agger, "Independents and Party Identifiers:
Characteristics and Behavior in 1952," in Eugene Burdick and Arthur G.
Brodbeck, eds., *American Voting Behavior* (New York, Free Press, 1959),
pp. 308–29; and Lester Milbrath, *Political Participation* (Chicago, Rand
McNally, 1965).

one another than to the independents. The latter were concentrated in the lower class—94 percent—compared with 64 percent of the autonomists and 62 percent of the leftists. A higher percentage of autonomists were lower lower-class (unskilled) while a higher percentage of leftists were upper lower-class (skilled). Middle-class members (professionals, teachers with university degrees, etc.) constituted a higher portion of the left than of the autonomist faction. (See Table 6-16.) But differ-

Table 6-16.   Members: Social Class, by Faction (in percent)

	Auton.	Left.	Ind.
Lower-lower	41	30	67
Upper-lower	23	32	27
Lower-middle	30	26	4
Middle	4	12	0
Not ascertained	2	0	2
	100	100	100
N	84	43	169

ences between the two groups of identifiers were not nearly as substantial as those between the identifiers and independents.

Occupational differences were, of course, closely related to differences in social class. Identifiers were more often found among tradesmen, professional men, and clerks, while independents were over-represented in the agricultural categories. Autonomists predominated over leftists among the unskilled and sharecroppers, while a higher proportion of leftists were skilled workers and tradesmen. But in this case, also, the two groups of identifiers were more similar to one another than to the independents (table not shown).

While the concentration of independents in the lower social classes suggests that this might account for their low level of participation, this turned out not to be the case. As Table 6-17 indicates, within each social class the substantial differences between identifiers and independents remained. Similar results emerged when participation was controlled for education (table not shown). It seems clear that the difference between the

Table 6-17. Members: Participation, by Social Class and Faction (in percent)

| | Social Class | | | | | | | | |
| | Lower-lower | | | Upper-lower | | | Lower-middle and middle | | |
	Autom.	Left.	Ind.	Autom.	Left.	Ind.	Autom.	Left.	Ind.
Nominal	6	0	27	0	0	16	3	7	14
Marginal	11	15	39	16	38	53	18	40	43
Participant	34	31	23	32	8	24	29	33	43
Militant	49	54	11	52	54	7	50	20	0
	100	100	100	100	100	100	100	100	100
N	35	13	112	19	13	46	28	16	7

identifiers and independents in their level of participation was not due to the unequal distribution of social classes and levels of education between them. Identifiers participated more regardless of social class and education.

Another major difference between the factional identifiers and the independents lay in the area of political knowledge. The independents achieved dramatically lower scores than the identifiers on eight questions designed to test the respondent's knowledge of Italian politics.[7] The identifiers had a virtual monopoly on political knowledge in the party. Autonomists dominated the highest category while leftist identifiers were concentrated in the middle. (See Table 6-18.)

Table 6-18. Members: Political Knowledge, by Faction (in percent)

	Auton.	Left.	Ind.
0–2 Right answers	25	23	84
3–5 Right answers	35	56	15
6–8 Right answers	40	21	1
	100	100	100
N	84	43	169

This superior knowledge was probably due in part to educational differences between the identifiers and the independents. Completion of elementary school (i.e. five years of schooling) is the normal minimum education to be expected in this part of Italy. Yet over half the independents had less than this amount, while many identifiers had more. (See Table 6-19.)

The identifiers were much more issue-oriented than the independents. Responses to open-ended questions concerning problems of Italian public life and perceptions of several political parties were coded as to whether they were issue-oriented or not.[8] Almost one out of four independents gave answers that could not be meaningfully coded; and another 44 percent of them—compared with only 28 percent of the leftists and 16

7. See Chapter 7 for a discussion of this measure.
8. This measure is discussed further in Chapter 10.

Table 6-19. Formal Education, by Faction (in percent)

	Members			Leaders	
	Auton.	Left.	Ind.	Auton.	Left.
Less than five years	22	16	53	3	0
Five years	47	56	41	33	33
More than five years	31	28	6	64	67
	100	100	100	100	100
N	84	43	169	36	15

percent of the autonomists—had no issue content in their answers. Four out of five autonomists and three out of five leftists gave issue-oriented answers. (See Table 6-20.)

Table 6-20. Members: Issue-Oriented or Not, by Faction (in percent)

	Auton.	Left.	Ind.
Issue-oriented	79	60	33
Not issue-oriented	16	28	44
DK, not codible	5	12	23
	100	100	100
N	84	43	169

The significant differences between the identifiers and the independents are further revealed by their differing sense of political efficacy. The independents were clustered toward the negative end of the index of political efficacy, while the two highest categories were dominated by the identifiers.[9] The sense of political efficacy of the group as a whole seems surprisingly low considering that all the respondents were sufficiently aroused about politics to join a party. Nevertheless, 31 percent of the autonomists, 24 percent of the leftists, and only 7 percent of the independents gave more than two answers indicative of a sense of political efficacy. (See Table 6-21.)

Two final differences between the identifiers and independents were their membership sections (whether urban or rural)

9. This measure is discussed further in Chapter 7.

Table 6-21. Members: Index of Political Efficacy, by Faction (in percent)

Number of Responses Indicative of a Sense of Efficacy	Auton.	Left.	Ind.
0	13	12	36
1	25	30	32
2	31	34	23
3	24	12	5
4	7	12	2
Not ascertained	0	0	2
	100	100	100
N	84	43	169

and length of membership in the party. Members of the single urban section were much more likely to be identifiers than those enrolled in outlying party sections of the commune: the section in the provincial capital (with 38 percent of the sample) contained 55 percent of the autonomists, 60 percent of the leftists, and only 27 percent of the independents.

There were also important differences in length of membership between identifiers and independents. Those who joined the party in 1960 or after were very likely to be among the independents. Those who joined before 1950 were also slightly more often identifiers than those who joined in 1950–59, but the difference between them was not great. (See Table 6-22.) Members with little seniority in the party were much less likely to identify with a faction than those who had been members for

Table 6-22. Members: When Joined Party, by Faction (in percent)

	Before 1950	1950–59	1960–
Autonomists	41	32	5
Leftists	18	20	4
Independents	41	48	91
	100	100	100
N	114	100	81

several years. The atmosphere of the party and the nature of the leadership when the individual joins the party seem to have an impact on the member's choice of faction. Thus one-third of the leftist members joined the party during the years from 1950 through 1955, compared with only 18 percent of the autonomists. These were years of close relations with the Communists, and the present leader of the left faction in the province was secretary of the federation during most of that period.

It was noted above that the factions have no meaning for more than 60 percent of the membership. This statement now needs to be amplified in the light of the data presented above. It is obvious that the politically competent—the more active, knowledgeable, issue-oriented, efficacious, urban, middle-class, and senior members of the party—were all heavily represented among the identifiers. Those who count among the members were concerned with factional affairs. It was largely the newer, less committed, and less politically competent members who were unaware of and unconcerned with factions. The operation and destiny of the party were in the hands of the identifiers, and the differences between the autonomists and leftists are more important than their numbers would indicate.

The following chapter will examine some aspects of participation and political competence in greater detail.

7.

Participation and Political Competence

PARTICIPATION AND VOLUNTARY ASSOCIATIONS

One of the best documented conclusions about participation in voluntary associations in the United States is that high education and high participation are closely related. Studies further demonstrate that participation in voluntary associations is associated with increased political competence even if the associations are themselves nonpolitical. And the evidence is overwhelming that political competence and association membership correlate highly in the United States.[1]

There is considerable evidence that these findings apply elsewhere. In their five-nation study, Gabriel Almond and Sidney Verba found that

> Organizational membership appears to have a cumulative effect. . . . Those who belong to an organization show higher political competence than those who are members of no organization, but the members of more than one organization show even higher political competence than those whose affiliation is limited to one. And in their political competence multiple members differ from members of a single organization about as much as, if not more than, single members differ from nonmembers.[2]

1. See Howard E. Freeman, Edwin Novak, and Leo G. Reeder, "Correlates of Membership in Voluntary Associations," *American Sociological Review*, 22 (1957), 258–83; Herbert Maccoby, "The Differential Political Activity of Participants in a Voluntary Association," ibid., 23 (1958), 524–32; Charles R. Wright and Herbert H. Hyman, "Voluntary Association Memberships of American Adults: Evidence from National Sample Surveys," ibid., 23 (1958), 284–94.

2. *The Civic Culture*, p. 320. Their measure of competence differs from that used in the present study.

Similar findings are reported from a Finnish study cited by S. M. Lipset: "Those participating in one specific type of organization were more likely to be active in others, to attend political meetings, to read more, to have more friends and so on."[3]

While social class and political competence are closely related, participation in voluntary associations is associated with higher political competence, regardless of class. Political competence is also closely associated with other, related, variables. One of the most important is education. Formal education is one method, albeit not the only one, of acquiring both the substantive knowledge and the feeling of personal efficacy that are essential to participation in politics. That the better educated have higher rates of participation, regardless of how participation is measured, is shown by a number of studies.[4]

But it is equally obvious that some lower-class individuals of low education are active in politics and that others who possess the opposite characteristics are not active. Level of social interaction can account for this observed relationship between status and participation as well as for the deviant cases. Thus it is not social class or education per se that accounts for the level of participation but rather the fact that people low in educational achievement or social class are less likely than others to achieve the high level of interaction that is associated with high levels of participation in voluntary associations. Thus farmers are less likely than workers of the same educational level to have the opportunity for repeated social interaction and are hence less likely to be participants.[5] Workers in industries or jobs that tend to set them apart, whether geographically as in the case of miners and lumbermen, or in regard to time as with typographers, are likely to interact more with one another and to develop political skills.[6] Education broadens contacts as well as knowledge

3. *Political Man* (Garden City, N.Y., Doubleday, 1960), p. 202.
4. For example, Almond and Verba, *The Civic Culture*, p. 304; Campbell et al., *The American Voter*, pp. 475–81; the evidence cited in Lipset, *Political Man*, pp. 187–89; and Milbrath, *Political Participation*, pp. 122–24.
5. Campbell et al., *The American Voter*, Chapter 15.
6. Lipset, Trow, and Coleman, *Union Democracy*, pp. 118–59.

and thereby facilitates communication. One's job may facilitate contact with a broad range of people, or it may reinforce identification with a restricted group, as in the case of the American farmer and the Italian peasant. In short, while high education and high social class increase the probability of high interaction, there are other variables that also affect it.

But if one's chances of acquiring political competence are not determined by class and education they are greatly affected by them; the characteristics associated with low political competence are found disproportionately concentrated in a particular subset of the population. Low education, low interaction, and low political competence are highly associated. Genevieve Knupfer, a psychiatrist, has written the following of American middle-class culture: "economic underprivilege is psychological underprivilege: habits of submission, little access to sources of information, lack of verbal facility . . . appear to produce a lack of self-confidence which increases the unwillingness of the low status person to participate." [7] Participation requires some minimum level of knowledge and sense of efficacy. Most people who are largely preoccupied with mere survival have neither the physical energy nor the time to develop the political competence that makes meaningful participation in politics possible. On the other hand, the middle class acquires through socialization a minimal political awareness and some general knowledge of economic and political relationships as a matter of course.

This is not to say that members of the lower class are not aware of basic economic and political realities. A peasant receives a lesson in economic relationships almost daily. And he usually understands the nature of political power. It is difficult, however, for him to articulate his attitudes and to develop the associations necessary to convert numbers into influence. In a society devoted to the preservation of the status quo, existing institutions do not serve him well.

Class distinctions are sharply drawn in Italy. The extremes of rich and poor, the social stigma attached to most nonwhite-

7. Genevieve Knupfer, "Portrait of the Underdog," *Public Opinion Quarterly, 11* (1947), 114.

collar occupations, and the unequal sharing in economic prosperity give to parties a distinct social significance. In such an environment differences among parties are widely if vaguely perceived within the electorate. Social and traditional impulses may motivate the voter to favor and join one party rather than another. It is possible to join a party without being highly politicized, without any real knowledge of politics, and without any feeling of political efficacy. As will be indicated, party membership in the formal sense, for many, does not necessarily represent a level of politicization and commitment qualitatively greater than that of a sympathizer or supporter. It may reflect only the coincidence of having a husband, brother, father, close friend, or work colleague who was a member and who recruited those closest to him. Indeed, this seems to be the case with a large part of the sample. Those who remain members for extended periods of time, however, are likely to become more involved, committed, knowledgeable, and efficacious.

There is considerable evidence that this is a general phenomenon of voluntary organizations. Research on participation in trade unions reinforces the contention that length of membership is associated with commitment. James March and Herbert Simon concluded, "There is evidence indicating that most union members become participants either more or less involuntarily or for limited special reasons, but that participation results ultimately in much deeper involvements." [8] Greater interaction among unionists was found to be associated with higher rates of participation.[9] *Union Democracy* carefully documents the same findings.[10] American trade unions are hardly "voluntary" organizations in the same way a political party in a democracy is a "voluntary" organization, so one could expect a similar or stronger association between commitment to parties and interaction, or what the authors of the *American Voter*

8. *Organizations* (New York, Wiley, 1958), pp. 72–73.
9. William Spinrod, "Correlates of Trade Union Participation: A Summary of the Literature," *American Sociological Review*, 25 (1960), 237–44; A. S. Tannenbaum and R. L. Kahn, *Participation in Union Locals* (Evanston, Ill., Rowe Peterson, 1958).
10. Pp. 118–269.

term "proportion of life in contact." These authors did indeed find it to be an important explanatory variable.[11] And, more nearly analogous to the PSI situation, Gabriel Almond found that recruits were attracted to the Communist Party by a wide variety of influences, but that those who stayed in the party became more knowledgeable and committed.[12]

As a subsequent chapter will show, the motivations for joining the PSI are varied. Many new members are singularly deficient in knowledge and sense of efficacy. Yet many party members of all classes develop political competence. This phenomenon was noted by Almond and Verba, though its implications for working-class politics were not developed.[13] Participation in politics is one of the few avenues open to members of the lower class for acquiring the political competence that the middle class acquires in the home and school. Lipset has written, "Granted that a group of people is suffering from some deprivation under the existing socioeconomic system, it does not automatically follow that they will support political parties aiming at social change. Three conditions facilitate such a response: effective channels of communication, low belief in the possibility of individual social mobility, and the absence of traditionalist ties to a conservative party." [14] Communication is the crucial variable, and membership in a party exposes the recruit to communication:

> Perhaps the most important condition is the presence of good communications among people who have a common problem. Close personal contacts between such people further awareness of a community of interests and of the possibilities of collective action, including political action, to solve the common problems. When informal contacts are supplemented by formal organization in trade-unions, farm groups, or class political movements, with all their machinery

11. Campbell et al., *The American Voter,* pp. 325, 369.
12. Gabriel Almond, *The Appeals of Communism* (Princeton, Princeton University Press, 1955).
13. Almond and Verba, *The Civic Culture,* pp. 300–22.
14. Lipset, *Political Man,* p. 261.

of organizers, speakers, newspapers, and so forth, political awareness will be intensified still more.[15]

My principal concern is to examine variables associated with participation and to show how these relate to political competence.

I do not believe that self-selection is the principal reason for the increased competence of the high participants. There is plausible evidence that many people join the PSI without prior development of political competence, and that competence results from participation and not the reverse. But cause and effect in social relations are difficult to establish with certitude. My argument is therefore not that participation results in increased political competence but rather that (1) they are closely associated; and (2) on some dimensions the association is stronger for members with low formal education than for those with high. More than this I do not claim.

THE MEASUREMENTS EMPLOYED

The model respondent had completed elementary school and therefore had five years of formal education. However, more than one-third of the sample had less than five years, and only one in six members had more. Consequently, the three categories of formal education are less than five years of school (low), five years (average), and more than five years (high). (See Table 7-1.)

Answers to two batteries of questions were utilized to construct indices of knowledge and efficacy. Respondents were asked whether each of eight questions about Italian politics was true or false.[16] To reduce guessing, respondents were asked whether they knew the answer to each question before replying

15. Ibid., p. 262.
16. The eight questions are the following: (a) Calabria has a special regional status. (b) Twenty-five is the minimum age for being elected a deputy. (c) There are seven countries in the European Common Market. (d) The PSI abstained on the vote of confidence for the center-left government (Fanfani, 1962). (e) AGIP is a private industry. (f) In the past the PCI has taken part in the government. (g) The Constitutional Court has yet to be established. (h) Everyone who has reached the age of twenty-one can vote for the Chamber and for the Senate.

Table 7-1. Formal Education of Sample

	N	N	%
Illiterate	8		
1 or 2 years of school	30		
3 years	78		
Total with less than 5 years (low)	116	116	39
Total with 5 years (average)	135	135	45
6 or 7 years	10		
8 years	20		
9–12 years	6		
13 years (secondary diploma)	3		
Some university	2		
University degree	7		
Total with more than 5 years (high)	48	48	16
Totals	299	299	100

Table 7-2. Number of Correct Answers Given to Knowledge Questions

Correct Answers	%
0	32
1	12
2	15
3	9
4	10
5	7
6	6
7	5
8	4
	100
N	299

true or false.[17] The distribution of the responses on the knowledge questions is shown in Table 7-2.

17. The items were machine tested for scalability using the Multiple Scalagram Analysis developed by James C. Lingoes, "Multiple Scalagram Analysis: A Set-Theoretic Model for Analyzing Dichotomous Items," *Educational and Psychological Measurement*, 23 (1963), 501–24. They were also tested for scalability by conventional counter-sorter procedures. As the

The four questions concerning political efficacy were treated in a similar fashion.[18] Table 7-3 gives the pattern of responses.

Table 7-3.   Number of Responses Indicative of a Sense of Efficacy

Efficacious Answers	%
0	26
1	31
2	27
3	11
4	5
	100
N	295

The measure of party participation was described in the previous chapter.

PARTY PARTICIPATION, KNOWLEDGE, AND EFFICACY

Previous findings of close association between education and knowledge are strikingly confirmed. A somewhat weaker association exists between education and efficacy, and between party participation, on the one hand, and knowledge and sense of efficacy, on the other. (See Table 7-4.)

However, when these relationships are broken down by educational levels, important distinctions emerge. I hypothesized that the association between participation and measures of competence would be stronger for those members in the low education category than for those in the two higher groups. The

items did not form an acceptable Guttman-type scale, the number of correct answers given by each respondent provided his position on an index of political knowledge.

18. The questions were as follows: (a) The average member has no influence at all on what the party decides. (b) Sometimes politics seems so complicated that it is difficult to understand it. (c) I don't think that public officials care very much about what people like me think. (d) Voting is the only way for the rank and file members of the party to influence the policies of the party. The questions were taken from SRC American electoral studies. Although none of the items were reversed, there is no internal evidence of distortion due to response set.

Table 7-4. Intercorrelation Matrix: Party Participation, Education, Knowledge, and Efficacy: Entire Sample[a]

	Education	Knowledge	Efficacy
Participation	.22	.44	.33
Education	—	.61	.42
Knowledge		—	.42

[a] All measures of association herein are gamma rank order coefficients. Gamma was chosen because it does not require N × N tables in order to reach the values of ±1.o. For a discussion of gamma, see William L. Hays, *Statistics for Psychologists* (New York, Holt, Rinehart, Winston, 1963), pp. 655–56.

better educated generally have better educated parents; apart from their formal education, they are likely to acquire some political competence at home and from their peers. The poorly educated often are caught up in a cycle of ignorance and political incompetence. With poorly educated parents and associates and a long tradition of alienation and cynicism, they can break out of the pattern only through great personal effort or good fortune. Participation in politics is one way for the poorly educated to acquire knowledge and a sense of efficacy; indeed, it may be the only avenue available. It is not nearly as important for the better educated.

Level of party participation, for example, is related to the

Table 7-5. Party Participation and Knowledge, by Education (figure is mean knowledge, 0–8 possible)

		Education	
Participation	Low	Average	High
Nominal members	.2	2.0	[a]
Marginal members	.8	1.8	4.6
Participant members	1.4	3.0	5.0
Militant members	2.1	4.4	6.1
N	116	133	47
Gamma	.52	.40	.35

Total N = 296

[a] Less than five cases.

knowledge and efficacy of all groups. However, the regularity and magnitude of the increase are more impressive for the less well educated, and the difference is greater for knowledge than for efficacy. (See Table 7-5.) The association between party participation and knowledge is stronger for the lowly educated (gamma = .52) than for the average (.40) or highly educated (.35). Nominal members with low education have a *mean* of .2 on the index of knowledge (i.e. only one out of five in this category could answer even one of the eight questions correctly) while the mean of the militants in the same category was 2.1. The importance of education is shown by the fact that the mean for nominal members with average education is 2.0, rising to 4.4 for militants with the same education. Those with high education scored much higher, from 4.6 for the marginal members to 6.1 for the militants. Marginal members of high education scored higher than militants of the lower two categories. The progression among the militants from 2.1 for the lowest educational category to 6.1 for the highest likewise demonstrates the importance of education for political knowledge even among the most active members. Further, while the association between party participation and knowledge is stronger in the low education group, the absolute differences between the mean levels of knowledge in the low and high educational categories are relatively constant within each level of participation. Thus, among marginal members it is 3.8, participants 3.6, and militants 4.0.

The association between party participation and sense of efficacy is roughly similar for all groups. The increase in sense of efficacy by level of party participation is monotonic for the lowest educational category; while there is an overall increase for the two other categories, it is an irregular one. Table 7-6 shows the mean sense of efficacy for each category, after the fashion of the above discussion of knowledge. It seems from these findings that knowledge about politics is very much a function of exposure to politics, as knowledge consistently increases with party participation and education. A sense of efficacy, on the other hand, may have several origins. While in

Table 7-6.   Participation and Efficacy, by Education (figure is mean efficacy, 0–4 possible)

		Education	
Participation	*Low*	*Average*	*High*
Nominal members	.4	1.0	a
Marginal members	.8	1.6	1.9
Participant members	1.0	1.6	1.5
Militant members	1.3	1.9	2.6
N	*112*	*133*	*47*
Gamma	.38	.24	.33

Total *N* = *292*

a Less than five cases.

general it exhibits the same patterns as political knowledge, there are irregularities that elude simple interpretation.

TOTAL MEMBERSHIPS, KNOWLEDGE, AND EFFICACY

The previous discussion of the relationships between party participation, knowledge, and efficacy has indicated that there are important differences among the three educational levels in the effects that are associated with participation. While substantial, these differences are not as great as those exhibited by these same three educational groupings when the total number of voluntary associations to which each respondent belongs (hereafter referred to as total memberships) is examined.

Those with a high level of participation in the PSI are also more likely to belong to other voluntary associations: the degree of association between the two is .43. This is compelling support for the findings cited earlier. Like party participation, total memberships are highly associated with knowledge (.44) and efficacy (.38). But there is even greater variation among educational levels in the relationships between total memberships and levels of knowledge and efficacy than between party participation and these variables. In fact, as Table 7-7 demonstrates, for political knowledge these differences are more impressive than those previously discussed dealing with party participation. The

Table 7-7. Association between Total Memberships and Level of Political Knowledge, by Educational Levels

Less than five years' education $= .42$ $(N = 116)$
Five years' education $= .30$ $(N = 135)$
More than five years' education $= .12$ $(N = 48)$

relationship between the respondents' level of knowledge and total membership is much stronger for the least educated than it is for those with more education. As was the case with party participation, however, the absolute differences in levels of knowledge between the extremes remain substantial. Those low on education who belong only to the party rank very low on the knowledge index; mean knowledge levels increase dramatically with increases in the number of organizations. The increase is regular but small for the best educated group. Nevertheless, the best educated group remains far superior to the other groups. (See Table 7-8.)

Table 7-8. Total Memberships and Knowledge, by Education (figure is mean knowledge, 0–8 possible)

	Education		
Total Memberships	*Low*	*Average*	*High*
Party member only	.7	2.1	4.8
Party + one other	1.1	2.9	5.1
Party + two others	2.5	3.5	5.3
Party + three others	a	3.6	5.4
Party + four or more others	a	a	5.8
N	*116*	*135*	*48*
Gamma	.42	.30	.12

ᵃ Less than five cases.

Although less regular, results are in general similar for the relationship between total memberships and efficacy. The regularity of the progression is slightly disturbed by the reversal of the group with the most education and the middle group. (See Table 7-9.) Examination of the mean sense of efficacy for each

123

Table 7-9. Correlations between Number of Organizational
Memberships and Sense of Political Efficacy, by
Educational Levels

Less than five years' education $= .59\ (N = 112)$
Five years' education $= .10\ (N = 135)$
More than five years' education $= .16\ (N = 48)$

category reveals surprising irregularities for the two better educated groups. While the least educated group progresses from
.5 to 1.1 to 1.6, the other two groups exhibit nonmonotonic
progressions up to the final set for that category, which in each
case has a smaller mean than the first set. (See Table 7-10.)

Table 7-10. Total Memberships and Efficacy, by Education
(figure is mean efficacy, 0–4 possible)

| | | Education | |
Total Memberships	Low	Average	High
Party member only	.5	1.4	1.9
Party + one other	1.1	1.8	1.6
Party + two others	1.6	1.8	2.6
Party + three others	a	.8	2.6
Party + four or more others	a	a	1.4
N	112	135	48
Gamma	.59	.10	.16

Total $N = 295$

a Less than five cases.

As in previous examples, the absolute differences between educational levels in each category remain substantial. The findings
concerning the relationship between total memberships and
political competence thus reinforce the conclusions derived from
a study of party participation and competence.

This discussion began with a review of other findings concerning participation and its impact on political competence.
The generalization that high rates of participation are associated

with high levels of political competence was confirmed. It is now possible to suggest refinements in the interpretations of this association.

Persons of low educational achievements are more dramatically affected by participation in a political party and in voluntary associations than are those of higher education. This strongly suggests that participation in politics is a significant way for the poorly educated to break out of the circle of political ignorance and low sense of efficacy. This seems especially important in a country such as Italy.

But the advantages of the better educated are strikingly confirmed also, for they rate high on political competence even when they are relatively uninvolved in associational activities, and their advantages increase with increases in levels of participation. Low participants with high education excel over other low participants with less education on both knowledge and sense of efficacy, and the absolute advantages of the better educated are maintained among the high participants. In other words, the poorly educated do not catch up through participation; they start behind and they stay behind.

This advantage of the better educated has vast ramifications for internal democracy in the PSI. The poorly educated majority does not acquire as high a level of political competence as the small group with more than average education even through intensive participation in the PSI and extensive participation in other associations. As differences in competence among the educational levels remain even among militants, the existence of formal opportunities to develop competence and leadership potential does not reduce the gap. While a few persons may largely surmount their poor education, in the party as a whole the lower classes are severely handicapped by their low political competence. Although participation in politics is undoubtedly a path to increased political competence, it nevertheless has severe limitations as a means to overcome the disadvantages of a poor education.

8.

Socialization and Recruitment:
Conventional and Ideological Socialists

In understanding the politics of a party it is useful to know how members acquired their orientations toward politics and why they joined that particular party. The latter assumes special significance where, as in the present case, individuals have numerous alternatives.

It is impossible to investigate all important areas of inquiry in a single interview schedule. In this study of participation, socialization was not emphasized. As a consequence, data are limited and findings are more suggestive than definitive. Despite these shortcomings, however, potentially significant generalizations can be tentatively suggested: (1) many members and leaders joined the party for conventional reasons, such as family tradition and the influence of family and friends; and (2) those who joined for nonconventional reasons are of exceptional importance in the party, as they participate more and hold many important leadership positions.

SOCIALIZATION IN THE FAMILY

The family is an important agent of political socialization everywhere. The tendency for people to continue in the political tradition of their parents has been widely documented.[1] This general finding is reinforced by the data from the PSI. Most members who knew what party their parents had favored re-

1. See Campbell et al., *The American Voter*; Philip E. Converse and Georges Dupeux, "The Politicization of the Electorate in France and the United States," *Public Opinion Quarterly*, 26 (1962), 1–23; Milbrath, *Political Participation*; Robert Lane, *Political Life* (New York, Free Press, 1960).

126

ported that it was the PSI.[2] Fathers were more political than mothers: the political sympathies of slightly more than one-third of the mothers and almost two-thirds of the fathers were known by the respondents. Consequently, the following analysis will concentrate on the fathers' political preferences.

The high degree of class consciousness existing in the province and its relationship to politics have repeatedly been emphasized. They are strikingly reflected in the similarity in the politics of the two generations, and especially in the near absence of support for nonleftist parties among the fathers of PSI members. (See Table 8-1.) Ignoring those who did not know the sym-

Table 8-1. Members: Political Sympathies of Father, by Social Class (in percent)

	Lower-lower	Upper-lower	Middle	Total
PSI	52	57	61	55
PCI	3	8	6	5
Other	5	3	8	5
Nonpolitical	9	8	6	8
DK	31	24	19	27
	100	100	100	100
N	161	80	51	292

pathies of their fathers and those with nonpolitical fathers, the support for the PSI is even more remarkable: 86 percent of the fathers were PSI, 7 percent PCI, and only 7 percent supported other parties. Especially striking is the absence of a strong class differential, as only an insignificant difference exists between lower-class and middle-class rank and file members. (See Table 8-2.) The membership is thus remarkably homogeneous in political background.

There are some factional differences, however. Leftists were much more likely to have had pro-Communist fathers: more

2. Converse and Dupeux found that while many Frenchmen did not know their father's political preferences those who did were overwhelmingly similar in allegiance ("The Politicization of the Electorate").

Table 8-2.   Members: Political Sympathies of Father, by Social Class (in percent)

	Lower-lower	Upper-lower	Middle	Total
PSI	87	85	82	86
PCI	5	11	8	7
Other	8	4	10	7
	100	100	100	100
N	96	54	39	189

Apoliticals and DKs eliminated.

than one out of four leftists who knew his father's sympathies had a pro-Communist father, and hence would be pulled to the left by family tradition. (See Table 8-3.) The pro-Com-

Table 8-3.   Members: Political Sympathies of Father, by Faction (in percent)

	Auton.	Left.	Ind.
PSI	59	54	54
PCI	5	21	a
"Left," other	8	4	4
Nonpolitical	13	0	8
Don't know	15	21	34
	100	100	100
N	84	43	169

a Less than 1%.

munist fathers were not concentrated in any social class among the leftists. The 13 percent difference between autonomists and leftists in the nonpolitical category is also interesting.

There is no evidence that the nonpolitical and DK categories were used by those with deviant parents to evade responding. The nonpolitical and DK responses can therefore be accepted at face value, especially considering the large number of members in these two categories who grew up under fascism. One would expect such answers from many of these respondents, since the political alternatives available to their fathers were limited during a twenty-year period.

Turning to the leadership interviews, a similar pattern emerges, except that there are proportionally more leaders than members who are middle-class, with the result that a higher percentage of fathers are non-PSI and -PCI. Also, there are only one DK and thirteen nonpoliticals. (See Table 8-4.)

Table 8-4.   Leaders: Political Sympathies of Father, by Social Class (in percent)

	Lower-lower	Upper-lower	Middle	Total
PSI	68	88	47	64
PCI	16	0	12	11
Other	16	12	41	25
	100	100	100	100
N	19	8	17	44

Apoliticals and DKs eliminated.

The importance of this 25 percent with deviant parents becomes clearer when they are analyzed in terms of their position in the leadership hierarchy. The higher the level the larger the percentage with non-PSI and -PCI parents. (See Table 8-5.) This

Table 8-5.   Leaders: Political Sympathies of Father, by Leadership Level (in percent)

	Exec. Comm. and Above	Directing Committee	Sec'y. of Section	Totals
PSI	36	62	100	64
PCI	14	14	0	11
Other	50	24	0	25
	100	100	100	100
N	14	21	10	45

Apoliticals and DKs omitted.

is a census, not a sample, so the fact that the fathers of so many of the top leaders supported parties other than the PSI is important despite the small numbers involved. These are the leaders who broke family tradition in choosing the party, and they differ from others in their motivations.

There are also important differences within the rank and file between those who knew their fathers' preferences and those who did not or whose fathers were nonpolitical. The former are significantly more militant, knowledgeable, and efficacious.[3] In short, they exhibit greater political competence than the nonpolitical and DK categories. There are no significant differences between the two groups on other matters: each group is roughly similar on programmatic position, conception of democracy, and level of ideological sensitivity. This suggests that the family affects general orientations rather than specific policy or ideological preferences. Of course, the reverse is possible: perhaps the more militant, knowledgeable, and efficacious tend to recall their fathers' preferences more often than others. Older members were more likely not to recall their fathers' preferences, which suggests that age, not competence, is the source of the failure to recall. But firm conclusions are unwarranted, as the size of the sample prohibits further breakdowns. In the absence of even ordinal data for the leaders on participation, knowledge, and efficacy, a comparable analysis cannot be made for them.

Respondents in the membership sample were asked whether their fathers were very, somewhat, or not much interested in politics, with the results shown in Table 8-6. Members with

Table 8-6.　Members: Father's Interest in Politics (in percent)

Very interested	17
Somewhat interested	16
Not much interested	46
DK	21
	100
N	301

more-involved fathers ranked significantly higher on participation, or at least high participants tended with greater frequency to recall their fathers as being more interested. But there are

3. All "significant" differences in this chapter refer to chi-square tests significant at least at the .05 level.

no significant differences between the two groups on efficacy, programmatic position, conception of democracy, knowledge, or ideological sensitivity. In other words, the level of the father's interest in politics seems to have no impact on the political competence or attitudes of the child.

This finding is surprising, because it was important whether or not the father was a party sympathizer. Two possible explanations merit attention. The first is purely statistical. If one examines a large number of relationships the probability is increased that some of them will turn out by chance to be significant; that is, the findings may be statistically significant but scientifically meaningless. While feasible, this explanation is unlikely to be correct, because the close association between the party of the father and child, participation, knowledge, and efficacy is what would be expected on the basis of the findings of other research.

The second and more likely explanation for the lack of an impact of the father's level of political interest is to be found in the importance of the political culture of the immediate environment. Lower-class members with pro-Socialist or -Communist fathers are also likely to have been socialized into a strongly leftist political culture and to have been subjected to roughly the same influences as their fathers. Those with non-political fathers or with DK answers are likely to have grown up in a less political atmosphere, or at least in a family environment largely isolated from the general political culture. The high percentage of the latter whose fathers were peasants suggests a culturally isolated childhood. Hence here too it is difficult to separate the influence of the father from that of the larger culture. Consequently, the greater or lesser interest in politics of the father would have little independent impact on the child. If it were otherwise, the greater political involvement of the father would have led not only to higher rates of participation, but also to greater political competence.

The importance for socialization of the subculture into which the individual is born is dramatically shown by the following simple analysis. Information was secured on the occupation of the father of the respondent and the sample was divided into those whose fathers had rural (peasant, farmer-owner, woodsman) and nonrural (all others) occupations. This was based on the assumptions (1) that the occupation of the father was the best general indicator of the sociocultural environment in which the respondent matured; and (2) that the isolation of rural occupations compared to nonrural in this part of Italy, especially when the present members were growing up, resulted in considerable differences in subcultures. Table 8-7 indicates

Table 8-7. Members: Subculture of Youth, Based on Father's Occupation (in percent)

	Rural	Nonrural
Ideologue or near-ideologue	7	31
Marxian conception of democracy	65	56
No efficacious response	33	15
One or no correct responses on eight knowledge questions	57	23
Militants in level of participation	21	35
Fathers not interested in politics	70	42
Education		
Less than five years	51	19
Five years	45	46
More than five years	4	35
Social Class		
Lower-lower	72	25
Upper-lower	24	34
Middle	4	41
N	169	105

the differences between the two groups on a number of important variables. Remember that the rural and nonrural categories are based on the occupation of the respondent's *father*. This suggests the great distinction between countryside and city that existed in Italy a generation ago, and that is still reflected in some behavioral characteristics of the sample. There is little doubt that the political subcultures of their youth socialized members differently, especially in the realm of political competence, and that those with urban backgrounds are a generation ahead of the others in acquiring competence. The data do not permit further speculation.

IMMEDIATE MOTIVATIONS FOR JOINING THE PARTY

A political party attracts members for many varied reasons. No simple explanation for the decision to participate is adequate to encompass the motivations of people of different backgrounds, unequal skills, and diverse levels of politicization. The following data present the reasons given by respondents for joining the party. One reason per respondent was coded from open questions to which the respondent could reply in his own terms. As the frame of reference varied from respondent to respondent, the categories lack taxonomic elegance. The replies, however, reproduce the self-proclaimed motivations of the respondents.

Many leaders and members spoke at length about their experiences under fascism. They indulged their desire for freedom of political action by joining the PSI as soon as possible, either when the party was formed in 1945 or when they returned from military service or captivity, which was sometimes a year later. These founders were coded together. Others responded that they joined the party as soon as they came of age, or because they had become persuaded through observation of the political scene. A few were disillusioned ex-Communists. (There were twenty-seven ex-PCI members in the membership sample; they formed roughly equal portions of the autonomists, leftists, and independents.) Others feared reprisals and joined only when they felt safe. Many pleaded no prior interest in politics, while a handful joined to facilitate obtaining employment. Still others answered that they were pre-Fascist Socialists, presumably considering that an adequate explanation. Four had come into the PSI when other parties merged with it. Finally, two important groups claimed that friends or family influenced them to join.

Leaders' responses required an additional category, that of the influence of leftist professors. Also, when possible, two responses were coded for the leaders. The reasons given by the two groups demonstrate that motivations, at least as recalled in memory, vary between leaders and members. Table 8-8 gives the results.

Table 8-8. Motivations for Joining

	Members		Leaders[a]	
	N	%	N	%
First opportunity for political action after fall of fascism	56	22	30	34
First opportunity after becoming of age	13	5	5	6
Convinced by observing politics	23	9	10	12
Left PCI because it was extremist	19	8	2	2
Feared reprisals earlier	8	3	0	0
Influence of friends	58	23	5	6
Influence of family	31	12	17	20
No interest in politics until PSI engaged his interest	14	6	5	6
Work made it opportune (get or hold a job)	5	2	0	0
Merger of other parties with PSI	4	2	5	6
Prewar member	20	8	0	0
Influence of leftist professors	0	0	7	8
	251	100	86	100

[a] Leaders based on more than one response when applicable.

The most important differences between the two groups involve the greater portion of the leaders who joined at the end of fascism and the reversal of the relative importance of family and friends. Over a third of the present leaders joined soon after the end of fascism, and 69 percent had joined by 1948; none, however, were pre-Fascist members of the PSI. As was noted earlier, the present top leadership is remarkably concentrated in the forty to forty-nine age group. They grew up under fascism, matured during the Second World War, and were young when the party was reorganized; 79 percent of them saw military service, and all were deeply moved by the Resistance whether they participated in it personally or not. It seems obvious that these experiences have a great influence on the party today, for it was then that the present leaders' attitudes toward the PCI, the Church, social and political revolution, and working-class unity were formed; and it is only against this background that the internal struggle of factions can be understood.

A second notable difference between leaders and members is to be found in the reversal of the influence of friends and family. Among the members, 23 percent mentioned friends and 12 percent family as the principal influences on their decisions to join the party; among the leaders, 5 percent mentioned friends and 20 percent mentioned family. As more leaders are middle-class and probably deviant from the point of view of family and friends, the overall greater influence of family and friends among the members is to be expected; it is in fact surprising that the portion is not larger. But the relative unimportance of friends among the leaders requires examination.

Lower-class leaders are likely to have Socialist friends as well as family; those of the middle class are more likely to be deviant. This turns out to be the most important explanation. No middle-class leaders mentioned either family or friends, while one lower middle-class leader mentioned both; all other references to friends and family were by lower-class leaders. Even more revealing than social class is education: none of the leaders who had attended a university mentioned either family or friends. Instead, they spoke of the influence of leftist professors and general ideological commitments. The top leaders of the party also avoided references to family: only two of seventeen references to family were made by members of the executive committee.

It is perhaps not as important that these references may reflect greater sophistication in fielding questions as that their choices reflect what leaders feel to be more noble or self-enhancing responses. These findings strongly suggest that different categories of leaders cite distinctive motivations for joining the party, with those of middle-class backgrounds, who also hold a disproportionate share of top leadership positions, much more often citing nonconventional motivations.

There is also evidence that similar dynamics are at work

among the members. Those members motivated primarily by the influence of family or friends were less well educated, active, efficacious, and so on, than others. (See Table 8-9.) As could be expected, a high portion of those motivated by family influences had pro-Socialist fathers. They also tended to be younger and poorly educated (despite the fact that in general the younger are better educated). These two groups influenced by friends and family participate little. They rank extremely low on ideological sensitivity. Few of them identify with either of the factions. Both these categories include a high percentage of people who selected the Marxian conception of democracy. They also included 64 percent of the codible responses of women in the sample. In short, these conventional Socialists make but a slight impact on the party despite their numbers. Their membership was seemingly instigated by friends and family, their commitments to activity for the party are minimal, and their political sophistication is extremely low. The more ideologically motivated, the deviants, the party switchers, the old-timers, carry a weight disproportionate to their numbers. Of particular interest is the fact that differences between leftists and autonomists are negligible. Although they differ systematically from the independents, the two factional identifiers are amazingly similar.

Exactly comparable information was not obtained for the leaders, but there is evidence that similar dynamics are to be found among them also. However, it is difficult to compare the leaders to the members, since most of the former are better educated, more active, and so on. There are some interesting differences relating to the internal politics of the party. As mentioned above, middle-class leaders often cite ideological reasons for joining the party, while only lower-class respondents mention being influenced by their family. Differences between leaders of the two internal party factions are slight, with a higher portion of leftists citing general ideological reasons. All five of those leaders who entered through the merger of other parties are autonomists, as are all five who cited the influence of friends.

Because so many middle-class leaders deviate from the point

Table 8-9. Members: Motivations for Joining x Several Variables (in percent)

	First Opportunity after Fascism	Because Became of Age	Followed Politics & Became Convinced	Disillusioned Communist	Feared Reprisals Earlier	Influence of Friends	Influence of Family	No Previous Interest	Reasons of Work	Merger of PSI and Other Parties	Prewar Member	Other and DK
Under 40	9	92	70	53	50	60	61	64	40	25	0	33
More than 5 years' education	18	31	26	10	25	10	9	14	0	75	20	15
Part. or militant	63	46	55	83	62	35	29	21	40	75	70	56
Above median on efficacy	46	69	56	58	38	43	42	28	40	50	40	54
Non-Marxian conception of democracy	45	47	35	47	0	31	15	15	40	75	60	43
Ideologues and near-ideologues	25	23	12	5	25	6	6	14	0	50	20	10
Without factional loyalties	36	46	42	37	62	77	68	85	80	25	50	63
With pro-Socialist fathers	54	69	43	42	33	46	71	64	80	50	55	61
N	56	13	23	19	8	58	31	14	5	4	20	51

of view of their parents, it is surprising to find the occupation of the father reflected in the internal political orientation of the son. But this is the case: among the leaders, six of seven sons of businessmen are autonomists, as are all three sons of clerks and the sole son of a professional man. One can only speculate that socialization in a middle-class family may not prevent one from becoming a Socialist, but it does encourage moderation. However, the structural basis of the leftists in the trade unions is an important influence, so it is difficult to isolate the effect of background from that of present occupation. But this kind of controlling is unnecessary, for present occupation is not independent of family background.

It is clear that Socialists come from many backgrounds and join for diverse reasons. It is equally obvious that the many conventional Socialists are counterbalanced by the smaller number who are ideologically inclined. And it is also apparent, especially among the leaders, that those Socialists who have rejected the politics of their fathers and social class are of particular importance in the party.

9.

Primary and Secondary Group Influences
on Membership Behavior

Previous chapters have indicated the relevance of knowledge and efficacy—political competence—for political participation. They have demonstrated that knowledge of politics and sense of efficacy are not closely associated with participation among the better educated members, while the contrary is true for those with less education. Ideological sensitivity and orientation toward democracy are in turn closely related to both political competence and level of participation.

While causation cannot be demonstrated, many people seem to participate prior to the acquisition of competence. Why do such people join and remain in the party? What leads people of little education, knowledge, and skills to enroll? Why do they persevere? The previous chapter has suggested that some join for conventional reasons and others for ideological ones, and that socialization experiences have a great impact on later behavior. This chapter examines the influence of primary and secondary groups on the behavior of members. It demonstrates the importance of some groups and the seeming irrelevance of others for participation.

Some people with little competence may join the party out of a commitment to its goals or desire to participate meaningfully in politics. That is, they may have been highly motivated before joining, despite their low level of competence. Their increase in knowledge and efficacy may be due largely to personal exertions to improve themselves. In other words, joining the party might be a result of a general activation of political interest, a variable that is prior in time and in logic to either political participation or competence.

As has been indicated in the previous chapter, there is considerable evidence that this is true of some of the members, especially those who became active at the end of fascism and the reorganization of the party in 1945. Politics was in the air, so to speak, and after twenty years of prohibition on political activity there was considerable enthusiasm for political parties. The PCI, PSI, and Action Party in particular were popular, for they were untainted by fascism and had been active in the Resistance. The memory of the Resistance and the mystique of the left attracted many middle-class individuals who ordinarily would not have been drawn to the left by self-interest. Interviews with middle-class members and leaders repeatedly demonstrate the importance of ideological and rational—nonconventional and nontraditional—motivations for these middle-class Socialists. In some cases the influence of professors in the ideological conversion of better educated members is evident; other members mentioned an anti-Fascist military commander, a particular Resistance figure whom they admired, or their sharp emotional and intellectual revulsion against fascism. In these cases it is evident that joining the party followed a more basic political awakening.

But this is not the dominant pattern. The interviews suggest that many, indeed most, of the rank and file members of the party did not join because they were highly motivated by considerations of ideology or the possibility of exercising influence. In fact, it is difficult to determine the difference between the nominal member and the party supporter.[1] It is probable that the former was presented with the opportunity to enroll without making any particular effort. The number of wives and relatives of members in this category suggests that many joined for what were probably nonpolitical reasons. There are other members for whom such simple explanations are not available. Why do people continue in the party? How does the network of associations affect participation? What is the impact of primary and secondary group memberships on participation? As there

1. The category of supporter corresponds to the use of the term by Maurice Duverger, *Political Parties* (New York, Wiley, 1954), pp. 101–09.

are many varieties of political motivation, no simple group determinism is adequate. But it is equally clear that group memberships influence the degree of politicization of the individual, his choice of allegiances, and his political attitudes. The group memberships examined in this chapter are the family, work associates, trade unions, and friendship cliques.

For most members of the party the effect of group memberships is cumulative and reinforcing. It is for this reason that one can speak of a conventional or traditional Socialist. In the province under study, social stratification and political orientation are so closely related that what needs to be explained is often not why an individual is leftist in his politics but why he is not. Yet the dominant political climate of an area does not determine the level of a person's interest in politics: it merely presents him with alternatives that are more or less acceptable, or predisposes him toward a particular party. It would have been desirable to be able to examine comparable data from other parties, especially the PCI. From internal evidence of PSI members alone, however, some important components of party identification can be indicated. The influence of the PSI within the family and other groups is evident, and it is also clear that these groups have considerable influence on the attitudes of the rank and file. An additional interest here is the impact of these groups on the internal divisions of the party. The influence of the family will be examined first.

FAMILY INFLUENCES

There are several ways in which the family can influence a member's political activity. The political orientation of his parents has been shown to be influential in socializing him into a set of attitudes and loyalties toward political objects. Parents seem to influence the level of political interest and the political loyalties of their children. The member's contemporary family is important also. It may reinforce or discourage his political initiatives. If other members share his political views and loyalties, participation is facilitated; if they are unconcerned or favor rival parties conflicts may easily arise. Withdrawal from the conflict situation is a common mechanism for dealing with incompatible loyalties.

The evidence from the PSI sample indicates that respondents' families reinforce their Socialist sympathies. Almost all married members indicated that the political sympathies of their spouses were for the PSI. (See Table 9-1.) Many respondents have other

Table 9-1. Political Sympathies of Spouses (in percent)

PSI	94
PCI	4
DC	1
Other	1
	100

$N=192$

members of their families enrolled in the PSI. There are two different types of family memberships involved here. One is that of a truly militant family in which several members are enthusiastically involved in party affairs. Although such families exist, they are rare. Women rank low on participation and there are few husband-wife activist teams in the party; while there are some father-child and brother-brother activist combinations, they are likewise rare. (The question asked was, "What other members of the immediate family were enrolled?," and only wife, husband, son, daughter, brother, and sister were coded.)

The second and more common type of family membership involved an activist, usually a husband or father, recruiting other members of his family. This is done for various reasons—swelling the membership rolls, increasing section and faction voting strength, expressing solidarity, facilitating political education, and others. The practice of enrolling members of the family is an old one that is not strongly encouraged at the present time; it is not, however, forbidden. The lukewarm nature of most such satellite memberships is recognized by party leaders and can be inferred from the data. It is somewhat obscured by the inclusion of both the activist and the satellite members, which tends to cancel out some of the differences in participation. But nominal members are more likely to have other members of the family enrolled than any other group, with militants having the next highest percentage. (See Table 9-2.) This suggests

Table 9-2. Level of Participation and Other Members of Family Enrolled (in percent)

	Nominal	Marginal	Participant	Militant
Other enrolled	67	36	33	47
Not enrolled	33	64	67	53
	100	100	100	100
N	43	102	79	74

that militants and others recruit many of the nominal members. This can also be inferred from an examination of sex differences on the variable of multiple family memberships. In the entire sample, 43 percent had other family members in the PSI while 57 percent did not. But the percentage of women with other family members in the party was very large, as Table 9-3 in-

Table 9-3. Other Members of Family in PSI, by Sex (in percent)

	Women	Men
Yes	85	36
No	15	64
	100	100
N	39	262

dicates. Women members of the PSI federation ranked very low on the participation scale, with 44 percent of them in the nominal category and 41 percent in the marginal: most fall into the category of recruited members.

On the other hand, the study provides no confirmation of the conventional wisdom that wives of members of leftist parties support the Christian Democratic Party. On the contrary, PSI wives seem to support the PSI overwhelmingly. But the fact that most of the respondents were males suggests caution. Perhaps Italian males do not like to admit to interviewers that their wives disagree with them; or perhaps wives say nothing and quietly vote Christian Democratic. Thus it cannot be stated with certainty that wives of PSI members follow their husbands in politics though there is no evidence that they do not. On the other hand, most women do not participate actively in the PSI even when they are formally enrolled as members.

Finally, a slightly higher portion of leftist identifiers (48 percent) than autonomists (38 percent) had other members of their families enrolled in the party.

To summarize, available evidence suggests that contemporary families reinforce the PSI sympathies of members. Few members are placed in conflict situations by family political loyalties. The political homogeneity of the environment is remarkable, however, and it is impossible to separate out the effects of the family from those of the political culture in general. The culture strongly reinforces the leftist patterns acquired in childhood and reinforced by the contemporary family. Perhaps the most important legacy of the family is party identification: in a province in which the Communists outnumber the Socialists more than two to one, joining the PSI rather than the PCI seems to be in large part a matter of family tradition.

THE IRRELEVANCE OF WORK

In studying the International Typographical Union, Lipset and his associates found that the work life of typographers set them apart from other workers and strongly reinforced their identification with the union.[2] Members spent much of their lives in close contact with other members in work situations that permitted extensive interaction. Work was thus an important factor in the integration of the union. But it is irrelevant for PSI members.

It is not surprising that employment should be more crucial for an association of trade unionists than for a political party. Respondents were asked if they worked closely with others; if

2. Lipset, Trow, and Coleman, *Union Democracy*, pp. 118–59.

yes, what were the first names of their work colleagues, their party sympathies, and, if PSI members, their factional preferences. In contrast to American typographers, the work community is of slight importance for PSI members. Only a minority claimed to have regular work associates (apart from members of the family), and these seemed to exert little influence on participation and attitudes.

There are important differences among occupations in the existence and importance of work associates. Farmers work alone or with members of the family. Many unskilled laborers also either work alone or with casual groups. Artisans and professional people often have no regular work colleagues; and, of course, neither do students, housewives, and the retired. Among those with work colleagues, consequently, there is a concentration of skilled workers from the few large enterprises of the commune. The PCI holds an electoral majority in the commune and in most individual plants, so it is to be expected that many PSI members work closely with PCI members or sympathizers. Although most workers in the province favor parties of the left, some do not; this too is reflected in the distribution of work colleagues. Most non-PCI-PSI workers support the Christian Democratic Party (which has a significant trade union wing). Of respondents with work colleagues 81 percent have either Socialists, Communists, or combinations thereof with whom to work. More than half of the total with work colleagues work closely with at least one Communist. Table 9-4 shows

Table 9-4. Political Sympathies of Work Colleagues, by Principal Occupation (in percent)

	Agri.	Nonagri. Unskilled	Skilled	White-Collar
PSI	50	29	37	18
PCI	50	55	44	30
Right	0	13	12	41
PCI and right	0	3	7	11
	100	100	100	100
N	4	31	41	17

the political sympathies of the work colleagues of different occupations.

Except for the general differences discussed below, neither the presence of work colleagues nor their political sympathies seems to have any independent effect on the behavior of the PSI member. All categories provide roughly similar portions of different levels of participation, knowledge, efficacy, and ideological sensitivity. Socialists with communist work colleagues are no more likely to support the left faction than others; nor do they more often choose the Marxist conception of democracy or exhibit unusual attitudes toward other political parties. In short, the politics of work colleagues seems to be irrelevant in the PSI.

There are, of course, differences in the amount and direction of the participation of various occupational categories. It seems, however, that the existence and attitudes of work associates have little to do with this. Rather, it is more likely that unequal opportunities for learning accounts for occupational differences in participation and competence. Peasants, for example, learn little of political value through their work, while lawyers, school teachers, and factory workers have opportunities to pick up relevant information in their daily contacts on the job. Occupation is closely related to socioeconomic status and education, and the interaction of these variables accounts for occupational differences in behavior without the additional variable of the political sympathies of work colleagues.

The political sympathies of the lower classes in the commune are overwhelmingly leftist. The PSI member encounters little in the work situation that contravenes his general leftist sympathies. On the other hand, he seldom is able to choose his close work associates. The numerical superiority of the PCI ensures that in any nonpurposeful distribution of assignments in plants of any size PSI members will be forced to work with Communists. It is doubtful that this is viewed as an imposition by the PSI member. While there are no data available on PCI members in the commune, an estimate based on a year's field work and informal contacts with PCI leaders and members is that there is probably little difference between the typical lower-class member of the two parties in this commune on most characteristics and attitudes. The Socialist would thus find little separating him from the Communist who works beside him, apart from party matters. As discussion of pressing political problems might find them taking different positions, these are evaded when possible: the way to harmonious on-the-job relations lies in avoiding controversy.

The nature of work-home relationships facilitates this separation of work and politics. The work community is often completely separate from the community of residence. Although the PSI organized the NAS (Socialist plant cells) to compete with the Communist plant cells, both have largely lost their vitality. The most important local unit of the PSI is the section, which is geographically based on residence, not the NAS. Many members live a considerable distance from their work, often remaining in outlying rural settlements (*frazioni*) and commuting to work. Party life revolves around the residential community, not the work community. This has important ramifications for trade union activity as well.

THE INFLUENCE OF TRADE UNION MEMBERSHIP

The PSI strongly supports the CGIL and requires that PSI members support and join a CGIL federation if they are eligible for membership. The other two important Italian labor confederations are the CISL (Confederazione Italiana Sindacati Lavoratori), which is in practice largely Christian Democratic in its political orientation, and the UIL, which is Social Democratic in its political preferences. The PSI is the minority partner of the PCI in the CGIL. In the province studied, however, the PSI seemed to exercise more influence in the CGIL than warranted by its portion of the membership; for example, the secretary of the provincial Chamber of Labor was a PSI leader. Trade unions provided the organizational foundation for the internal opposition in the PSI. It was also an important channel of communications with the workers of the province for the PSI as a whole.

Considering the strong ties between trade unions and parties it is not surprising that all PSI members who claimed trade union membership listed the CGIL. However, only 47 percent (142) of the respondents claimed union membership. The portion of various occupation groups claiming membership is shown in Table 9-5.

Table 9-5. CGIL Membership, by Principal Occupation (in percent)

	Agri.	Nonagri. Unskilled	Skilled	White-Collar
Not union member	53	42	38	50
Member only	46	51	54	34
Member and leader	1	7	8	16
	100	100	100	100
N	60	55	76	32

Like PSI membership, joining a trade union in Italy may mean a variety of things. In contrast to American unions, Italian unions seldom possess a highly articulated structure and dues-paying membership. There is a universal open shop. Union strength is best measured by the votes received in elections to plant grievance committees or by ability to mobilize mass support for union demands. Union members are expected to buy a union card and pay monthly dues, but fully paid-up members are exceptional.[3] The importance to the unions of the political party is obvious. It is almost certain that party members provide the hard core of union activists and leaders.

A PSI member who claims CGIL membership probably is an above-average unionist in his level of commitment and willingness to work for the organization. Even so, data from the sample indicate that party members devote relatively little attention to union affairs. Caution should be exercised in interpreting the findings, however, for it is activity in times of crisis that is crucial for Italian unions, not routine meetings or collective

3. See Joseph LaPalombara, *The Italian Labor Movement* (Ithaca, Cornell University Press, 1957); and Horowitz, *The Italian Labor Movement.*

bargaining. PSI union members may devote little attention to union matters over a considerable period of time and yet take an active role in demonstrations and strikes. This suggests the obvious, that it is difficult to separate union and party activity. Nevertheless, the following analysis will indicate some dimensions of party-union relations that emerge from the study.

Union membership is highly associated with party participation. The portion of the PSI members who are also union members rises in each succeeding level of participation. Participation is thus a generalized phenomenon, with those active in the party being also active in the union. (See Table 9-6.) The ease

Table 9-6. Party Participation and Union Membership (in percent)

Nominal	20
Marginal	40
Participant	55
Militant	66

with which one can affiliate with a union is not independent of occupation, but there are very few occupations whose practitioners cannot find some relevant union to join if they are sufficiently determined. The Federmezzadri, for example, organizes sharecroppers; pensioners can maintain earlier affiliations; with ingenuity, students, teachers, lawyers, and artisans can find some CGIL affiliate relevant to their interests. Nevertheless, it is much easier for an industrial worker to join than for individuals in the above categories. Indeed, industrial workers who are PSI or PCI members are under continued pressures to join. They likewise tend to participate more in party activities.

It is impossible to say whether industrial work facilitates joining both the party and union, whether union or party activity precedes the other, or whether political competence causes or is the result of participation. In the absence of time series the direction of causation must be left undetermined. What is evident is that these are strongly associated with one another.

Undoubtedly the sequence varies for different individuals. Information gathered on social relationships in the area suggests the following as the most common pattern. Most lower-class individuals are exposed early and often to the PCI and PSI in the form of social contacts with members and supporters of the parties. Few people have to "seek out" the leftist parties; they are omnipresent in this area. Some people are encouraged by friends, family, fortune, or ambition to seek a closer relationship. They do not have to be politically competent and highly motivated to do this. For most, joining the PSI rather than the PCI is probably a matter of personal relations with members of the two parties rather than ideology or perceptions of different policies and goals.

After joining, some develop political skills and take a more active interest. Involvement is cumulative; in this province union and party work do not form neatly separated compartments. The parties closely control unions and use them virtually as integral units of the parties, jointly administered by the PSI and PCI leadership. Union positions are interchangeable with party positions; no one can advance in the union hierarchy without the sponsorship of one of the two parties. It is to be expected, therefore, that party activists likewise take an interest in union affairs.

The unions provide the structural basis of the opposition faction in the PSI. It is surprising therefore that in the rank and file sample union membership is not associated with any particular position on the variables dealing with internal party differences. Thus union members are no more likely than nonmembers to be leftist in internal party politics, to take more leftist programmatic stands, to have non-Socialist friends, to choose a particular conception of democracy, or to exhibit attitudes toward other parties that deviate from the overall PSI pattern. Union members do reflect the differences that are associated with high participation in general. They are more knowledgeable and efficacious, and more often identify with one of the two internal factions; but they divide between the two factions exactly as does the party as a whole. Thus union membership is associated with increased political competence and higher levels of participation, but it is not significantly related to internal factions except as increased competence and participation are reflected in an increased awareness of and involvement in internal factional matters.

When not mere membership but attendance at union meetings is examined the following conclusions emerge. Not unexpectedly, party militants and factional identifiers attend more union meetings. Although both are equally likely to belong to unions, leftists participate slightly more than autonomists in union meetings, and both participate more than independents. While statistically significant, the differences between the two factions are small.

Being active in the union is thus largely a function of party participation. Those members who participate more in the latter participate in the former. And factional identifiers are also more likely to be union members, though there is not much difference between autonomists and leftists on either union membership or level of union participation. However, this is true of the members only, not the leaders.

THE INFLUENCE OF FRIENDS

The political homogeneity of the party environment has repeatedly been emphasized. Nowhere is this more apparent than in the friendship network that incorporates the PSI member into a leftist political culture. As in the case of work colleagues, respondents were asked the first names of their two closest friends, and then questioned about their friends' political associations or sympathies, their factional adherence (if PSI members), their occupations, and the amount and nature of political discussions with them. These figures underestimate the number of PSI friendships, because if one was non-PSI his party was coded. Few PSI members had nonleftists among their two closest friends. Many had Communist Party members or sympathizers as close friends, however, and there are some interesting variations in their portion within different levels of PSI participation. As Table 9-7 indicates, militants and nominal categories had

Table 9-7. Participation and Political Sympathies of Friends (in percent)

	Nominal	Marginal	Participant	Militant
Both friends PSI or apolitical	80	64	50	78
At least one friend PCI	8	24	35	14
At least one friend right of PSI-PCI	12	12	15	8
	100	100	100	100
N	25	83	74	68

more members whose contacts were limited to Socialists. The high portion of participant members and, to a lesser extent, marginal members with at least one close friend with Communist sympathies is of interest. The high level of PSI integration of the nominal members is understandable in terms of their probable reasons for joining the party: most are almost certainly enrolled for social or family reasons, not because they are highly politicized. It is therefore not surprising that a high portion of them have Socialist friends; this is one of the principal reasons why they are enrolled in the party.

The influence of friends is also evident in matters reflecting internal factional loyalties. Most members have friends who agree with them on internal party matters. Thus of the ninety-eight members who listed their friends and who also admitted to a factional allegiance, eighty-eight said that both friends supported the same faction and only ten stated that even one close friend was of the opposing persuasion.

The relationship between party participation and integration into a PSI subculture is also shown by the amount of time devoted to party matters. This approaches the question of friendship from a somewhat different direction, seeking to ascertain the relative amount of energy devoted to discussing party matters with friends. According to their own recollections, participants spent significantly more time discussing party matters with friends and took a much more active part in the discussion. Also, members whose close friends were Socialists spent significantly more time discussing party matters with their friends: 31 percent of those with Socialist friends, 40 percent of those with Communist, and 57 percent of those with friends sympathizing with parties to the right of the PSI and PCI stated that they never discussed politics with their friends.

The more active party members more often spent their time with party colleagues and also more often with the same group. Thus 75 percent of the militants, 62 percent of the participants, 51 percent of the marginal, and only 40 percent of the nominal members associated habitually with the same group of party colleagues. As would be expected, the same differences were found between factional identifiers and independents. But the autonomists and leftists are remarkably similar to one another, is indicated in Table 9-8. Between 20 and 25 percent of each

Table 9-8. Faction and Association with Party Colleagues (in percent)

	Ind.	Auton.	Left.
Never associate with party colleagues	28	5	10
Same group	51	70	70
Different group	21	25	20
	100	100	100
N	163	83	40

group circulate among different groups of party colleagues; distinctions emerge only in the greater amount of time spent with the same group of colleagues by the identifiers. The importance of a homogeneous environment is demonstrated anew by the large portion of autonomists and leftists who associate with party colleagues.

The family, work, union, and friendship associations of the respondents generally serve to reinforce loyalties to parties of the political left and, in most cases, the PSI in particular. Supporting the political left is often a family tradition, and preferring the PSI over the PCI is likewise usually a matter of following the example of the family. However, as the general orientation of the political culture is leftist it is difficult to separate the influence of the family on participation from that of the culture in general. This is especially true of level of participation and attitudes toward internal party matters.

Work associates likewise reinforce the leftist sympathies of the respondents. They do not, however, seem to influence either the level or the direction of their PSI participation. The strength of the PCI and the separation of work and party activity seem to be the most important reasons for this. Union activity is closely related to party activity, without exercising much of an independent influence in party matters. However, leftists do take a slightly more active role in union affairs than autonomists. Friends likewise are of the left. The higher the level of participation the more homogeneous the circle of friends (except for the nominal members, who are enrolled for affective reasons anyway). The overall evidence from the influence of associates is that it is very easy in this commune to be a psi member for traditional and social reasons. One can join and remain in the psi without being ideologically inclined, highly motivated, or politically competent. The family and the political environment make socialism a traditional loyalty for most of the membership. However, ideology is generally assumed to be of considerable importance in Italian socialism. We will now investigate its relevance for an understanding of the politics of this federation.

10.

The Relevance of Ideology

Few concepts in political science are as important and yet as ill-defined as ideology. That ideology is relevant to the study of politics is seldom denied. But what is meant by ideology and how the concept might be operationalized have given rise to a debate that has served to underline the importance of the problem without contributing much to its solution.[1] In this study of democracy in a Socialist party the beliefs of party members are of great importance; understanding them will contribute to an assessment of the meaning of ideology within a party based upon a clearly articulated ideological position. Furthermore, it affords the opportunity to study the impact of ideology on different categories of members.

IDEOLOGICAL SENSITIVITY

The PSI is a classic Marxian democratic Socialist party, perhaps the last major one in Europe. At a time when most European Socialist parties were re-examining their philosophical foundations, rejecting doctrinaire Marxism, and vehemently proclaiming their anticommunism, the PSI remained loyal to the Marxian creed, the unity of the working class, and the Italian Communist Party. Only slowly and reluctantly did the PSI move away from its close ties and unity of action with the PCI. At the time of this study the PSI still cooperated closely with the PCI in trade unions, local governments, and other areas, while collab-

1. For a review of the different usages of the term "ideology" see David W. Minar, "Ideology and Political Behavior," *Midwest Journal of Political Science*, 5 (1961), 317–31; for the present author's analysis of the concept see Barnes, "Ideology and the Organization of Conflict," *Journal of Politics*, 28 (1966), 513–30.

orating with the center parties on the national level. Although there is evidence that some of the party's elite and rank and file are in fact revisionists similar to the Social Democrats of Italy and other European countries, the split between the PSI and the PSDI discussed in Chapters 3 and 4 eliminated many, though not all, moderates from the party and left it in the control of its more doctrinaire wing.

Unlike American and British parties, which have provided the subject matter of so many analyses of ideology, the PSI is formally committed to a particular world view. The party *Statuto* reaffirms its adherence to the Genoa program of 1892, which proclaimed that society was divided into two antagonistic classes of workers and capitalists, that the political system defended the socioeconomic dominance of capitalists, and that only through the socialization of the means of production could the working class attain freedom. "Only through the action and power of the proletariat organized in a class party, independent of all other parties" could this goal be achieved. Both industrial activity by unions and political party organization were necessary to capture power and transform it "into an instrument for the economic and political expropriation of the dominant class."[2]

The disunity of the working class that contributed to the rise of fascism and the experience of struggle and eventual victory against the common enemy contributed to the mystique of working-class unity that has exerted such a powerful attraction for the PSI. It is thus impossible to distinguish ideological influences from the requirements of strategy and tactics. Nor is it completely necessary. For ideological presuppositions conditioned the selection of means, and the events of the twentieth century seemed to confirm, for many Italian Socialists, the correctness of the original Marxian analysis. The retarded development of Italy, the uneven impact of development, the persistence of precapitalist social relations, the peculiar position of the Catholic Church, and the impact of fascism left Italy socially fragmented and devoid of political consensus.[3]

2. *Statuto*, 1957 text, article 1.
3. For an elaboration of this point see Samuel H. Barnes, "Oppositions

Contemporary Italy consequently is one of the most badly fragmented countries in Europe in terms of social structure and ideological commitment. The PSI represents one of these ideological currents, which range from "pro-Chinese" communism to clericalism and fascism. There is no doubt of this: Italian politics can be and often is viewed in ideological terms, and for many Italians these ideologies have behavioral consequences.

The concept of ideology has several components and can be approached in diverse ways. It has been demonstrated that education makes a big difference in political participation. Not surprisingly, it also affects the level of ideological understanding. Education is especially necessary for conceptions of ideology that emphasize abstractions and articulateness. Given the low level of educational achievement of PSI members, some formulations of ideology are simply beyond the members' frame of reference.

The significance of ideology for a political party thus may not lie in its salience for and diffusion through the bulk of the membership but rather in its meaning for leaders and the nucleus of militants. Party decision making may be heavily influenced by ideological considerations even though rank and file members possess little ideological sophistication. Consequently particular attention will be devoted to the significance of ideology for specific categories of the party.

Ideology is not an undifferentiated concept; it has many interpretations and dimensions. These all probably refer to different dimensions of a single concept, ideology, which is the underlying framework, the analytic a priori, an individual utilizes to bring order into sensory experience, whether received first or second hand. Although a thorough discussion would lead into the unfamiliar field of perception, some guidelines need to be indicated.[4] Most people seem to order their experiences in terms of past experiences. When confronted with

in Italy: Left, Right, and Center," in Robert A. Dahl, ed., *Political Oppositions in Western Democracies* (New Haven, Yale University Press, 1965), pp. 303–31.

4. For an elaboration see Barnes, "Ideology and the Organization of Conflict."

something new they tend to be bewildered and uncertain; they lack a wider frame of reference and training in reasoning by analogy and extrapolation. This means, of course, that I am building an intellectual bias into the concept of ideology. I think that this is justifiable. The wisdom of experience is not ideology, nor is constraint in belief and action stemming from rigid adherence to tradition. On the other hand, these may, like ideology, contribute to constraint and stability in belief systems.

Catholicism may serve as an example. The natural law of Catholicism represents a well-developed ideology, an analytical framework for ordering most of human experience. Theologians, priests, and even educated laymen understand natural law teachings and can apply them to new subjects such as space travel and birth control pills. The devout Catholic who is not trained in natural law acquires attitudes toward right and wrong through socialization, but he does not necessarily become conversant with the underlying rationale for these choices. Indeed, one of the advantages of participation in an association or group is the possibility of acquiring ideology by proxy. And traditionalism may be viewed as ideology by repetition. The provision of a wider frame of reference is one of the functions performed by churches, political parties, and investment counselors. For a party to have ideological significance it is not necessary that even the bulk of the membership be ideologically sensitive. It is sufficient that the leaders exhibit sensitivity and that these ideological views influence the behavior of the membership.

Consequently, it is to be expected that high ideological sensitivity will be closely associated with education and knowledge, for ideologues possess a frame of reference that is difficult to acquire without the ability to deal in abstractions and to benefit from experience second hand. While it is important to keep ideological sensitivity separate from constraint in belief systems, it is difficult in practice to separate the two; but it is not impossible even with the crude means of measurement used in this study. For it is one thing for an individual to express positive or negative judgments on policy questions and another to express himself on open-ended questions concerning problems of contemporary politics and the nature of other parties in the political system. The person with genuine ideological sensitivity will view these problems in terms of his frame of reference; the ideologist by proxy, suddenly cast adrift from the anchor of party platform and policy, either spouts clichés or is rendered inarticulate. I maintain, therefore, that the measure of ideological sensitivity used in this chapter taps any underlying ideological analytical framework that is there.

The presence or absence of constraints in the belief systems of individuals is another dimension of ideology.[5] This taps the degree to which the individual's beliefs are internally consistent. There is no simple way of determining whether this consistency is due to an ideological framework, family background, or personal organizational loyalties. From the narrow viewpoint of constraint in belief systems perhaps it does not matter, but for the student of political parties and the role of leaders in mediating between the governmental system and mass publics it has vast ramifications. Thus it is possible that only elite attitudes are, in general, ideologically derived, though these may likewise be formed by other sources.

Contrary to the conventional wisdom, it is probable that ideologically sensitive individuals are more apt than others to modify their policy preferences over time; for as the situation changes, their frame of reference should lead them to adapt to changed conditions, while the constraints stemming from tradition and organizational loyalties are not so easily altered. Thus can the "conservatism" of many working-class organizations be understood: explanations of the world acquired at great effort and sacrifice are not easily abandoned for merely intellectual reasons.

There is a third dimension of ideology, a substantive one, that will be discussed in the next chapter and consequently will merely be introduced here. The importance of the unity of the working class in the official outlook of the PSI was emphasized

5. For a discussion of this approach see Philip E. Converse, "The Nature of Belief Systems of Mass Publics," in David Apter, ed., *Ideology and Discontent* (New York, Free Press, 1965), pp. 206–61.

above. Its economic goals and basic class loyalties are similar to those of the PCI. Yet, the PSI has maintained its separate existence, even when it ran joint candidates with the Communists; and after 1956 pre-existing tendencies toward autonomy were accelerated. The basic doctrinal differences between the two parties involve contrasting conceptions of democracy. The PSI is devoted to achieving and maintaining power by democratic means. For a majority of its leaders, a democratic system of government is necessary regardless of the economic system; socialism without democracy would be a monstrosity. The PCI, on the other hand, is prepared to use the democratic system as a means to power, but it has never proclaimed its intention to adhere to the democratic rules of the game once in power.

There are also great differences in practice in internal democracy in the two parties. The PCI, like other Communist parties, encourages a high level of participation by the membership. However, the doctrine of "democratic centralism" combined with a numerous and efficient bureaucracy result in a "manipulatory democracy" in which participation is utilized primarily as a device for indoctrination rather than local initiative. The PSI is not wholly dissimilar in its avowed aims. It encourages participation, but the formation of "factions" is prohibited, unity is stressed, discipline can be applied against deviants, and, as has been noted, a strong bureaucracy was planned as the moving force in the party. However, the reality is different. The PSI is in practice a stratarchy in which echelons are relatively autonomous. De facto factions have historically divided the party. Leaders are reluctant to discipline opponents. The bureaucracy is small and inadequate to the task of running the party without volunteer assistants. The PSI is thus in fact internally democratic. While similar close examination of the PCI would undoubtedly reveal that it too is hardly as monolithic as it outwardly appears, the difference between the two parties on the issue of internal democracy is considerable.

In the remainder of this chapter I will examine the first two dimensions of ideology. The first of these is ideological sensitivity. Who in the party exhibits the ability to interpret political questions in ideological terms and who sees them in terms of class or group benefits or simply good and bad? The relationship between patterns of responses to five questions relating to party policy—constraint in belief systems—and several variables will also be examined. The third ideological dimension—the view of democracy held by the members—will be taken up in the next chapter, which deals with attitudes relevant to internal democracy.

LEVELS OF IDEOLOGICAL SENSITIVITY

Ideological sensitivity refers to the capacity to view political events in terms of some analytical scheme of values. The concept was operationalized by coding answers to open-ended questions into several categories of responses. Respondents were asked, "In your opinion what are the most important problems of Italian public life today?" and, "If you had to explain Italian political parties to someone who had spent all of his life in another country, in a few words, what would you say about the PCI? About the Christian Democratic Party? About the PSI? About the Social Democratic Party?" Respondents who exhibited a great deal of ideological sensitivity, who used ideological terms seriously and meaningfully, were coded high on ideological sensitivity.[6] While only this group can be considered without reservations as exhibiting ideological sensitivity, only eight of the respondents, a number too small for analysis, met the original standards. Consequently, the interviews were re-examined, requirements for inclusion were relaxed, and an additional thirty-four respondents whose answers included references to democracy, totalitarianism, a planned economy, and similar concepts with ideological implications were coded as exhibiting some ideological sensitivity. The remainder of the respondents were divided into four categories. Those who saw parties in terms of general group or class benefits, such as favoring the working class or being the party of capitalists, were separated from those who gave more limited or programmatic

6. Adapted from Campbell et al., *The American Voter,* Chapter 10.

answers, referring, for example, to the interests of farmers or industrial workers. Many respondents held a simple good-bad view of the parties, saying merely that "The PCI is bad," or "I don't like Saragat." These were placed in a single category of respondents who viewed politics in terms of personal ties or simple likes and dislikes. Finally, many respondents were simply unable or unwilling (and the former seems to be the case most often) to articulate anything about the parties that could be meaningfully coded. The patterns of responses is given in Table 10-1.

Table 10-1.   Levels of Ideological Sensitivity

	N	%
High ideological sensitivity	8	3
Some ideological sensitivity	34	11
General group or class benefits	45	15
Limited benefits or programmatic	64	21
Personalities or simple likes and dislikes	100	33
Not codible	50	17
	301	100

This indicates a surprising lack of ideological sensitivity. As this sample omits those members who held formal PSI leadership posts in the commune, it undoubtedly slightly under-represents the overall ideological sensitivity of the total membership. Many of the leaders, especially the well-educated ones, exhibited a great deal of ideological sophistication; other leaders, however, especially secretaries of sections, were not attuned to the ideological dimensions of issues. And as this is a one-of-three sample, inclusion of the leaders could not have greatly altered the above distribution. The conclusion must be that the PSI in the commune does not contain many members who view political questions in ideological terms, despite the fact that the PSI is a Marxian party with a well-defined ideological tradition.

A previous chapter has demonstrated that ideology was important in motivating a crucial segment of the party to join; this segment is important precisely because it contains the deviant members of the party, those whose Socialist affiliation contrasts with their traditional class ties. These members are important to the party because they possess many of the qualities of education, knowledge, and sense of efficacy that are so lacking in the remainder of the party, and hence these ideologues occupy key positions in the party. As we will see, this distinction between the ideologues, who are disproportionately middle-class and high in participation, and the nonideological rank and file is basic within the party. Consequently, it can be maintained simultaneously that an overwhelming majority of the rank and file are not sensitive to ideological issues and that ideology plays an important role in the PSI, for it is an important variable in attracting and retaining the loyalty of those with skills that are scarce in the party. This is, of course, not the only source of such skills; the PCI very effectively and the PSI less successfully trains leaders from within the working class.[7]

The following analysis will suggest, however, that the most important factor in the development of ideological sensitivity is education; except for the well-educated, participation is not highly associated with ideological sensitivity.

CORRELATES OF IDEOLOGICAL SENSITIVITY

It has already been acknowledged that the conception of ideology as constraint in belief systems has an intellectual bias, that it requires the ability to apply general concepts to concrete problems. Training in dealing with abstractions and generalities is typically one of the products or by-products of formal education. As is to be expected, ideological sensitivity is closely associated with education (gamma = .49).[8] Only 4 percent of those with less than five years of formal education exhibited any ideological sensitivity; 15 percent of those with five years did so; 44 percent of those with more than five years qualified for the ideological categories. Although the numbers are too small to

7. On this phenomenon within Communist parties, including the PCI, see Almond, *The Appeals of Communism*.
8. As explained in Chapter 7 the gamma correlation summarizes the degree of association between ordinal variables, with limits of ±1.0.

justify conclusions, these percentages rise to 55 percent of those with at least a technical school education (eight years) and 72 percent of those with at least some high school (nine years or more).

If the respondents are examined as an undifferentiated sample, the intercorrelation of education with knowledge, participation, and several other variables is very high. In this sample, in which attributes tend to cluster to a high degree, it is difficult to separate education from social class, occupation, residence, and other variables. The overall patterns are what were to be expected; of particular importance are the differences in the patterns of specific groups. And here some rather surprising divergences from the overall patterns emerge. A previous chapter has demonstrated that participation can serve as a substitute for education in developing political knowledge and a sense of efficacy. Participation is also highly associated with ideological sensitivity, *but only for those with considerable education.* In other words, ideologues are those members who have attained a high level of education *and* who rank high on participation. Poorly educated militants are not ideologues: only those high on participation who have a strong educational base rank high on ideological sensitivity. The association between level of participation and ideological sensitivity for the three educational groups is shown in Table 10-2. This is not to say that participation has no impact on the member's view of politics. It may increase the sophistication of all educational levels, though the increase for the lowest level is slight; but its impact is far more dramatic for the best educated group.

The implications of these findings are important. Participation increases the ideological sensitivity of all educational groups. Its impact, however, is less on those with less education; and, while it slightly raises their consciousness above the simply good and bad level, it does not convert them into ideologues. Participation seems to increase political competence (knowledge and efficacy) and hence makes political action possible. Insofar as the goals of political action are conditioned by a sensitivity to ideological considerations, however, individuals with low edu-

Table 10-2. Participation and Ideological Sensitivity, by Educational Level

A. LESS THAN FIVE YEARS' EDUCATION

Level of Participation	Ideological Sensitivity					Totals
	Low				High	
	1	2	3	4	5	
Low 1	9	4	1	1	0	15
2	18	8	3	1	0	30
3	13	2	4	2	0	21
High 4	11	9	3	0	0	23
Total N	51	23	11	4	0	89

Gamma = .09

B. FIVE YEARS' EDUCATION

Level of Participation	Ideological Sensitivity					Totals
	Low				High	
	1	2	3	4	5	
Low 1	2	2	4	1	0	9
2	21	8	9	4	0	42
3	13	7	7	6	0	33
High 4	6	13	6	5	2	32
Total N	42	30	26	16	2	116

Gamma = .17

C. MORE THAN FIVE YEARS' EDUCATION

Level of Participation	Ideological Sensitivity					Totals
	Low				High	
	1	2	3	4	5	
Low 1	1	1	0	0	0	2
2	2	2	3	2	2	11
3	3	4	1	1	0	9
High 4	0	1	4	8	7	20
Total N	6	8	8	11	9	42

Gamma = .43

cational achievement are dependent on others for the analysis and casuistry involved in applying ideological concepts to specific problems. Since most members seem to affiliate for non-ideological reasons, and many acquire their sense of competence from the party, leaders who are ideologically sophisticated have an important weapon in the internal power struggle. They are in a position to interpret events, choose the alternatives presented to the membership, deal in dialectical niceties, and defend theoretically their actions. Although often competent in practical politics, in fact sometimes more so than the ideologues, the low-status member is severely handicapped in dealing with abstractions and problems of general orientation. Even leaders of low-status origins are more likely to prefer the simplicity of traditional solutions—close ties with the PCI, working-class unity, and an end to factions (i.e. no internal debate over goals)—for they are at a disadvantage in debate and abstract reasoning. Ideological sensitivity is a virtual monopoly of the educated member.

CONSTRAINT IN BELIEF SYSTEMS

The limited ideological sensitivity of the rank and file and the importance of education in the development of this sensitivity have been demonstrated. The ideologues have been identified. Constraint in belief systems will now be considered.

By constraint is meant the existence of a pattern in the opinions held by individuals. Beliefs are not held at random; rather, they tend to cluster, to be compatible with one another. However, this can not be assumed: the degree of constraint is an empirical question. Not all belief systems are necessarily internally consistent. In the analysis that follows the degree of coherence is the dependent variable: it will examine the variables associated with high levels of constraint.

In distinguishing ideology from constraint in belief systems it must be recognized that there are several possible sources of constraint, and that ideology is but one of these. While participation in an organization may not convert an individual into an ideologue, it may provide him with a set of beliefs that exhibits far more constraint than would otherwise be the case. Education might also provide constraint quite apart from the impact of party. It must be recognized that constraint might derive from education, from party-induced attitudes, or from ideological sophistication. The following analysis will examine these sources of constraint.

Respondents were asked to select an attitude—agree strongly, agree, uncertain, disagree, disagree strongly—that was closest to their own on five statements expressing opinions about the psi and its role in Italian politics. These statements covered some of the major sources of controversy within the party and the Italian polity, and hence were salient and current for any involved party member. The distribution of responses will be analyzed in the next chapter. The questions and the letters used to identify them are as follows:

a. The psi must maintain its friendship with the pci in local administrations regardless of what happens.
b. The psi must always maintain its friendship with the pci in the trade unions.
c. It is impossible to carry forward any effective social reforms with the participation of the dc in the government.
d. With the center-left government the psi runs the risk of losing its ideological identification and of becoming social democratic.
e. Unification with the psdi would strengthen the party.[9]

As previously, gamma is used as the measure of association among the statements, as it is sensitive to scalar as well as correlational constraints.

Table 10-3 shows the strength of the association between responses on one of the questions and responses on others. As this matrix makes clear, the party is badly divided on most of these issues, a division that strikes at the roots of the party's

9. Responses to this question were reversed to bring it in line with the other questions on the left-right dimension within the party.

Table 10-3. Constraint in Policy Questions, Total Sample

	B	C	D	E
A	.75	.02	.19	.28
B		.00	.08	.16
C			.20	.02
D				.04

orientation in Italian politics, its choice of friends, its hopes for reform, its commitment to the left. The choice facing the party is the same one faced by the respondents—it can retain a doctrinaire leftism or it can pragmatically adapt to the accommodating hand being extended by the center parties. While the questions are not merely ideological, they involve ideological ramifications as simple and transparent as those faced by any party at any time. Consequently, if ideology is the principal source of constraints one would expect the most ideologically sensitive to exhibit the greatest amount of constraint. But, as Table 10-4 demonstrates, this is not the case; no group clearly exhibits more constraint than any other.

Slightly different results obtain when constraints by educational level are analyzed. As education is closely related to both social class and occupation, constraints deriving from these sources should be apparent. There is a slight hint of greater constraints among the better educated. In none of the ten cells do the better educated exhibit the smallest amount of constraint, while in six they are intermediate and in four they show the greatest amount of constraint between two items. The most poorly educated, on the other hand, had the least constraint in seven of the ten cells; and of the two pairs on which they were highest, one (C x E) revealed insignificant differences and the other (A x B) showed them simply as exhibiting most strongly a tendency common to the entire party—agreement between the necessity for continued cooperation with the Communists both in local government and in the trade unions. Significantly, these are the issues that have the most immediate meaning for the poorly educated members; the other issues relate to national politics, on which the poorly educated rank and file are ill-in-

Table 10-4. Constraints, by Level of Ideological Sensitivity

	B	C	D	E
A	.54	−.01	.35	.57
	.68	.26	−.09	.49
	.86	−.13	.33	.46
	.76	.08	.17	.06
B		.10	.21	.07
		.34	−.15	.28
		−.23	.18	.25
		.08	−.04	.16
C			.39	−.03
			−.08	−.01
			.30	.10
			.17	.14
D				.20
				.12
				.08
				−.08

Top figure in each cell is gamma for ideologues and near-ideologues combined; others are the decreasingly sensitive categories as in Table 10-1.

Table 10-5. Constraints, by Educational Level

	B	C	D	E
A	.70	−.09	.30	.47
	.70	.11	.22	.24
	.87	−.06	.06	.21
B		−.04	.40	.12
		.06	.21	.20
		−.02	−.15	.10
C			.23	.00
			.28	.02
			−.01	.07
D				.31
				.04
				−.16

Top figure in each cell is more than five years' formal education; middle, five years'; bottom, less than five years' formal education.

formed. Table 10-5 shows the distribution. Although inconclusive, these results suggest that the better educated exhibit slightly more constraint in their belief systems. This is not surprising, given the low political competence of the sample.

But what emerges most clearly from the analysis is the organizational base of constraints within the party. For the greatest constraint of all is exhibited by members who identify with the left minority within the federation. And this is true only of the left, as the autonomists on most pairs of questions reveal even less constraint than the independents. Thus the responses of the majority of autonomists reflect no consistent ideological position; they exhibit leftist as well as autonomist viewpoints on many of the major policy questions. This is quite consistent with my own impressions gathered from interviews with the leaders—autonomists are much more ambivalent than leftists in their attitudes toward the future orientation of the party.

Leftists, on the other hand, show a great deal of constraint. It is tempting to attribute differences between leftists and autonomists to ideological origins, for doctrinal differences certainly do exist. But there are sufficient differences to suggest caution. The leftists, for example, are no more ideologically sophisticated than autonomists; in fact, they are slightly less so. If the principal sources of the division were ideological, the autonomists, at least, should also have exhibited constraint in their policy preferences. Thus I suspect that it is the structural position of the left in the party, especially its dependence on cooperation with the Communists, that gives rise to its constraints. These ties are sufficient to cause leftists to respond with remarkable consistency to questions that contain hints of a reorientation of the party on both the local and national levels that might jeopardize these good relations. However, the organizational and ideological sources of constraint cannot be completely untangled.

Table 10-6 indicates the differences in constraint among leftists, autonomists, and independents. In all but two pairs $(A \times E; D \times E)$, the leftists exhibit the greatest constraint. In half the pairs the leftists rise above .50 in constraint, and a sixth

Table 10-6. Constraint, by Factional Identification

	B	C	D	E
A	.91	.23	.47	.31
	.53	−.20	.11	.38
	.80	.12	.04	.11
B		.60	1.00	.54
		−.15	.12	.06
		.06	−.12	.08
C			.56	.09
			.17	−.06
			.07	.06
D				.02
				.03
				−.09

Top figure is leftists; middle, autonomists; bottom, independents.

is .47. Factional adherence seems to be the major source of constraint in belief systems within the party. While it will not surprise students of Italian socialism that factional divisions are fundamental, it is striking that *only* the leftists are in substantial agreement on these points; autonomists and independents exhibit much less constraint.

As I have indicated, ideology seems to be important in the recruitment of middle-class members, many of whom emerge as party leaders. It is probably of negligible importance for the rank and file member. The level of ideological sophistication in the party is extremely low, and few of the members are ideologues or near-ideologues. And those who do exhibit some ideological sensitivity are sharply divided in their policy preferences. Yet the leftist members show markedly more constraint than the autonomists or independents. I conclude, consequently, that constraint derives from organizational as well as ideological sources.

11.

Membership Attitudes Toward
Party Politics

In a study of internal democracy, members' expectations assume primary importance. These expectations largely determine the interpretations that members place on the actions of leaders. The attitudinal variables studied are members' attitudes toward internal party democracy and the leadership, their general satisfaction with the party, and their policy preferences.

Those members who believe a democratic party to be one in which rank and file participation is widespread will hold expectations different from those who do not relate democracy to participation. Thus the distribution of members' attitudes toward party democracy may serve to restrict or liberate the freedom of action of the leadership. Widely shared norms requiring consultation with the membership are restrictive; the opposite is true if the members judge the party by results (ends), not processes (means). The significance of the distribution of such attitudes within a party is obvious.

Equally clear is the importance of members' trust or distrust of the leaders and their general satisfaction with the party. While distrust and dissatisfaction may lead not to opposition but rather to disaffection, associations in which they are widespread are undoubtedly more difficult to manipulate than those in which they are at a low level. Throughout this chapter close attention will be paid not only to the levels of disaffection but also to its distribution within particular categories. Special concern will be devoted to differences between the attitudes of those who rank high and low on participation, for the inner core of militants has been shown to be very important in party matters. And, where important, factional differences will likewise be analyzed.

CONCEPTIONS OF PARTY DEMOCRACY

The Hungarian revolt and the revelation of Khrushchev's denunciation of Stalin triggered, but did not cause, the open dialogue between the PSI and the PCI on the issue of democracy. The general importance of this debate about the nature of democracy in the party and state plus its relevance for this analysis of participation in the PSI render conceptions of democracy held by respondents central to this study of party democracy.

In investigating the meaning of democracy, members of the party were asked to select one of three statements reflecting differing conceptions of democracy. Pretests had demonstrated that it was extremely difficult for the rank and file to articulate their opinions and attitudes on open-ended questions. But a forced choice between set alternatives also involved some difficulties. The statements themselves, for example, are neither completely unambiguous nor necessarily mutually incompatible. It could be argued that they tap different dimensions of the notion of democracy. Furthermore, there is no way of knowing how they were interpreted by the respondents: people bring different frames of reference to the act of choosing and consequently employ various criteria.

However, in one respect this is an advantage, for it corresponds to the situation in real life; even if people choose their parties for ideological reasons, assuming that parties have well-defined ideological positions as revealed by statements of programs or historical evidence, they have to choose the most satisfactory of existing alternatives. And while it is true that most people probably select their party for a variety of reasons, of which ideological affinity may or may not be one, it is equally valid to maintain that, at least in Italy, the ideological implications of their choice have ramifications for the political system. Choice of party has an ideological significance whether particular members are aware of it or not.

The three statements were printed on separate cards, which

were shuffled between interviews. The respondent could study and rearrange them at will. The statements were designed to reflect the "classic" conception of democracy as participation, the "neoliberal" notion of democracy as choice between alternative sets of leaders and policies, and the "Marxian" view of democracy as the dominance of the interests of the neediest and most numerous class:

> Classic—A political party is democratic when the members are able to participate and influence the policies of the party.

> Neoliberal—A political party is democratic when the members have the possibility of choosing among various leaders and political policies that are proposed.

> Marxian—A political party is democratic when it represents the true interests of the most numerous and needy class of the population.

It is not surprising that a large portion of the respondents in a Marxist party such as the PSI selected the third statement. As the following analysis will demonstrate, however, selection of alternative views of democracy was not random. The pattern of the responses casts considerable light on the meaning of democracy for people of low political competence. It suggests that participation itself affects one's notions of democracy, that participation and political sophistication, not ideology, encourage respect for opposition and other components of conventional notions of democracy. Although there is widespread acceptance among respondents of democracy as a goal rather than a process, a higher portion of those who are deeply involved in party politics are concerned with democratic processes.

Of the 272 members who responded to this question, 169 (62 percent) chose the Marxian conception. When this group is broken down by level of participation, important differences emerge, as Table 11-1 indicates. The drop in the percentage selecting the Marxian conception is particularly remarkable be-

Table 11-1. Conception of Democracy and Level of Party Participation (in percent)

	Nominal	Marginal	Participant	Militant
Classic	12	12	24	36
Neoliberal	18	17	16	16
Marxian	70	71	60	48
	100	100	100	100
N	33	93	74	69

tween the first two categories, neither of which is active in party life, and the two highest categories. Equally important is that the increase in those preferring the non-Marxian categories is due solely to the increase in those choosing the classic conception. The proportion choosing the neoliberal is remarkably constant, suggesting a certain randomness in selection of this category.

Similar findings emerge from an examination of the relationship between total associational memberships and conception of democracy. Less than half of the PSI members who belong to two or more associations preferred the Marxian conception, while 71 percent of those who belonged to no association apart from the party preferred that conception. (See Table 11-2.)

Table 11-2. Total Memberships and Conception of Democracy

	Party Only	Party + One Other	Party + Two Others
Classic	13	20	33
Neoliberal	16	14	21
Marxian	71	66	46
	100	100	100
N	104	92	60

Considering that the PSI is a Marxian party, perhaps it is not surprising that almost half of the militants chose what we consider to be the Marxian conception. It should not be assumed that these members are unconcerned with internal democracy;

for example, they could have chosen the Marxian conception for ideological reasons. There is some evidence that they did not, for the more ideologically sensitive members tended more often to select non-Marxian conceptions.[1] (See Table 11-3.)

Table 11-3. Conception of Democracy and Ideological Sensitivity (in percent)

	Ideologues and Near-Ideologues	Group Benefits	Personalities
Classic	32	19	20
Neoliberal	23	20	12
Marxian	45	61	68
	100	100	100
N	41	103	89

Some categories are combined.

It is unfortunate that the small number of respondents does not allow further breakdowns. There is confirmation from another source that ideology is not the major determinant of the respondents' choice of conception of democracy. As discussed previously, the party is internally divided into autonomist and leftist factions plus the independents (who are in fact merely uninformed and unconcerned).

In selecting a response to this question, leftists would be expected to choose the Marxian conception more often than the autonomists if ideology were significant. This turns out to be true; but the independents, who would be expected to lie between the two factions by this logic, in fact chose the Marxian conception more than either group of factional identifiers. (See Table 11-4.) The autonomist identifiers have a somewhat higher rate of participation than the leftists (and of course the independents), so when participation is held constant roughly half the difference between the two factional groups disappears. Controlling for participation has less effect on the independents, as their level of participation is low: as would be expected,

1. The measure of ideological sensitivity was discussed in the previous chapter.

Table 11-4. Faction and Conception of Democracy (in percent)

	Auton.	Left.	Ind.
Classic	33	31	12
Neoliberal	25	9	14
Marxian	42	60	74
	100	100	100
N	81	42	149

most high participants were also identifiers. Thus leftists are slightly more likely than autonomists to choose the Marxian conception. While this may be attributable to factional allegiance it may also be explained away by reference to social class, union participation, and the like. But to do so would be to engage in the recurring temptation to overcontrol, for these are exactly the bases of factions. Consequently, it is preferable to let the differences stand: leftists choose the Marxian conception more often than the autonomists and less often than the independents.

An examination of the relationships between several indices of political competence reinforces the conclusion that ideology does not play a large part in the choice of conceptions of democracy. The more knowledgeable and efficacious the respondent, the more likely he is to fall into the non-Marxian categories. When the total sample is divided into three roughly equal categories on the knowledge index the portion choosing the Marxian conception is reduced from three out of four to less than one out of two. (See Table 11-5.) The percentage of those

Table 11-5. Knowledge and Conception of Democracy (in percent)

	Low (0)	Medium (1–3)	High (4–8)
Classic	12	12	36
Neoliberal	14	19	17
Marxian	74	69	47
	100	100	100
N	73	103	96

high in knowledge who selected the classic conception is three times that of those in the low and medium group; those choosing the neoliberal, however, form roughly similar portions of each knowledge category.

The relationship between sense of efficacy and conception of democracy is similar to that just examined. The portion choosing the non-Marxian conception increases with increases in efficacy. (See Table 11-6.)

Table 11-6. Efficacy and Conception of Democracy (in percent)

	Number of Efficacious Answers			
	0	1	2	3 and 4
Classic	10	19	25	33
Neoliberal	19	17	13	21
Marxian	71	64	62	46
	100	100	100	100
N	63	84	76	48

Knowledge and efficacy, as has been demonstrated, are closely related to education; consequently, it is not surprising that the better educated also prefer the non-Marxian categories. But an unanticipated regularity is that the percentage preferring the classic category doubles with each education level, from 10 percent in the lowest group to 22 percent in the middle and 40 percent in the highest category, those with more than five years of formal education. The portion favoring the neoliberal conception, on the other hand, declines slightly with increases in educational level. (See Table 11-7.)

It is thus clear that all these measures are related. Those who participate little, who are poorly educated, who know little, who rank low on sense of efficacy, and who are not ideologically sensitive chose the Marxian conception of democracy in greater portions than those with the opposite characteristics. As this conception emphasizes democracy as a goal rather than a process, this means that a majority chose a view that said nothing about the importance of participation or choice on the part of

Table 11-7. Education and Conception of Democracy (in percent)

	Less Than Five Years	Five Years	More Than Five Years
Classic	10	22	40
Neoliberal	20	18	11
Marxian	70	60	49
	100	100	100
N	94	131	47

the individual member. This could mean that the leadership encounters little concern on the rank and file level for internal democracy. On the other hand, the minority that did choose the conception granting influence to the individual member includes most of the members who do participate. Two conclusions may be drawn from this evidence. First, the minority of active members contains a majority that values participation and choice as criteria of internal party democracy. Second, it is probably participation itself, rather than ideology, that is primarily responsible for these preferences. Actual participation is probably more important than ideological abstractions as a source of respect for internal democracy.

ATTITUDES TOWARD PARTY FACTIONS

There is one attitudinal dimension that, upon first examination, seems to contradict the foregoing analysis but that can be explained in terms of federation politics. That is the existence of ambivalent attitudes toward the existence of factions even on the part of many who approve of participatory democracy. Table 11-8 shows the relationship between conception of democracy and attitudes toward factions.

It is clear, however, that most of the members (and leaders too, for that matter, though their views are not analyzed here) do not relate their attitudes toward factions to the question of democracy but rather to more mundane issues of intraparty politics. It will be recalled that the national leadership of the PSI in the period 1950–56 opposed internal divisions and attempted

Table 11-8. Conception of Democracy and Attitudes toward Factions (in percent)

	Approves of Factions	
	Yes	No
Classic	37	22
Neoliberal	23	15
Marxian	40	63
	100	100
N	73	59

to construct a monolithic party with only one slate of candidates and only one general resolution presented to the members and delegates at various party elections. Only with the changes made in 1956, when the autonomists came to power, was it possible for a minority viewpoint and slate to be presented. Despite the handicaps that would have accrued to the leftist minority if the PSI had reverted to democratic centralism (without altering the distribution of power within the party, of course), leftists strongly preferred the pre-1956 system. Responses to the question "Do you think the existence of factions in the PSI is a good thing?" indicated that three out of five leftists disapproved of factions. (See Table 11-9.)[2] Although they were in the majority

Table 11-9. Approval of Faction, by Faction (in percent)

	Auton.	Left.	Ind.
Yes	62	33	5
No	31	60	4
DK	7	7	91
	100	100	100
N	84	43	169

2. This is indirectly relevant for May's argument that Michels was more concerned with furthering the interests of the rank and file than in advancing organizational democracy; the left, the more revolutionary (romantic?) faction, was less supportive of internal democracy than the right. See May, "Democracy, Organization, Michels," American Political Science Review, 59 (1965), 429.

(and hence did not directly depend upon internal democracy), almost two out of three autonomists approved of factions. A similar pattern can be seen in the response to the related question, "Do you think that the existence of the factions weakens the party?" This was a control question asked later in the interview. The slight changes in the pattern are interesting: considerably more autonomists *and* leftists approved of factions than thought that they did not weaken the party. (See Table 11-10.)

Table 11-10. Do Factions Weaken the Party? by Faction (in percent)

	Auton.	*Left.*	*Ind.*
No	51	19	5
Yes	35	72	3
DK	14	9	92
	100	100	100
N	*84*	*43*	*169*

These findings strongly suggest that, whatever an outside observer might think, many PSI members are able to conceive of a participatory intraparty democracy without factions. Their attitudes toward the existence of factions are greatly influenced by their factional loyalties and the policy preferences resulting therefrom. This is further evidence of the greater importance of organizational as opposed to ideological constraints.

ATTITUDES TOWARD THE ROLE OF THE RANK AND FILE

Another related attitudinal variable concerns members' perceptions of their influence in the PSI. Respondents were asked whether the rank and file member had a great deal of influence, not much influence, or no influence at all on what the party did. Table 11-11 indicates the pattern of response. Of the fifty-six respondents who did not answer the question, fifty were independents, most of whom were of the lower-lower social class. The other responses are randomly scattered throughout several categories; chi-square tests of the significance of the relationship between this variable and several of the party cate-

Table 11-11.   Influence of the Rank and File

	N	% Total N	% Reduced N
Great deal of influence	136	45	56
Not much influence	98	33	40
No influence	11	3	4
Did not respond	56	19	—
	301	100	100

gories previously used do not attain even the .05 level. In other words, while many party members feel that the rank and filers do not exert much influence on party matters, they are not concentrated in any particular category. High and low participants, independents, leftists, and autonomists, middle-class and lower lower-class members all divide roughly equally among the three categories. The only possible exception to this observation arises from the concentration of the nonrespondents in the independent and lower lower-class categories. Had they responded they might have swelled the uninfluential categories of these two groups, thus altering the results. But this is only a "perhaps." Feelings that the rank and file member is influential seem to stem predominantly from individual idiosyncratic attitudes not directly related to socioeconomic or internal factional differences within the party.

Asked whether the rank and file should have more influence, the same influence, or less influence, the respondents replied as indicated in Table 11-12. It is a bit surprising that so many individuals who thought that the rank and file members had a great deal of influence thought that they should have still more. As in the previous question, many lower lower-class re-

Table 11-12.   Influence Rank and File Should Have

	N	% Total N	% Reduced N
More influence	191	64	78
Same influence	49	16	20
Less influence	6	2	2
Did not respond	55	18	—
	301	100	100

spondents did not answer this question. Even so, lower lower-class members were more inclined than others to think that the rank and file should have more influence. While differences among the categories are slight, they are statistically significant. They are politically significant only in that they indicate that lower social classes are a bit more prone than higher to want greater influence in the party. This probably derives from a vague feeling that they are disadvantaged in party affairs, and this is indeed objectively the case. (See Table 11-13.)

Table 11-13. Social Class and Influence Desired (in percent)

	Lower-lower	Upper-lower	Middle
More influence	87	77	58
Same influence	12	22	38
Less influence	1	1	4
	100	100	100
N	125	66	50

These findings can be summarized as follows: A majority of party members think that the rank and file have a great deal of influence but a majority also feel that they should have more. Aside from a tendency for lower-class members to prefer more influence, these attitudes seem to have few ramifications for the internal politics of the party.

MEMBERSHIP SATISFACTION WITH PARTY

The fourth dimension of membership attitudes toward party democracy concerns general satisfaction with the party. While it is difficult to relate a generalized feeling of satisfaction or dissatisfaction to specific behavioral consequences, it is perhaps a measure of underlying discontent. A leadership faced with widespread discontent undoubtedly must act with greater circumspection than one that is not. Satisfied members are less likely to obstruct the leadership, undermine it, or seek to overthrow it than are those who are dissatisfied. It is not merely a question of rank and file revolt; rather, it is the opportunity, the lever, that such dissatisfaction provides to opponents of the leadership. It is much easier for dissident leaders to combat the formal leadership if there is a widespread malaise, whether the rank and file are sufficiently aroused to oppose the incumbents actively or not.

All associations probably contain both dissatisfaction and potential leaders ready to exploit it. The degree of dissatisfaction that is compatible with security of leadership tenure is an important question. Unfortunately, it requires comparative data, preferably over some considerable time span; in the absence of such data, that larger question cannot be dealt with here. It is possible, however, to examine the relationship between dissatisfaction and internal party politics. This indicates that the large body of nominal and marginal members form a contented cushion seemingly untouched by the opinions of the discontented left.

When satisfaction was analyzed it was evident that the small number of discontented rendered a detailed breakdown unwarranted. Instead, the familiar chi-square test of significance was utilized to discover which differences were unlikely to occur by chance alone. This is a dangerous procedure, for if a sufficient number of tables are examined some of them can be expected to evidence significant differences in distributions by chance alone. This danger is minimized by establishing a very high significance level of .001. Confidence in the results is increased by referring these findings to other data, gathered through leadership interviews and observation, that bear on the topic of satisfaction. The findings of the membership interviews are thus reinforced by other, independent, sources.

Respondents were asked whether they were in general very satisfied, satisfied, uncertain, dissatisfied, or very dissatisfied with present party politics, with the results indicated in Table 11-14.

Only forty-seven did not express satisfaction. These were scattered throughout the levels of participation, with the militants being neither more nor less satisfied than other groups. Only the relationship between several indices of status and faction and satisfaction reach significance at the .001 level.

The first area of discontent involves status. Respondents of

Table 11-14.   Satisfaction with Party

	N	%
Very satisfied	78	27
Satisfied	157	55
Uncertain	30	11
Dissatisfied	15	5
Very dissatisfied	2	1
	282	100

higher social class express less satisfaction; this is also true of those with higher education and more total associational memberships. One suspects that these groups may merely be less prone to give conventional answers. It is also probable that persons with these characteristics who join the PSI do so at least in part out of general dissatisfaction, and that its manifestation in response to this question may owe as much to nonparty feelings as to immediate party politics. While the different response patterns of these groups are statistically significant, it is difficult to determine with security their political significance.

This is not the case with the second arena of discontent, that relating to programmatic position and faction. Respondents with leftist positions on the programmatic index express dissatisfaction much more frequently than those with more rightist positions. When the scale of satisfaction is dichotomized into those expressing satisfaction and those uncertain or dissatisfied the different programmatic positions are progressively more satisfied from left to right. (See Table 11-15.)

Table 11-15.   Programmatic Position and Level of Satisfaction with Party (in percent)

	Extreme Left	Left	Moderate	Right	Extreme Right
Satisfied	55	80	84	94	100
Dissatisfied, uncertain	45	20	16	6	0
	100	100	100	100	100
N	33	107	31	78	21

Similar findings emerge from an examination of the responses of the adherents of the leftist and autonomist factions. The leftists express far more dissatisfaction than the autonomists. This is what would be expected, as the leftists are the minority in opposition to the present leadership and its policies. Of particular importance is the high level of satisfaction of the independents, those who do not identify with either faction. (See Table 11-16.) The independents express almost as much satis-

Table 11-16. Faction and Satisfaction (in percent)

	Auton.	*Left.*	*Ind.*
Satisfied	92	48	88
Dissatisfied, uncertain	8	52	12
	100	100	100
N	*84*	*41*	*156*

faction as the autonomists, indicating that the party members who say they do not engage in factional activities do not seem unhappy with the way the present majority runs the party.

Satisfaction with the party is thus widespread. Only members of the minority faction express dissatisfaction. This was to be expected, given the structure of conflict within the party. The similarity between autonomists and independents on this variable is important, as it seemingly indicates strong support among the rank and file for the leadership in office.

ATTITUDES TOWARD CURRENT POLICY QUESTIONS

The final dimension to be discussed concerns specific policy issues. An index of programmatic position, computed from five questions dealing with attitudes toward current issues within the PSI, revealed what one would intuitively expect: the leftists took the leftist position and the autonomists the rightist position on these issues. The party as a whole was somewhat left of center on the index: 37 percent of the autonomists were in the two leftist categories while only 7 percent of the leftists were in the two rightist categories. Furthermore, 47 percent of the independents were leftists and only 34 percent were rightist in their responses. (See Table 11-17.)

Table 11-17. Index of Programmatic Position (in percent)

	Auton.	Left.	Ind.
Strongly leftist	4	35	11
Mildly leftist	33	46	36
Indeterminant	11	12	11
Mildly rightist	39	5	27
Strongly rightist	13	2	7
DK, not ascertainable	0	0	8
	100	100	100
N	84	43	169

Programmatic position is one variable on which the independents were much closer to the autonomists than to the leftists, and it seems likely that the viewpoints of autonomists in the commune coincided closely with those of the party as a whole on the major issues facing the party. This relationship is even stronger when social class and education are held constant: that is, when the three categories are compared within particular social classes and educational levels, the independents are even more similar to the autonomists than the gross figures indicate.

This can be seen in Tables 11-17 and 11-18, in which the strongly leftist and mildly leftist categories are combined and the mildly rightist and strongly rightist categories are likewise considered together. Table 11-17 would thus look like Table 11-18 when the categories are collapsed and DKs eliminated.

Table 11-18. Index of Programmatic Position, Categories Collapsed (in percent)

	Auton.	Left.	Ind.
Leftist	37	81	52
Undetermined	11	12	12
Rightist	52	7	36
	100	100	100
N	84	43	150

When similar tables for each social class were examined, the magnitude of the differences between autonomists and independents was reduced considerably, though the independents remained slightly more leftist than the autonomists in all except the lower-middle and middle class (and note that the number of independents in that category is only seven, too small to provide reliable estimates). It is also of interest that the percentage of autonomists and independents taking a leftist programmatic position declined with a rise in social class, while it was the reverse for the leftists. In other words, the lower social classes were more similar to one another than were the higher, at least on the variable of programmatic position. (See Table 11-19.)[3]

A second interesting pattern emerged when programmatic position was controlled for education. Within each of the factional categories, the better educated were less leftist in their programmatic position. (See Table 11-20.)

As stated above, the programmatic index was constructed of five separate items. These were statements of points of view current in the party on several painful choices that have confronted or might in the future confront the party. Respondents were asked whether they agreed, agreed with reservations, were uncertain, disagreed but not completely, or disagreed completely. Of course the leftists took the leftist position on each of these more often than did the autonomists. But there are very great differences in the responses to individual questions that shed light on the present significance and potential divisiveness of various issues within the party. Thus there was substantial accord between autonomists and leftists in their attitudes toward the possibility of reform with the Christian Democrats: no more than 4 percentage points separated them in each category. (See Table 11-21.)

Differences emerged, however, on the question of the possible

3. This is similar to the findings of Herbert McCloskey et al., concerning partisans of American parties: that is, that the rank and file of the two parties are more similar to one another than are the elites ("Issue Conflict and Consensus Among Party Leaders and Followers," *American Political Science Review*, 54 [1960], 406–27).

Table 11-19. Social Class, Faction, and Programmatic Position (in percent)

| | Social Class and Faction | | | | | | | | |
| | Lower-lower | | | Upper-lower | | | Lower-middle | | |
	Autom.	*Left.*	*Ind.*	*Autom.*	*Left.*	*Ind.*	*Autom.*	*Left.*	*Ind.*
Leftist	43	69	58	37	85	44	25	88	14
Indeterminant	11	8	10	11	15	15	11	12	14
Rightist	46	23	32	52	0	41	64	0	72
	100	100	100	100	100	100	100	100	100
N	35	13	98	19	13	46	28	16	7

Table 11-20. Education, Faction, and Programmatic Position (in percent)

Faction and Years of Formal Education

	Autom.			Left.			Ind.		
	0–4	5	5+	0–4	5	5+	0–4	5	5+
Leftist	56	35	27	86	84	73	53	53	30
Indeterminant	5	20	0	14	8	18	12	12	0
Rightist	39	45	73	0	8	9	35	35	70
	100	100	100	100	100	100	100	100	100
N	18	40	26	7	24	11	79	66	10

Table 11-21. It is impossible to carry out any effective social reform whatever with the Christian Democrats participating in power (answers by percents).

	Auton.	Left.	Ind.
Agree	19	21	22
Agree, with reservations	17	14	13
Uncertain	17	14	26
Disagree, but not completely	23	19	11
Disagree completely	23	27	18
DK, not applicable	1	5	10
	100	100	100
N	84	43	169

effect on the PSI of the center-left government. Responses to the question "With a center-left government, the PSI would run the risk of disqualifying itself ideologically and of becoming social-democratic" reflected these differences, with three out of four autonomists believing that such a government would not damage the PSI ideologically, while only half the leftists held such a belief. (See Table 11-22.)

Attitudes toward unification with the Social Democrats exhibited a somewhat similar pattern. The autonomists and in-

Table 11-22. With a center-left government, the PSI would run the risk of disqualifying itself ideologically and of becoming Social Democratic (answers by percents).

	Auton.	Left.	Ind.
Agree	7	23	6
Agree, with reservations	4	12	5
Uncertain	12	12	25
Disagree, but not completely	8	12	12
Disagree completely	67	37	33
DK, not applicable	2	4	19
	100	100	100
N	84	43	169

dependents were to be found toward both extremes; the autonomists, however, still dominated in the rightist category. (See
Table 11-23.)

Table 11-23.   Unification with the Social Democrats would
reinforce the PSI (answers by percents).[a]

	Auton.	Left.	Ind.
Disagree completely	21	44	24
Disagree, but not completely	7	7	7
Uncertain	17	26	21
Agree, with reservation	13	9	8
Agree	41	12	25
DK, not applicable	1	2	15
	100	100	100
N	84	43	169

[a] Order is reversed to retain comparable ideological dimensions.

Two crucial issues in this province in the Italian Red Belt
concerned continued cooperation between Communists and
Socialists in local administration and trade unions (that is, even
if the Socialists coalesced with the Christian Democrats on the
national level). Feelings ran strong on these two questions, with
an extraordinary 91 percent of the leftists agreeing strongly that
the PSI must maintain friendship with the Communists in the
trade unions regardless of what happened. Lesser majorities of
both the autonomists and independents also took this point of
view. (See Table 11-24.) Only 17 percent of the entire sample
disagreed, completely or not, with this statement.

A similar, if more complex, pattern emerged on the question
of continued cooperation with the Communist Party in local
administration. The leftists were heavily concentrated on the
leftist position as in the question above, but the autonomists
spread over all the categories, as did the independents to a
lesser extent. While the leftists felt almost as strongly on this
issue as on the one above, the other two groups did not. (See
Table 11-25.)

Table 11-24. The PSI must maintain its friendship with the Communists in trade unions regardless of what happens (answers by percents).

	Auton.	Left.	Ind.
Agree	46	91	44
Agree, with reservations	24	5	16
Uncertain	5	2	11
Disagree, but not completely	15	0	6
Disagree completely	10	2	11
DK, not applicable	0	0	12
	100	100	100
N	84	43	169

The foregoing analysis leads to the conclusion that there is little in the attitude structure of the membership that acts to restrain the leaders in their freedom of action. Members are generally well satisfied with the party, its leaders, and its policies. Those members who hold participatory notions of democracy tend to be the ones who participate most; there seem to be few frustrated members whose behavior is out of harmony with their attitudes toward party democracy. Only the leftists are exempt from this conclusion, as they do reflect negative attitudes

Table 11-25. The PSI must maintain its friendship with the Communists in local administration regardless of what happens (answers by percents).

	Auton.	Left.	Ind.
Agree	18	70	35
Agree with reservations	32	21	20
Uncertain	7	0	8
Disagree, but not completely	24	5	9
Disagree completely	19	2	17
DK, not applicable	0	2	11
	100	100	100
N	84	43	169

toward the current leadership and its policies. The evidence suggests, however, that internal party politics exercises more influence in this regard than more abstract notions of democracy and the role of the member.

12.

Communications and Party Politics

The strategic factor in democracy has been operationalized as the existence of multiple autonomous communications channels. The uneven distribution of political competence and many factors that affect the decision of a member to join and participate in the party have been examined. The importance of these factors for the internal divisions in the party has also been indicated. These divisions render possible a sustained and viable alternative to the official channel of communication.

In this chapter behavioral characteristics of the members will be related to the communications networks of the party. There are in reality two major types of networks that merit close attention—the party structure and the sources of information of the members, especially the mass media. The former involves the local party organization and its direct impact on the members; the latter includes extraparty sources of information as well. The importance of political competence for involvement in communications networks has already been indicated; how it is related to party structure and other communications networks will now be shown.

PARTICIPATION AND PARTY STRUCTURE

Considerable research demonstrates a relationship between organizational structure and participation rates.[1] In this study, the most important structural unit with extensive rank and file contacts is the local section, and it forms the basic unit of the following analysis.

Local sections vary greatly in size in the commune under

1. See Lipset et al., *Union Democracy*, pp. 160–226, 306–47.

study. It would be desirable to be able to isolate and study size of section employing controls for the size of the community in which it is located and the characteristics of the individual members, but this is impossible. Sections tend to be organized wherever there are enough members to sustain them and they are permitted to grow until there are compelling reasons for subdividing them. These reasons usually are related to participation problems, especially those deriving from the distances involved in attending meetings; thus the smaller sections are often those whose members find it troublesome to frequent a larger section. On the other hand, a secretary who has inherited a large section or who has built one up himself is reluctant to see it partitioned, as section size is closely related to influence in the party. This relationship between size and influence is the principal reason why the federation leadership has always been reluctant to subdivide Mascagni section, the only one in the city of Arezzo itself.

The size of the section, then, tends to be determined by the size of its potential clientele—which is primarily but not exclusively determined by the size of the community—plus the energy and skill that have been devoted to realizing this potential. The degree to which the potential is achieved, of course, is affected by how long the section has been established, and other variables, and the potential is itself related to the social composition of the community. Size of section is consequently not independent of other variables: it is related to the needs of the leadership, the occupational structure of the commune, the distribution of leadership skills, and even the physical geography of the commune. All these factors interact, and insight into this interaction is necessary for an understanding of party communications patterns.

The first step is an examination of the relationship between participation and section size.

Participation and Section Size

Each respondent was coded by his local section and then the sixteen sections were divided by size into five categories ranging from one containing only the largest section, that of Arezzo, with 117 respondents represented in the sample, to the smallest sections grouped into a single category with only 37 respondents in the sample. The categories are far from equal in number of respondents, but the wide range of section sizes makes this necessary.

When the levels of membership participation in the five categories are examined it is clear that the relationship between section size and general participation, at least as measured in this study, is not a strong one. The pattern is irregular, suggesting that many other factors are more important. (See Table 12-1.)

Table 12-1. Participation and Size of Section (in percent)

	Less than 40	40–49	50–99	100–199	200+
Nominal	14	13	16	23	10
Marginal	43	32	28	31	36
Participant	19	39	23	23	29
Militant	24	16	33	23	25
	100	100	100	100	100
N	37	32	52	62	117

Indeed, an analysis of variance performed with the factors of education, age, length of party membership, and size of the section to which the respondent belongs reveals that section size is much less important than the other three factors. Table 12-2

Table 12-2. Some Determinants of Participation

	Unadjusted Association	Adjusted Association
Education	.24	.33
Age	.28	.28
Length of party membership	.33	.28
Size of section	.12	.15
Multiple association		.38

shows, first, the association between each of the factors and participation, and, secondly, the adjusted (partial) association of each factor with the others controlled.[2] Thus size of section accounts for less of the variance in participation than the other three determinants.

If another indicator of participation, whether the respondent had attended a section meeting in the last year, is examined similar results emerge. This variable is not independent of the general participation variable, of course, but it responds somewhat more directly to the question of participating in a particular local section. But the results are the same as for general participation: size of section seems to make no systematic difference (the gamma association is .007!). The percentage of the respondents that had attended a section meeting, from the smallest to the largest group of sections, was 51, 44, 40, 47, and 42, an irregular progression to say the least.

There is another and more definitive approach to participation and size that relies on voting at precongressional assemblies of the sections. These assemblies, it may be recalled, are the most important of the section meetings, for they elect the delegates to the provincial congress and thereby determine the factional division within the federation organs and, ultimately, in the party as a whole. These figures were obtained not only for the sixteen sections of the commune under study but for the entire province as well. The only assemblies for which complete voting records for the entire province could be obtained were the crucial ones preceding the provincial and national congresses of 1947, 1948, 1949, 1961, and 1963. The product moment correlation coefficients (Pearsonian Rs) for *total membership* in the section and the *percentage* of the members voting are shown in Table 12-3. While there is considerable variation in the strength of

2. These measures are generated by a Multiple Classification Analysis Program. When squared, they indicate the portion of the variance in participation explained by the variable. Thus education alone accounts for less than 6 percent of the variance; with controls this rises to 10 percent. The fact that the adjusted measure is larger than the simple association for both education and size of section indicates that these are rather sturdy, if unexciting, determinants of participation.

Table 12-3. Voting and Size of Section in Some Federation Precongressional Assemblies

Year	Product Moment Correlation (R) Size x Turnout	Number of Sections
1947	−.29	35
1948	−.52	49
1949	−.43	63
1961	−.21	95
1963	−.27	98

the correlation in different years, the correlations are definitive in one respect: they are all negative, that is, in every election the turnout rate declined with increase in the size of section. The smaller sections have higher rates of turnout, at least in the province of Arezzo, and in the years 1948 and 1949 the differences were dramatic indeed. It may be recalled from Chapter 4 that these were crucial election years for the party, years in which the leadership was overturned. It can be inferred from these figures that an important component of the two defeats was the large turnout in the smaller sections. It can also be suggested that the facilities that enabled the opposition to reach these sections were crucial, especially in 1949, the year in which Ferri, aided by Communist and Communist-front ties, recaptured the leadership from the former Action Party leaders.

Membership Characteristics and Section Size

Section size is closely related to several important characteristics of the membership such as social class and occupation. This is not to imply a complete stratification of the party by section, as the developmental patterns of the commune ensure that some urban workers, for example, reside in even the most isolated communities. Nevertheless, the smaller sections are severely handicapped by the composition of their membership, which tends toward the low end of most indices. Table 12-4 demonstrates some of the differences among the various sized sections on several variables.

Table 12-4. Section Size and Several Membership Variables (in percent)

	Less Than 40	40–49	50–99	100–199	200+
Above median on efficacy	38	19	50	54	41
Lower-middle and middle-class	8	0	8	10	33
More than 5 years' formal education	17	0	10	10	29
More than one correct answer on knowledge index	62	28	52	45	71
Ideologue or near-ideologue	16	0	11	11	26
Marxian conception of democracy	62	62	52	57	55
Belonging to more than one nonparty organization	30	6	14	19	37
PSI fathers	41	53	50	57	62
Apolitical and DK fathers	51	47	40	32	26
With other members of family enrolled	32	44	40	58	39
N	37	32	52	62	117

It is clear from Table 12-4 why it is difficult to separate out the effects of section size alone. Membership characteristics are unevenly distributed among the sections, though the higher rankings of the smallest sections on several of the indices indicate that size itself is hardly the principal reason. It is, rather, the relationship between the social geography of the commune and the structure of the party that is most important. In fact, some of the smaller sections may rank higher precisely because they are small; that is, they have not expanded widely among their potential members, as a consequence of which they contain more of the highly motivated and better informed members. Middle-sized sections, on the other hand, have probably grown by incorporating more and more borderline members. Table 12-1 suggested that this is the case, as the percentage of nominal members increased from 14 percent in the smallest to 23 percent in the fourth category, dropping down to 10 percent in Mascagni (Arezzo). This hypothesis finds support in an examination of the percentage of section members with other members of their families enrolled, which, as Table 12-4 indicates, rises from 32 percent in the smallest to 58 percent in the fourth category, only to fall back to 39 percent in Mascagni.

This analysis by section size suggests why Mascagni is so important in the party. It held only 39 percent of the sample, yet contained 88 percent of the middle-class and 72 percent of the lower middle-class members. It had more than its share of the knowledgeable and ideologically sophisticated; its members belonged to more organizations and it contained more than its share of the very young as well as the older members. It enrolled six of the seven PSI members in the membership sample who possessed a university degree, and in addition, of course, it carried most of the top leaders on its membership lists. As a result, it exerted its dominance not through size alone—though that might have been sufficient—but also through its clear superiority in political skills. This is not to imply that the other sections were devoid of skills, but their concentration in one section of the party clearly handicapped the smaller sections. As will now be suggested, this concentration was as much the result of conscious choice as it was of the size of the city of Arezzo itself.

THE SECTIONS AND FACTIONAL POLITICS

One of the most important reasons for the continuance of Mascagni as a single section is its importance in factional disputes within the federation. Its size and centrality render it crucial to the party leadership; the majority and, probably, the minority as well find it easier to deal directly with the most important section in the province. In fact, Mascagni is administered directly by the federation headquarters; its secretary in 1963 was a university graduate and the only secretary of section to be included within the top leadership of the federation.

Size of Section and Factional Politics

The close relationship existing between federation politics and Mascagni politics is reflected in the greater involvement of Mascagni members in factional affairs. With but 39 percent of the sample, Mascagni contained 50 percent of the autonomist and 61 percent of the leftist identifiers of the commune. Because of the uneven distribution of the variables associated with factional identification, this concentration in Mascagni should of course not be attributed to section size alone. Nevertheless, factional identification is higher for Mascagni than the other sections, which form an irregular pattern on this variable. (See Table 12-5.) It is obvious that much of the factional politics of

Table 12-5. Factional Identification and Section Size (in percent)

	Less Than 40	40–49	50–99	100–199	200+
Independents	57	69	65	76	42
Autonomists	35	25	27	11	36
Leftists	8	6	8	13	22
	100	100	100	100	100
N	37	32	52	62	117

the federation takes place in Mascagni. The centrality of Mascagni was recognized by all the leaders with whom this question was discussed; although a few suggested that it might be better for the opposition if it were broken up, the present concentration on this single section seemed in general to please autonomists and leftists alike.

But if Mascagni is dominant it is not clear what the contribution of size alone is to this state of affairs. It is, in fact, impossible to treat the question of size in an adequate manner with the interview data. Fortunately, the voting records utilized for examining the relationship between size and voting turnout also permit an analysis of the relationship between size and voting for the various factions. These voting records were analyzed for the entire province, with up to ninety-eight sections represented in the last year analyzed. This line of analysis suffers from the same limitations as the data from individual interviews: size of section is not unrelated to other variables, and merely analyzing a larger number of sections does not eliminate the problem. It does, however, reduce the effect of the small number of sections represented in the interviews.

Moreover, the characteristics of the members of larger sections, *if they are similar to those of Mascagni, which cannot be assumed,* suggest that larger sections should have *higher* participation rates than smaller sections, if size has nothing to do with it. And including a larger number of sections for analysis will tend to reduce the idiosyncratic factors relating to the quality of leadership, section cohesion, and other intervening local variables. It cannot be argued that it eliminates these disturbances; there is no basis for claiming this. But it became obvious during the field work that there were small old sections and relatively large new ones, well-administered small ones and incompetent secretaries of large sections, small sections with strong factions and large one-faction dominated sections. And there is no reason to assume that these cancel out one another, though increasing the number of sections by expanding the universe undoubtedly reduces their impact. Finally, it should be recalled that this involves a census, not a sample. Table 12-6 shows the relation-

Table 12-6. Voting for the Opposition and Size of Section in
Some Postwar Federation Elections

	Less Than 40		40–49		50–99		100–199		200+	
	%	N	%	N	%	N	%	N	%	N
1948	53	17	100	4	43	23	75	12	86	7
1949	21	28	29	7	66	9	82	11	84	6
1961	69	46	78	9	87	23	100	12	100	5
1963	79	47	85	13	95	19	100	13	100	6

Percentage is of sections in which the opposition received at least one vote.

ship between size of section and factional voting for the province.
Although none of the years shows the impressive differences of
1949, the relationship between intraparty competition and size
of section is clear. In 1949 the winner in each section polled an
average of 90 percent of the section's votes, despite the fact that
the winning faction received only 70 percent of the total vote,
indicating that the smaller sections voted overwhelmingly for
one faction or the other. The average percentage of votes in
each section received by the winner in the other elections (there
was no opposition in 1947), with the percentage of *total* vote
received by the provincial victor in parentheses, is as follows:
84 in 1948 (70), 76 in 1961 (60), and 74 in 1963 (61). This
seems conclusive evidence that the opposition does poorly in
the smaller sections; individuals in small sections tend to vote
as their colleagues in that section vote, which is not, of course,
necessarily the way the provincial party as a whole votes.

The Sections and the Leftist Potential

In Chapter 11 the attitudes of the rank and file toward
a number of important issues currently facing the party were
discussed. It will be recalled that there are some dramatic differences between the two factions in this respect, with 37 percent
of the autonomists, 81 percent of the leftists, and 52 percent of
the independents holding either a strongly leftist or moderately
leftist position on the Index of Programmatic Position. It will

also be recalled that the less well-educated tended to be more leftist in orientation than the better educated. Finally, the center of gravity within the party was slightly leftist, with an impressive portion of the independents and even autonomists taking that position, so that on this dimension, at least, the leftist faction has an unrealized potential.

The percentage favoring the leftist programmatic position entered an irregular decline with decrease in section size; the decline, however, was not nearly as sharp as the decline in the percentage claiming to identify with the left faction. (See Table 12-7.) The consistency of the responses to a question relating

Table 12-7. Size of Section and Some Factional Differences (in percent)

	Satisfied (Extremely or Moderately) with Party Policies	Leftist (Extreme or Moderate) on Index of Programmatic Position	Leftist in Factional Identification
Less than 40	81	43	8
40–49	81	44	6
50–99	81	40	8
100–199	81	60	13
200+	74	52	22

to satisfaction with the present policies of the party is remarkable, with every category except the largest (Mascagni) expressing the exact same percentage; but this too indicates that the left has not achieved its potential in the smaller sections, as the portion not expressing satisfaction in Mascagni is quite close to the portion identifying with the leftist faction. It will be recalled from Chapter 11 that only 48 percent of the leftists expressed satisfaction, compared with 88 percent of the independents and 92 percent of the autonomists. Thus it seems likely that the left does not reach its potential in the smaller sections, assuming that expression of dissatisfaction combined with a

COMMUNICATIONS AND PARTY POLITICS

leftist programmatic position indicate good prospects for the internal party opposition.

A final note about voting and party politics concerns the characteristics of voters and nonvoters at the precongressional assemblies for the provincial and national congresses of early 1961 (some of the section assemblies were held in late 1960). As would be anticipated, those who attended were the high participants, the efficacious, the knowledgeable, and the well-educated. Only 28 percent of lower lower-class respondents voted, compared with 39 percent of the upper lower-class and 52 percent of the combined lower middle- and middle-class categories. Moreover, as would be expected, identifiers turn out in larger proportions than independents: the autonomist turnout was 58 percent, the leftist 52 percent, and the independent 17 percent. Seemingly, neither faction did a very good job of "getting out the vote" for these assemblies; and, obviously, neither seems to make much of an effort to mobilize the independents. Given sufficient effort and some contentious issues, it would seem possible to alter considerably the relative strength of the two factions in a single campaign. But this is not easily accomplished, probably due primarily to the difficulty of reaching the membership.

The importance of communications in sectional politics is thus obvious. In small sections, the meager political skills of the membership, their isolation, and the absence of a structural basis for opposition render the existence of an internal opposition precarious. For these reasons, small sections can man the official networks only with difficulty, and parallel networks are a dispensable luxury. Consequently, the leftist in most small sections (and perhaps the autonomist in small leftist sections) is likely to be an isolate politically and probably in other ways as well. Without colleagues to reinforce him, the social and other pressures of a small community make nonconformity difficult to sustain, especially for the many who join and participate for social and conventional reasons. In many respects, the dynamics of internal party democracy are disruptive of the social cohesion and solidarity that are among the basic appeals and strength of socialism. Only in large, more fragmented, sections can the two be easily reconciled. And as the following analysis will indicate, the contemporary opposition is further handicapped by the lack of interest in alternative sources of information on the part of the independents.

ALTERNATE CHANNELS: SOURCES OF INFORMATION

Until this point the analysis has concentrated on the impact of the sections on the internal politics of the party. Now the relative importance of various sources of information as alternate communications channels will be examined. The principal tool of analysis will be a series of questions in which the respondent was asked to evaluate the importance to him of each of these sources; he was asked whether he relied on each for a "great deal," "fair amount," "little," or "none" of his information about politics. The sources discussed were radio, television, friends, party rallies, newspapers, party circulars, party books, and party section meetings. Table 12-8 presents the pattern of responses and the interrelationships among them.

These figures indicate that there is considerable variation among the respondents in the importance assigned to the several sources of information, and there is also variation in the association between the different sources, as the matrix demonstrates. Respondents who rank one source as important do not necessarily rank all others as important. In fact, the matrix is largely undistinguished. Nevertheless, when these figures are broken down for analysis of specific groups within the party it becomes obvious that information is to a large extent cumulative, that people who participate, who are efficacious, who are knowledgeable consider all these sources of information to be important. Respondents who are active in the party are open to multiple sources of information; conversely, those who are not involved in and committed to the party are relatively impervious to communications from any of the sources investigated, and probably from others as well. The relationships between participation and several of the sources of information are shown in Table 12-9.

Table 12-8.   Sources of Information

	Radio	TV	Friends	Rallies	Newspapers	Party Circulars	Party Books	Section Meetings
None	18%	28%	28%	30%	30%	38%	44%	37%
Little	26	23	27	30	25	13	13	20
Fair amount	26	23	28	20	18	15	14	13
Great deal	26	20	9	14	17	18	13	12
DK, NA	4	6	8	6	10	16	16	18
	100	100	100	100	100	100	100	100

$N = 301$

	TV	Friends	Rallies	Newspapers	Party Circulars	Party Books	Section Meetings
Radio	.36[a]	.32	.36	.22	.22	.24	.25
TV		.39	.33	.39	.40	.38	.42
Friends			.45	.41	.41	.45	.47
Rallies				.35	.31	.31	.37
Newspapers					.59	.60	.52
Party circulars						.90	.66
Party books							.68

[a] These are all gamma measures of association as used in previous chapters.

Fortunately, these relationships can be investigated more precisely by using the Multiple Classification Analysis introduced earlier in this chapter. This analysis permits one to examine the association between participation and each of these sources of information, and then to determine the association for each one while controlling for that part of the association also accounted for by the other variables. It obviously is not being argued that these sources of information *cause* participation; but the analysis does indicate the strong association between participation and

Table 12-9. Participation and Sources of Information;
Percent Rating the Source as Used a Great Deal
or Fair Amount

	Radio	TV	Friends	Rallies	Newspapers	Party Circulars	Party Books	Section Meetings
Nominal	27	15	3	16	10	14	8	3
Marginal	57	47	36	28	28	36	29	11
Participant	68	47	42	39	39	32	24	39
Militant	53	62	64	55	70	67	60	65
N	289	283	278	283	271	252	253	247

information, and permits inferences as to the more basic sources.
(See Table 12-10.) It should be noted that the reference to section meetings is completely independent of the measure of attendance at section meetings, which was one of the components
of the measure of participation, so there is no relationship between the two deriving from the mechanics of coding.

Several comments about these findings are in order. The
first is that high participants consider section meetings to be very
important; not surprisingly, this shows the strongest association

Table 12-10. Association between Participation and Some
Sources of Information[a]

	Unadjusted Association	Adjusted Association
Radio	.23	.02
TV	.38	.07
Friends	.49	.19
Rallies	.43	.13
Newspapers	.47	.19
Section meetings	.64	.45
Multiple association	.68	

[a] The small size of the sample made it advisable to omit party circulars and party
books—relatively minor sources—in order to increase confidence in the other measures.

of all, and this is especially impressive when controls are instituted for the other factors. The measure of party participation used in this study thus seems to reflect the respondents' own estimates of the importance of attending section meetings. The strength of the association between participation and friends, rallies, and newspapers indicates that these are also important; but, for the activists, these contribute little not already explained by the section meeting. The weaker association between radio and television and participation, however, combined with its importance for all groups (see Table 12-9) suggest that many low participants are reached solely or largely through these media, over which the party exercises no control and which are, indeed, closely controlled by its national opposition, the Christian Democratic Party. If large numbers of PSI members rely primarily on these two media for information it has considerable ramifications for internal party affairs. But this is passing over into speculation: it is not known what they watch or listen to, how much time they spend at it, or what the effects are. Other aspects of the analysis of sources of information will now be considered.

If the index of knowledge is an adequate measure of information received by the respondents, some interesting conclusions are possible. The first is that analysis of variance (by means of the Multiple Classification Analysis Program) demonstrates the primacy of education. When the relationship between knowledge and sources of information are controlled for education most of the association disappears, while the adjusted association between knowledge and education remains .57, down only from the unadjusted .61.

Another conclusion is that knowledgeable people in the PSI read a great deal; they are not limited only to the party paper *Avanti!* When the relative contributions to knowledge of the organizational memberships, total newspapers read, and the regularity with which the party paper is read are analyzed it is evident that the regularity with which respondents claim to read *Avanti!* does indeed associate highly with the knowledge index, but total number of newspapers read and the total number of organizations to which the individual belongs are much more powerful predictors of knowledge.[3] The portion of the variance explained independently by each of these can be obtained by squaring the adjusted measure of association in Table 12-11. This plus an examination of the crossbreak between to-

Table 12-11.   Some Predictors of Knowledge

	Unadjusted	Adjusted
Total organizational memberships	.41	.23
Total number of newspapers read	.61	.51
Frequency of reading *Avanti!*	.47	.12

tal newspapers and readership of *Avanti!* suggest that those who read *Avanti!* regularly are also avid readers of other papers, and hence are among the best informed of the members. Faithful readers of the party press are precisely the members who are least dependent on it for information. And an examination of which newspapers they read indicates considerable affinity for the conservative press, in this case especially the Florentine conservative daily, *La Nazione,* as Table 12-12 suggests. This table

Table 12-12.   Political Sympathies of Newspapers Cited by Respondents (in percent)

Importance of Newspapers as Source	Reads None	PSI Only	PSI-PCI	PSI- Conservative
None	91	24	22	9
Little	9	38	39	32
Fair amount	0	31	17	28
Great deal	0	7	22	31
	100	100	100	100
N	70	42	18	141

implies that those who read only the PSI and PCI press attach less importance to newspapers than those who read the conserv-

3. Total organizational memberships are simply added for that measure, as are total newspapers; respondents were asked whether they read *Avanti!* never (41 percent), rarely (9 percent), sometimes (24 percent), often (16 percent), or always (10 percent).

ative press in addition to the PSI papers (who constitute well over half of those who responded to the question), as the latter place much more emphasis on newspapers as a source of information. This analysis could be extended to other sources of information, but the point will not be belabored further: it is obvious that the well-informed are not limited to the official communications networks, and the well-informed are, by and large, also participants and militants. Their activities serve to diffuse knowledge within the party, so that it is impossible for the party elites to restrict the members to the official networks.

It is probably different for the marginal and nominal members, for they seem not to be plugged into any political communications network. And despite their inscription in the PSI, they seem hardly politically involved at all.

13.

Democracy in the Provincial Federation

In this study the strategic factor in democracy is the existence of multiple autonomous communications channels connecting the citizenry with political decision makers. Numerous factors facilitate or frustrate the maintenance of these channels and affect the breadth of their coverage of the population. Cultural and environmental factors—mediated through behavior and structure—are important in establishing the framework and boundaries of the system. The maintenance of communications networks likewise requires extensive political competence; if this is not present in the population the best democratic intentions of leaders are unlikely to be realized. Attitudes and expectations compatible with democracy are also crucial. Finally, structural bases for multiple channels are necessary. This is the insight of political pluralism, and it applies to organizations as well as polities.

It is better not to say that a unit is democratic or undemocratic but rather that it is more or less democratic, depending upon how large a portion of the population is able meaningfully to influence decision makers. Thus democracy is at least in principle a quantifiable variable. Its presence depends not only upon the goodwill of elites—though this is probably essential—but also upon the availability of political competence and effective structures. The existence of competence is essential for the existence of structures, but the former is no guarantee that the latter will emerge: it is a necessary but not sufficient condition.

Democracy is therefore never wholly achieved. There are always factors that favor and others that limit democracy. Until

214

the millennium it will probably be true that eternal vigilance is the price of liberty. This is the "cruel game" to which Michels referred in the quotation at the beginning of this study.

Elements of this cruel game certainly are present in the Arezzo PSI federation. The leaders and members of the party are explicitly committed to democratic norms; the formal structure of the party reflects democratic practices. Yet, there are many factors that thwart the impact of democratic norms and structure and undermine democratic intentions. Some of these are special characteristics of the party under study; most, however, have more general implications.

LIMITING FACTORS

Belief Systems

In an examination of the belief systems of members and leaders, two different and sometimes contradictory components emerge. There is the formal ideology of Italian socialism with its Marxian conception of democracy and egalitarianism. Existing side by side with this formal ideology is Italian tradition with its strong component of hierarchical subordination and clientelism. Marxian and traditionalist beliefs coexist within the federation and within most individuals in it.

The subculture into which PSI members are socialized is a modernizing or transitional one. In this part of Italy, the peasantry has shaken off the lethargy and resignation of centuries and is changing its outlook toward authority. Many peasants and sons of peasants have become industrial workers, and the rural socioeconomic system is being profoundly transformed by the demands of those peasants who remain. As a result, the breakdown of the antithesis between town and countryside, peasant and worker, is readily apparent.

But if agricultural workers are acquiring modern outlooks, many traditional views remain among workers as well as peasants. These traditional views encourage a respect for authority and an acceptance of hierarchical relationships. The bases of authority, moreover, are not merely traditional; education, party position, and instrumental abilities all serve as sources of authority. Party officials, especially those who rank high in position, education, social class, and interpersonal skills, benefit greatly from all these sources of authority.

As they were not specifically investigated, it is difficult to evaluate the importance of traditional views within the party. The reality of their existence, however, emerges from many questions in the interview schedule and even more from the observations of members of the research team. There are important differences in the saliency of these attitudes for various segments of the party. They assume less significance for the better educated, the high participants, the more urban, and those of higher social class. But the numerous others often defer to the office holders. As previous chapters have demonstrated, there is no widespread dissatisfaction with the party leadership and little sentiment that internal party democracy is inadequate.

The low level of political competence of much of the membership is of course quite apparent to the leaders. Given the social distance between classes in Italy, exaggerated in rural and semirural areas, egalitarianism requires a strong commitment for its realization. Leaders are perpetually tempted to talk down to the rank and file, to ignore their frequently ill-informed and poorly articulated comments and complaints, and to rely heavily upon the authority of office and personal status. That they seldom do so demonstrates the depth of their commitment to the ideals of egalitarianism; most of the leaders are remarkably patient and gentle in their relations with the rank and file. They know their culture and clientele well, and can deal with the most ignorant peasant without patronizing him and yet without abandoning their own dignified position of authority. This is of course a universal talent of the professional politician but it is perhaps more difficult to sustain in an intimate organization with such disparate talents and statuses involved. In short, traditional attitudes toward authority facilitate the retention of power by the office holders.

Another aspect of general cultural patterns that benefits those

216

in office is the elitest nature of Italian political culture. It is almost as difficult to leave the "political class" as it is to enter it. Elites come to symbolize their organizations in the public image; long tenure and little mobility is the dominant pattern. Differences between Italy and, for example, the United States on this point are only of degree, and working-class organizations in both countries are characterized by long tenure of top leaders. But general cultural patterns are probably more important as the explanation in Italy; as Italy is more highly personalized in society and polity, often for practical purposes an organization *is* its leadership.

Thus leaders are very important to the provincial PSI. Many local leaders have such a strong position in local government and unions that they cannot easily be coerced by the party. These satraps, with their vote-getting ability and clientelistic following, are needed by the party as much as they need the party. Since open conflict is in the interest of neither, accommodation is the pattern. They are unrestrained in their own bailiwicks: yet their independence serves to limit the power of higher echelons. Despite its formal structure, the party is a stratarchy.

The above aspects of culture and belief systems have nothing specifically to do with socialism. But there is an aspect of Marxian socialism itself that discourages internal democracy. That is its emphasis on democracy as a goal, an end, rather than as a process. Although mass mobilization is important in Marxian socialism, the goal is predetermined: it is the achievement of a classless society in which private ownership of the means of production has been eliminated and social justice achieved. Of course, this does not exhaust its final goals, and there are numerous tactical and intermediate aims, including the elevation of the consciousness of the proletariat. But "real" democracy is possible only within a classless society; until then other goals remain secondary. As this goal is well defined, debate centers on how to achieve it. This enhances the roles of the tactical experts, the professionals, and even in the PSI these are likely to be bureaucrats or office holders. They thus have an advantage over the nonprofessional, especially when their expertise is joined with ideological sophistication. An examination of factional conflict in the PSI illustrates the importance of goal conflict for internal democracy and also illustrates the ambivalent role of ideology in facilitating internal democracy.

A relationship between the Marxian conception of democracy and internal party politics was apparent in the analysis of conceptions of democracy. The Marxian conception of democracy —the defense of the interests of the neediest and most numerous segment of the population as opposed to opportunity to participate or choose between alternatives—has a wide appeal within the federation. Some respondents undoubtedly selected the Marxian conception for ideological reasons; but many of the ideologically unsophisticated chose it too, probably because of its simple attractiveness. This latter group includes those low on indices of knowledge, efficacy, participation, and education, as well as ideological sophistication. In other words, a very large portion of the rank and file selected a conception of democracy that contained no reference to participation or choice. The close relationship between political competence and choice of classic and neoliberal conceptions of democracy suggests that the unsophisticated are not greatly concerned with democratic processes. Even if the rank and file do not reject internal democracy they certainly form a feeble bulwark against antidemocratic tendencies.

Nor are the ideological Marxists—those high on competence who selected the Marxian conception of democracy—an adequate bulwark. This is especially true of adherents of the leftist faction. Paradoxically, though the very existence of a minority faction requires internal democracy, these doctrinaire leftists more often than the autonomists viewed internal party factions as unnecessary and undesirable. Many leftists admired the seemingly monolithic structure of the PCI and considered internal factionalism to be a major source of the weaknesses of the PSI. It is clear that a commitment to Marxian conceptions of democracy is no guarantee of a concern for internal democracy; furthermore, it may actually discourage such an interest. This commitment encourages egalitarianism but not internal democracy. Democracy as operationalized in this study finds an ambivalent ally in Marxian ideology.

As this analysis has indicated, there is little in the belief systems of the majority of members that requires democracy. For most, democracy means equality and more of everything. It is not a process but an end product. If nondemocratic means are more effective for achieving this end, then they are quite acceptable.

Other Characteristics of Members and Leaders

An analysis of other characteristics that limit democracy must begin with a recognition of extensive class differences in political competence and the superior social class of many local PSI leaders.

Many analysts of working-class parties have noted the antidemocratic implications of the political incompetence of the masses. Many have emphasized that education would tend to overcome this incompetence and lead eventually to democracy. This study reinforces these conclusions. All indices of competence used in the study suggest that where talents are distributed extremely unevenly in a population it is difficult to distribute influence and authority evenly. With the best of good intentions, it is a formidable task to involve the politically incompetent in the decision-making process of an organization. And few organizations are dominated by saints.

Paradoxically, one of the results of the expansion of a mass organization is the enrollment of an increasing portion of the politically incompetent who can be more easily manipulated by the leadership. Communist organizational principles have long recognized this. The mobilization of masses facilitates the maintenance of tight control as long as deviants cannot gain control of the intermediate structures that tie the party to the masses. And party manipulation of its mass membership through its communications networks in unions, party, and press makes it difficult for deviants to gain a hearing. The inability of the PSI leadership to control all the networks reaching the membership is a major factor facilitating democracy. But the behavioral characteristics of the members of the PSI provide a weak defense against antidemocratic tendencies. The majority of the members simply do not possess the political competence to oppose the leaders.

With skills in such short supply, there is no overt effort to restrict entry into the leadership group. On the contrary, considerable effort is devoted to recruiting and "bringing along" promising members. The elite form an open stratum. The consequence for internal democracy is that talent is co-opted into the leadership. There are simply not enough people with the requisite skills in the party to mount and sustain a rank and file opposition or revolt. A common complaint, and perhaps a well-founded one, is that the existence of internal factions dissipates the limited leadership resources in intraparty politics, leaving an insufficient amount for external affairs. The maintenance of an opposition requires extensive political competence, and it is often in short supply. This is a lesson being learned by parties and polities alike in the mid-twentieth century.

As this study has demonstrated, there is a strong association between education, knowledge, efficacy, and ideological sensitivity. Lack of education seems to be the chief fountain of the other inadequacies, though participation can compensate in part for poor education. People with rural fathers were especially low on education, knowledge, efficacy, and ideological sensitivity. With little knowledge of political affairs and no feeling of efficacy it is impossible for an individual to play much of an active role in party life. It is impressive that so many people from poor backgrounds do acquire considerable political competence; but most do not. It is of course also impossible to play a meaningful role without participating in party activities. Roughly half of the membership contributed little time and energy to the party, and 14 percent did absolutely nothing.

In summary, when political competence is in short supply its value, as of any other commodity, rises sharply. The leaders recognize this and seek to co-opt talent. This leaves few superfluous competents to oppose the elite. Apart from the left opposition—whose leaders, after all, are granted recognition as part of the party elite—malcontents are likely to be isolated and disorganized. As the section that follows demonstrates, apart from unions and local government, there are few secure places from which an opposition can be mounted.

Party Structure

Elite control over access to formal positions in the organization limits democracy. Occupancy of formal positions provides the time and mobility necessary to dominate the organization. Control of the party structure also provides the leadership with legitimacy, visibility, and information.

Occupants of formal leadership positions possess legitimacy. This facilitates leadership in any organization, and it assumes even greater importance in working-class structures, for the poorly educated respond to the authority of office, which endows its holder with both charismatic and bureaucratic authority.

A major problem of those low on political competence is the selection of trustworthy leaders. Long experience with incompetent, blundering, and disloyal spokesmen makes for political alienation and cynicism. One of the achievements of the bureaucratic mass party, apart from its instrumental merits, is that it provides an institutional control over the idiosyncrasies of leaders. It does not, of course, prevent incompetents and opportunists from reaching positions of influence; but it is bigger than any single leader and can survive the replacement of any individual or group of individuals. Its integrity and survival over time assure the PSI legitimacy among a substantial portion of the Italian population.

This legitimacy also adheres to its leaders. Upon assuming office, they become the heirs and spokesmen for the Italian Socialist tradition. Where disunity has been endemic and factionalism is a chronic weakness, many members, especially those of little sophistication, resolve problems of orientation by following the formal leaders. The task of conversion, in other words, lies with the opposition, and it is sometimes a heavy burden indeed. In the mutual interplay between leaders and followers it is difficult to weigh the extent to which leaders follow the policies favored by followers and the latter adopt the lines proposed by the former. Leaders are more than instructed delegates; they are also molders of opinion, and legitimacy is an important weapon in this process.

A by-product of holding a formal leadership position is the visibility it affords. This is related to, but different from, legitimacy. Because of sharp class distinctions and the isolation of so many party members, it is difficult for leaders, especially those of a different social status, to contact rank and file members. Holding a formal position in the party is one of the few, albeit not the only, method of becoming widely known within the party. The publicity effort required to achieve visibility, not to mention support, among the membership is a formidable one; few can sustain it without some position in the formal structure of the party. As will be seen, there are functional equivalents of party position in the unions and elsewhere; but even these are controlled by the party elite, though not necessarily by leaders of the majority. Thus a revolt led by someone not a member of the party elite faces almost insurmountable obstacles.

The visibility of the incumbent leaders is therefore a great asset, except in those rare instances when the rank and file are led by extraordinary events to repudiate the party's policy and its proponents. This has happened only once in Arezzo—when the elections of 1948 resulted in severe losses for the PSI. In this instance there seems to have been widespread revulsion against the leaders who were responsible for the disaster. As a result, the federation's leadership core was repudiated and a new group elected. Having collaborated with the previous leadership cost some lower-echelon leaders their positions. Thus visibility was a handicap. However, when the new leaders tried to purge supporters of the deposed office holders from all party positions, the attempt failed, suggesting that the rank and file showed considerable discretion in assigning responsibilities. And the ensuing disruption of party affairs caused by the leadership struggle reduced the possibility of future upheavals of that magnitude: the federation's experiences with party revolts have not been happy ones.

Incumbent leaders have great advantages in information available to them. Control over information is not complete, but formal leaders inherit resources for gathering and disseminating information that others can acquire only at great cost. Leaders have party records at their disposal; they have an established intelligence network; and they can make known their points of view more easily than any opponent.

In addition, in this province as in most others, the official line of the national party as reflected in leaders' speeches, party newspapers and other organs, and parliamentary activities re-inforces the local majority leadership. Most important of all, however, is that incumbents control the official communications channels of the party. In competition with an internal opposi-tion, they have the battle half won at the beginning; they al-ready have access to the rank and file through official channels, whereas an opposition faces the difficult task of constructing net-works.

Finally, holders of paid positions within the party have the mobility and time to work at party affairs. Much political ac-tivity consists of the time-consuming task of building and mend-ing fences. In politics as in athletics, the professional has great advantages over the amateur; paid employees are able to devote most of their time to this task. Others lack adequate leisure to cultivate opinion leaders scattered over a sprawling mountain-ous province. The task is almost impossible for people living outside the provincial capital and difficult for those located at the center. Few Socialists are sufficiently well off to forego paid employment; even were this the case, transportation and other routine but necessary expenses require a substantial outlay of money. Although politics in this province is inexpensive by American standards, the area is a poor one. Only the incum-bents habitually have sufficient time and mobility to devote to politics.

FACILITATING FACTORS

The foregoing has pinpointed some of the factors that restrict democracy in the PSI federation. The view of democracy as a quantifiable variable leads to a search for factors that serve to facilitate democracy. As there are counterforces at work, the theorist of democracy must seek to identify these forces and suggest how they might be strengthened. As in the previous section, they will be discussed under the headings of belief systems, other characteristics of members and leaders, and structure.

Belief Systems

If it is true that both the traditional belief system of the province and the Marxian conception of democracy do not necessarily encourage democracy, it is equally relevant that democracy in the abstract is highly valued by some within the PSI. And though democracy for many party members does not necessarily require active membership participation, this is less true of those most active in party affairs.

As was demonstrated in the analysis of membership conceptions of democracy, adherence to non-Marxian notions is associated with higher levels of participation. Those members who are most active in party politics value internal democracy; as a result, they tend to offset the viewpoints of the passive members who view democracy as economic equality rather than a decision-making process.

The importance of these activists cannot be overestimated, for they set the style of the party. From interviews with leaders and other evidence, it seems that PSI activists view the issue of internal party democracy as the most important single difference between the PSI and PCI. Certainly most leaders prefer the PSI to the PCI precisely because of its more democratic nature. Autonomist leaders and identifiers—who did not particularly benefit from internal democracy—favored it strongly; minority adherents (leftists)—who could organize as a faction only because of internal democracy—were less supportive. This paradox re-

224

sults from the latter faction's esteem for the seemingly monolithic organization of the PCI.

There is an aspect of an emerging Italian belief system that,
however difficult to evaluate, is probably of some importance to
this discussion. The elitist and traditional biases of Italian belief
systems have been emphasized. They are of greatest importance
among the least modern segment of the population—the poorly
educated and rural; different attitudes are developing in more
modern sectors. Democracy itself increasingly has positive con-
notations among broad segments of the industrial working class
and educated people. Toleration of opposing viewpoints is growing as a norm, especially among university students, whether
Catholic, liberal, or Marxian in their viewpoints. Acceptance
of pluralism, whether ideological or organizational, is difficult
in this home of the Vatican; but few observers doubt that it is
making headway among the minority with political skills. These
norms of toleration have even made a substantial impact on the
PCI, which is struggling to adjust to doctrinal and organizational
conflict.

As a result, PSI activists who support internal democracy have
strong cultural norms to support them. They typify that expanding sector of the Italian population that is educated, modern, and democratic. Since the PSI leadership itself comes from
this sector, internal democracy is in principle strongly supported
by most incumbent leaders. Only leftists questioned its desirability, and then usually in terms of supposed inefficiency and
internal quarreling that dissipated the limited resources of the
party.

Party democracy is a major raison d'être of the PSI. Undoubtedly in part because of this factor it has recruited a somewhat
better educated membership than the PCI in most of Italy
(though not necessarily in the province studied), and the evo-
lution of Italian society should sustain the bases of democracy
in the party. The changes taking place in the PCI can be interpreted as an attempt to adapt to the changing nature of Italian
society and its emerging democratic norms. The PSI has a head-

start in this process; whether it will actually benefit from it in the long run is uncertain.

Thus from the democratic point of view perhaps the most important ingredient of party belief systems is that both activists and leaders generally favor internal democracy. Only some leftists claimed to oppose it. It is consequently not only their skills and party positions that encourage activists and leaders to support internal democracy: they are also the ones most ideologically committed to it.

Other Characteristics of Members and Leaders

There are several characteristics of leaders and led that serve as substantial restraints on antidemocratic tendencies within the party. The most important one is that the membership cannot be coerced: it must be led.

Leaders must exercise authority without antagonizing the rank and file. There are numerous alternative courses of action available to the dissatisfied member. He can vote with his feet by refusing to work for the party, or he can go further and actually leave the party. In the latter case he can withdraw in silence and lapse into political apathy or he can join one of several other parties catering to those of a leftist inclination. Depending upon the nature of his discontent, he might find the PCI, the Social Democrats, the Christian Democrats, or other parties eager to accept him and perhaps even capitalize on his defection. ("Perhaps" is a necessary qualification, for the PCI and PSI for many years did not proselytize members from one another, and accepted each other's apostates only prudently and without fanfare. At the time of research this reluctance was still evident, but was in decline.) Or, of course, he might remain in the PSI and support an opposition.

These alternatives underscore some major differences between various political systems. The disenchanted American unionist (unlike his continental counterpart) usually must retain his membership in order to obtain or hold a job. Indeed, some American unions are primarily employment agencies, often possessing a monopoly over an entire occupation. In such a case meaningful alternatives do not exist: the members must remain in the union. Apathy and noninvolvement may be the only way out of a distasteful situation.

A comparable situation is found in those countries such as the United Kingdom where one party effectively monopolizes the political voice of a social grouping, as the Labor Party does for the working class. Although an alternative may exist in the Conservative Party, it is an unconscionable option for many people. The party in a single-party system is likewise the only vehicle for political action. Democracy in the polity thus requires democracy in the party as well.

But one result of the multiplicity of parties catering to low-status Italians is that the lower classes are presented with several alternatives. Although one consequence is to fragment and weaken the voice of the left, another is to facilitate choice. If the PSI member is not happy with his party he can search out a more congenial one. Consequently, leaders must continually anticipate the reaction of the rank and file. Paradoxically, this reduces the flexibility of the party, because the rank and file are often quite conservative about party policies. Leaders hesitate to inaugurate new courses of action for fear of membership opposition. For this and other reasons, internal democracy may be viewed by sincere and conscientious leaders as disfunctional for the achievement of the "real" goals of the membership. For better or for worse, however, alternatives are available, and leaders must therefore prepare the membership carefully for changes in orientation. The skillful leader knows how fast he can proceed; he stops short of driving the rank and file into rebellion or apathy.

The PSI relies heavily on its activists; compared with the PCI it has a small bureaucracy and limited financial resources. Even though both parties rely heavily on activists for carrying out party responsibilities, the PCI has far more professionals who depend on the party for a livelihood and who consequently can be ordered about as employees. Volunteers are otherwise; they must be convinced and cajoled since they seldom can be commanded. As the PSI relies heavily on its activists, they are a major deterrent to antidemocratic tendencies.

This is true because PSI activists are more likely than non-activists to favor internal democracy. Activists also possess other personal characteristics that facilitate democratic participation, for they are better educated and more efficacious, knowledge-able, and ideologically sensitive than nonactivists. Moreover, as will be examined below, they have wider sources of information and are less dependent on the party for interpretations of events. Finally, this economic independence of the party gives them a high degree of autonomy. Whatever the psychological costs, the material deprivations that can result from opposition are, for most members, quite limited. As a result, they can withdraw from party activities if dissatisfied; they can also remain in the party and merely not work for what they do not support. There are numerous examples of programs and drives that never made headway because of noncooperation by the activists. The PSI simply cannot command its activists in the same manner as the PCI. And this applies to most PSI leaders as well: except for the handful who are functionaries of the party and associated or-ganizations, Socialist leaders do not submit easily to pressures from the party hierarchy, for they are occupationally independ-ent.

Thus the coherence of any potential ruling group is limited by the independence of individual leaders. Although leaders can be analyzed as a group in contradistinction to the rank and file, they differ among themselves in several ways. The most important and obvious internal division is that between factions. Most internal conflicts are pressed into this mold even though their origins may lie elsewhere. The existence of factions means that the party leadership at most levels is split; and, if the party is hierarchical in structure, there are parallel hierarchies rather than a single one.

But factional divisions do not exhaust the possibilities for intraleadership conflict. Personality differences and, more im-portant, conflicting personal ambitions give rise to cliques within each faction. Policy choices affect the fortunes of leaders differentially, so policy cleavages sometimes reflect factional and sometimes personal conflicts. A recurring and seemingly institutionalized party role is that of the majority faction leader who remains close to the minority in policy preferences, sentiment, and personal contacts. At various times different individuals and cliques have occupied this crucial position on both the national and local levels. The trimmer occupies a good strategic position, for he can shift with changes in party orientation and serve as the link between outlooks as well as the vital margin of victory for the majority. Internal party competition is thus isomorphic with the classic spatial model of party competition, with factions occupying policy space on a left-right continuum. The persistence of the continuum despite changes in personalities and issues suggests that it derives from internal party processes, especially competition among leaders.

A third line of cleavage is between federation officials and leaders from the important population centers of the province. The leading commune is administered directly from federation headquarters; its leaders also hold important provincial positions. But many other local leaders have a high degree of autonomy. This does not result in a periphery-center conflict, for these local leaders have weak ties among themselves. But it does tend to convert the party into a stratarchy, in which the several levels of organization are relatively independent of one another. These local leaders—often mayors, assessors, or union officials—cannot be easily disciplined. They seldom owe their positions to the federation leaders and would be difficult to replace. Their support and votes are in turn essential to the incumbent provincial administration. As a result, relations tend to be of a bargaining nature, and federation leaders must work through local leaders. Attempted purges are rare and successful ones rarer still. Thus internal democracy may make it possible for incompetent or unaggressive local leaders to remain in office indefinitely.

A by-product of internal democracy in the PSI is that the rise of a particular type of leader is facilitated. The pragmatic broker, unbound by strong ideological commitments, able to work with diverse types of people, and, above all, sensitive to the egos and interests of others, has advantages over the ideologue, the strong-man, the organizational technician. Perhaps this is true in all political parties; but significant, if only vaguely known, differences between the PSI and the PCI undoubtedly exist on this point. It is improbable that the local PCI in fact approached the monolithic ideal, but it was undoubtedly less of a stratarchy than the PSI federation.

These characteristics of leaders and followers thus serve to restrain antidemocratic tendencies in the PSI. These tendencies are also restricted by the limitations imposed by the party structure.

Party Structure

The most severe limitation on antidemocratic tendencies is the inability of the leadership to dominate all communications channels reaching the membership. Complete domination is of course possible only when elites can control not only intraparty channels but those of the entire society as well—in other words, only in a totalitarian society. In the absence of this measure of control, communications channels are circumscribed only by the talents and opportunities of those necessary to maintain them. Among a membership as politically unsophisticated as the one under study, talent and opportunity constitute a severe but not absolute limitation on the existence of multiple channels.

The bulk of the nonparticipants are not deeply enmeshed in any communications network. But the activists are, and they are people least dependent on party sources of information. They are informed by a variety of media, including radio, television, nonparty newspapers, friends, and so on. They thus acquire wide perspectives on party affairs and cannot be deprived of independent, or at least divergent, interpretations of intraparty matters.

The press is a major source of information for everyone. The party newspaper, *Avanti!*, is widely read by party activists and of course supports the majority leadership. But the very members who read *Avanti!* most faithfully also read other newspapers. For example, the most widely read non-Socialist paper is

La Nazione of Florence; it is an independent conservative paper with special pages devoted to local events in the province of Arezzo, a feature duplicated by few other papers. Many activists also read the Communist paper, *Unità*. And radio and television, both of which receive widespread attention, of course do not present Socialist interpretations of events.

Other parties are an additional source of alternative communications. The importance of the PCI to the internal opposition in the PSI during many crucial periods has been demonstrated. The Chambers of Labor and trade unions, both Communist-dominated, serve as the essential structural basis of opposition in the PSI. Furthermore, Communists and Christian Democrats are numerous in the factories and fields of the province. In their day-to-day contacts with friends, neighbors, and work colleagues, PSI members are repeatedly exposed to nonparty views.

The structure of the PSI itself, even apart from the factions, is not monolithic. Differences among leaders filter down to the rank and file. And the stratarchical nature of the party ensures that many viewpoints can survive within it.

A final structural restriction on the leaders is the limited impact of the party on the membership. Due to the conservatism of the rank and file in many matters, leaders often must communicate what the members want to hear; as they have such slight control over the formation of attitudes and opinions, leaders must exercise restraint in altering established policies and procedures. This factor severely limits the leaders' ability to innovate and partially accounts for the slowness in effecting the opening to the left and in moving away from the PCI. The party is simply not an adequate instrument for the implementation of the decisions of the leaders. Although it is an important agency in the formation of the views of members, the party is only one of several influences and it is sometimes counterbalanced by other agencies such as the PCI.

There are factors that encourage internal party democracy in the PSI federation and others that frustrate it. The cynical leader concerned only with enhancing his own power finds many weapons at his disposal. However, unless he is extremely skillful he will triumph over a shell of a party, for he can coerce few of the leaders and members. An idealistic democrat, on the other hand, can be driven to despair, for he will find many apathetic members and even more unsophisticated ones. If he too is not skillful he may render his party "democratic" but at the same time so disorganized and inefficient that it cannot effectively pursue membership goals.

The dilemma facing the party is how to survive and prosper while permitting and encouraging internal opposition. Although some members claim that the party would be better off without an internal opposition, the majority of members and especially leaders do not feel this way. Internal democracy is one of the chief differences between the PCI and the PSI and it is highly valued. The system of organized factions probably maximizes both meaningful opposition and organizational vitality.

There is still the objection that this system keeps party affairs in the hands of an elite, albeit a dual elite. This objection would have merit only if the elite were closed and if its interests differed from those of the rank and file. The shortage of political competence among the members has been amply demonstrated. This shortage is responsible for the differences in social class between leaders and rank and file. Few lower-class members possess the requisite skills for leadership, but no one who does is barred from the leadership group; indeed, great effort is devoted to recruiting and promoting promising lower-class members. This problem results more from the social structure of the province than from antidemocratic tendencies of the party elite.

Whether the interests of elite and rank and file differ is a more difficult, even metaphysical, question. Leftists, both in the PSI and PCI, claim that the PSI is in danger of becoming middle-class and Social Democratic. However, the social composition of the PSI leadership is not cited as the cause. There is merit in the charge; but at a time when the PCI is itself becoming more revisionist and moderate, and when the Christian Democrats are willing to enter into a dialogue, to many observers the present policies of the PSI do not seem unreasonable. At any rate, the PSI members who felt that the party was abandoning their interests had alternative courses open to them (and indeed they did form another party in 1963). There seems to be little evidence that PSI leaders form a ruling elite in any but the arithmetical sense of the term.

A more fundamental question concerns the suitability of the PSI's system of organization for achieving membership goals. This is a part of the larger problem of democracy and the organization of political parties.

14.

Democracy and the Organization of Political Parties: Some Speculations

This study has investigated some of the factors that facilitate and restrict internal democracy in a mass political party. Democracy, which depends upon the maximization of some kind of meaningful participation, is not something achieved once and for all. When political realities make such participation difficult or impossible to achieve, democratic norms are likely to be violated. A theorist of democracy therefore should do more than clarify democratic norms, important as that task may be: he should also deal with the behavioral factors affecting the operation of democracy.

The strategic factor in democracy is the existence of multiple autonomous communications channels that tie together the diverse elements of a unit and permit the extensive exercise of influence. This is the crucial intervening variable between democracy and the factors conducive to it. Democracy exists to the extent that members of a unit are plugged into autonomous communications channels that can transmit messages from the basic unit to the highest decision-making authorities. The unit and level of analysis thus become crucial variables in the discussion of democracy. For democracy at one level may rest on multiple autonomous communications channels that are made possible by units that are themselves internally anything but democratic. Yet these may contribute to democracy within the larger unit.

UNITS AND LEVELS OF ANALYSIS
AND THE STUDY OF POLITICS

The problem of unit and level of analysis is fundamental. Are generalizations valid at one level of analysis applicable to another level? Do the political processes of a nation-state and of a trade union or party correspond sufficiently to justify treating them as homologous? Is it useful to do so? For certain purposes it seems both justifiable and useful to combine them in a single analytical scheme.[1]

Are generalizations about political systems as wholes expected to apply, ceteris paribus, to their component parts? Does a democratic political system require, for example, that its subunits be organized in a particular manner?[2] Is a predominantly authoritarian family structure compatible with democracy? Is a surfeit of authoritarian personality types conducive to authoritarian political relations? The evidence is contradictory and inconclusive. Due to the compartmentalization of research, people interested in these different areas are seldom equally concerned with all of them. The problem of unit and level of analysis is rarely confronted directly. Two courses of action seem to have predominated. Some researchers have simply implied that what was true of the individual or experimental group could be generalized to units at other levels of the political system.[3] Others—and not only legalists and institutionalists—have treated states and organizations as if they were not composed of smaller units at all, the "black box" approach. The former assumes what needs to be demonstrated; the latter ignores that the problem exists.

The term "unit" is used as an analytic construct. It is any recurring interaction so patterned that communications among its constituent actors relevant to the subject under discussion are more important than the volume between them and actors outside the unit. Whether any collection of individuals forms a unit can thus be determined empirically for the purpose at hand

1. In this I agree with Robert A. Dahl, *A Preface to Democratic Theory* (Chicago, University of Chicago Press, 1956), p. 74; and Lipset et al., *Union Democracy*.

2. For a suggestion that this is the case see Harry Eckstein, *A Theory of Stable Democracy* (Princeton, Center for International Studies, Woodrow Wilson School of Public and International Affairs, 1961).

3. Theodore W. Adorno et al., *The Authoritarian Personality* (New York, Harper, 1950); and Kurt Lewin and Ronald Lippitt, "An Experimental Approach to the Study of Democracy and Autocracy: A Preliminary Note," *Sociometry*, 1 (1938), 292–300. Lewin himself did not assume this.

by their patterns of internal and external communications. A unit could therefore be an informal group, a formal organization, or a polity. Level of analysis differentiates individuals, small groups, complex organizations, and polities. Although the concepts of unit of analysis and level of analysis are related, both are essential, as there can be many units at any particular level. These distinctions are important for the sections that follow.

NORMATIVE AND EMPIRICAL THEORIES OF DEMOCRACY

Democracy means many things to many people. Rather than debate what it *really* means, it is more important, first, to distinguish normative and empirical theories of democracy; and, second, to isolate the factor that distinguishes, in conventional terms, present democratic from nondemocratic political units. This latter has been labeled the strategic factor in democracy.

Normative theorists have emphasized diverse aspects of democracy. The following list is intended to be merely suggestive: Democracy means majority rule; democracy is possible only in city-states; democracy is a way of life requiring a belief in the equality of man and individual participation in civic life. Democracy is individualistic, hence only the middle class with its individualism, self-discipline, and avoidance of extremes is fitted for democratic political life. Democracy is possible only with democrats, hence a system dominated by authoritarian personality types could not function democratically. G. D. H. Cole, for example, exhibits the normative theorist's concern when he writes: "Democracies have either to be small, or to be broken up into small, human groups in which men and women can know and love one another." [4]

These notions perhaps were relevant to the city-states of Greece and later times. But as empirical criteria for distinguishing contemporary states conventionally considered democratic they are merely quaint, as most normative theorists would probably agree. Majorities do not rule anywhere.[5] Modern democ-

4. G. D. H. Cole, *Essays in Social Theory* (London, Macmillan, 1950), pp. 94–95.
5. For an elaboration of this point, see Dahl, *A Preface to Democratic Theory,* pp. 124ff.

racies are large and complex; none is a city-state in which people "can know and love one another." They encompass belief systems and ways of life of great diversity; while some belief systems may be incompatible with democracy, there seem to be at least a limited plurality of viable democratic forms. Most evidence suggests that belief in equality is not deeply rooted, at least in the United States,[6] and European democracies all exhibit varying degrees of class consciousness. Participation in politics is low in all countries for which data are available, and few democracies seem to have attained the level of mass participation achieved by Fascist and Communist dictatorships. A propos the middle-class nature of democracy, it should be remembered that lower-class groups have sometimes been the backbone of democracy in several countries. And, finally, while the very notion of "authoritarian personality" is open to criticism, the presumed relationship between personality and politics is an important subject about which little is known, and definitive statements are at least premature.

This is not to argue that normative considerations are irrelevant to the functioning of a democratic political system; research on the relationship between ethics and politics deserves high priority. However, no particular ethical system is absolutely necessary for the existence of democracy: if it were crucial, it would be the strategic factor in democracy.

It is conceivable that no single strategic factor exists. On the level of face-to-face democracies this is probably the case. Anyone may hold any normative conception of democracy he wishes, and any particular existing state can thus be labeled democratic or nondemocratic according to the value preferences of the individual. Some would probably deny that democracy is possible in modern nation-states on the grounds that complex organization, especially bureaucratic organization, and democracy are incompatible.[7] Rather than quarrel with this point of view, it

6. Robert E. Lane, "The Fear of Equality," *American Political Science Review*, 54 (1959), 35–51.
7. Apart from Michels' *Political Parties*, see Alvin W. Gouldner, "Metaphysical Pathos and the Theory of Bureaucracy," *American Political Science*

might be better to adopt some other label for the reality under discussion. But that reality is a familiar type of political system found in Western Europe and North America, though not limited to these areas, and generally referred to as democratic. And the crucial differences between these and totalitarian and authoritarian systems are to be found in their communications patterns.

COMMUNICATIONS MODELS OF THE POLITY

A communications model of a democratic system can best be identified by contrasting it with models of other types of political systems. Existing political systems can be divided into three types according to how their communications networks channel conflicting demands. As all polities are "mixed," these three types should be considered as analytic constructs. Actual political systems (and other units) can be described in terms of the particular patterning of the mix of these models found within them. The authoritarian and the totalitarian will be discussed first.

In the authoritarian model only one or a greatly restricted number of communications channels are permitted to influence governmental policy. A system is authoritarian to the extent that subunits remain unmobilized and are barred from influencing the authoritative allocation of values of the system. There is no logical incompatibility between authoritarianism and constitutionalism (in the sense of effectively limited government). Indeed, some authoritarian systems have also been constitutional systems, for example, eighteenth-century England, perhaps contemporary Spain and Portugal, and some Latin American dictatorships. Nor, as the examples mentioned above would indicate, is authoritarianism incompatible with pluralism if by pluralism is meant the existence of autonomous communications networks. The networks exist—in churches, universities,

Review, 49 (1955), 496–507; and Peter M. Blau, "Critical Remarks on Weber's Theory of Authority," American Political Science Review, 57 (1963), 305–16.

business, ethnic communities, and various associations—but most simply have no political influence. Throughout most of its history India was an example of a society that was pluralist in this sense and yet authoritarian politically. When only a limited segment of the population is mobilized, the political system as a whole is generally authoritarian even though intraelite relations may be quite democratic.

A totalitarian system is similar in that only communications issuing from a single channel have authority. But the totalitarian system goes further—it seeks to control all the communications channels of a society. Those channels it cannot control it destroys; and if channels do not exist to bind all the subunits together, it creates them. It is total in its control of communications, so that every subunit is "plugged in" the network in some way through an officially sanctioned channel.

An authoritarian system seems to function best where political competence, which is essential to the operation of communications channels, is not widely distributed. The importance of education has been demonstrated. The combination of authoritarianism and a wide diffusion of political competence leads to rising frustration, anomic means of communicating demands (demonstrations, strikes, assassinations, and so on), and, in turn, repression. Although mankind has lived under authoritarian systems throughout most of history, this form without adaptation is unlikely to survive the entry of the masses into politics. The logic of mass mobilization leads either to democracy or to totalitarianism.

The totalitarian system manipulates consent or at least acquiescence through control of communications channels. Contemporary systems differ from the totalitarian polar ideal in several ways. The first concerns the depth of the penetration of the communications networks into the subunits. In the U.S.S.R., for example, subunits such as the family seem to be achieving greater autonomy; other subunits also seem to be increasingly independent. Significantly, these tendencies have emerged first in areas less overtly political, as in the family, arts, and religion; and the autonomy tolerated is not permitted to threaten the political system. A second variable is the degree to which communications channels are in fact effectively controlled. In National Socialist Germany, for example, and even more so in Fascist Italy, many networks, such as the state bureaucracy, the army, the Catholic Church, and some economic channels, were only superficially controlled. Insofar as this was the case, Germany and Italy veered toward the authoritarian pole, though the Fuhrer and the Duce and their respective parties certainly had totalitarian intentions.

The communications networks of democratic political systems are characterized by the existence of multiple autonomous channels connecting subunits at all levels of the system both vertically and horizontally. A channel is autonomous to the extent that its communications are not externally controlled.[8] These channels permit and facilitate the building of coalitions binding together levels in order to aggregate the demands of subunits, filter them, and translate them into policy alternatives. The existence of multiple channels renders difficult the blocking of communication, for the "outs" are generally receptive to potential coalition partners. And autonomy prevents the channels from being manipulated for the benefit of the "ins."

It should be emphasized that communication is two-way in all types of political systems. Feedback exists in all of them; the differences lie in the role played by feedback.[9] The content of communications is constantly being affected by feedback. This is why repeated communications in a system with open and free channels at best leads to adjustment of demands, to compromise. At the very least, communications and feedback increase rationality, for information reduces uncertainty and hence the extent of miscalculation and unintended consequences. In Deutsch's terms, it results in learning. It also, in Deutsch's terms, requires "good will," the willingness to learn, to adapt; and it is in this respect that some belief systems may be more

8. This is similar to Dahl's conception of autonomy in *A Preface to Democratic Theory*, p. 78.
9. See the discussions of feedback in Karl Deutsch, *The Nerves of Government* (New York, Free Press, 1963).

conducive to democracy than others, because some emphasize
"will" as opposed to "learning."[10]

PARTIES AND COMMUNICATIONS NETWORKS

Multiple autonomous communications channels are the strategic factor in democracy. In a formal sense these channels need
not be political parties. However, due to the division of labor
that characterizes complex societies it is difficult for a contemporary polity to function without a political party or parties. The
political party is the communications network that functionally
specializes in the aggregation of political communications (that
is, communications relating to the authoritative allocation of
values) for a polity. It is the political communications channel
par excellence, and in democracies parties generally sustain
multiple autonomous channels.

Different party systems are associated with different communications patterns. Where existing political elites have aggregated
demands from new units entering the political communications
network, two-party systems have emerged in which both parties
are in principle open to demands from almost all subunits. The
degree to which parties even in two-party systems are receptive
to communications from all subunits is an empirical question.
Certainly parties are not equally responsive to communications
from all subunits even in two-party systems, and the tendency
toward restrictiveness is more pronounced in multi-party systems.

There is probably no single historical explanation for the
emergence of multi-party systems. They are associated with discontinuities that inhibit communication across critical boundaries of the polity, such as religious divisions, class antagonisms,
regional boundaries, and ideological differences. Their common
feature is the inability of channels to aggregate communications
from across the critical boundaries. The unwillingness of those
who dominated existing channels to heed demands of the new
subunits entering into political consciousness, at least until too
late, has resulted in the establishment of new parties to serve
as channels.

10. Ibid.

In totalitarian polities the party is a principal channel for political communications. It is an instrument of mobilization in a system in which all subunits must be "plugged in" a communications network. The party infiltrates all structures but maintains its identity. In authoritarian systems, on the other hand, the primary goal of elites is to set limits on behavior rather than to mobilize the population, and governmental bureaucracies, police, and army are generally adequate for these purposes. Hence the party tends to lose its position as the dominant communications channel; it mingles with other networks within the machinery of state, thereby becoming only one of several competing channels. Compare, for example, the Communist Party of the Soviet Union with the Italian Fascist Party in its later years or some of the single-party regimes of the developing nations.

This conception of the party as a communications channel connecting politically relevant subunits places cadre, mass, totalitarian, and democratic parties within the same analytical framework. All of these parties serve as communications channels, but within political systems that structure communications networks differently. For example, in the past parties of notables have been able to incorporate all politically relevant units; but they have lost ground to mass parties in countries where the electorate has expanded greatly, for mass parties are unequaled for maintaining wide communications networks.

Two-party systems probably incorporate more people into influential communications networks than multi-party systems. The coalition-building process in two-party systems makes it difficult for either party to ignore completely communications from any weighty unit. The "outs" in particular exploit the grievances of disaffected units. The multi-party system, on the other hand, generally restricts the spread of communications received by any single party. A governmental coalition often can ignore communications from units outside the coalition, as has been the case with the extreme left in France and Italy and the conservative parties of several countries. But even when conservative parties are denied formal participation, the superior communications facilities available to the upper classes often assure them alternative means of access while the inadequate communications resources of the lower classes render formal channels indispensable. Hence multi-party systems often deprive some units of de facto influence, though comparable units may have more formal representation than in two-party systems.

Multi-party systems complicate choice. Two-party systems reduce policy alternatives, and the dynamics of coalition building tend to ensure, even require, a majority preference for one policy. A party that cannot succeed at this over time flounders. Most policy is made by politicians as skilled in weighing intensity and influence—the weight to be attached to communications received—as mere votes. The debate over policy serves to clarify and polarize alternatives, at least among those concerned with the issue, so that one policy has a majority. But when there are more than two choices a curious inconsistency can result. Assuming that choices are transitive, it is quite possible that regardless of which policy is adopted, a majority would have preferred another one. This "paradox of voting," sometimes referred to as the "Arrow Problem," deserves more attention than it has received from students of parties.[11]

Some ramifications of these characteristics of a multi-party system deserve mention. If inputs are relatively similar, if there is a high degree of consensus, especially on the "rules of the game," then a multi-party system based largely on differences in inputs in the socioeconomic sphere may function quite well, as in the Scandinavian countries. Also, where party communications channels cut the polity vertically, as in some religious parties, few units will be completely denied consideration. But horizontal blocks in communications channels, as in class-based party systems, serve to fragment rather than to integrate the

11. See Kenneth Arrow, *Social Choice and Individual Values* (New York, Wiley, 1951); William A. Riker, "The Paradox of Voting and Congressional Rules for Voting on Amendments," *American Political Science Review*, 52 (1958), 349–66; Anthony Downs, *An Economic Theory of Democracy* (New York, Harper, 1957); Duncan Black, "The Decisions of a Committee Using a Special Majority," *Econometrica*, 16 (1948), 262–70; and Dahl, *A Preface to Democratic Theory*.

communications networks and important units may be blocked from communicating with the authoritative networks. Parties in two-party systems possess wider communications networks.

THE ORGANIZATION OF WORKING-CLASS PARTIES

The significance of the level and unit of analysis for the study of political parties can now be indicated more clearly. Units can be either polities or subdivisions of polities. A democratic polity can contain democratic, authoritarian, and even totalitarian subunits within it as long as they serve to provide the multiple autonomous communications channels that are essential to democracy. Business organizations, for example, are usually authoritarian in their communications patterns. The Catholic Church, with its multiple channels serving specific groups in the church, veers in the totalitarian direction. Even in democratic polities the Communist Party seeks a total control over the channels dealing with the member or supporter—party, union, press, recreation, and so on. However, the experiences of both these associations demonstrate that without control over the official networks it is impossible to sustain a communications monopoly even over limited segments of a population. Compare the Communist parties of Britain and the U.S.S.R., for example, or the Catholic Church in contemporary Spain and France.

Even in a democracy some groups are more likely to have their demands effectively communicated by authoritarian or even totalitarian networks than by democratic ones. The reasons for this are important to an understanding of working-class parties and thus merit a brief analysis.

Class differences in communications patterns reflect the unequal distribution of political competence. Although research is limited, there is strong evidence that socioeconomic status correlates highly with education, knowledge, and sense of political efficacy. The ability to communicate political information is indisputedly related both to a sense of efficacy and to some minimal skill in articulating and transmitting demands. People find it difficult to articulate their feelings, much less to feed them in a refined form into a communications network; on the other hand, they can respond to the formulations of others, and hence are available for political mobilization.

Most elites possess a well-developed group life, wide personal contacts, superior communications resources, and an elevated sense of political efficacy. Elites thus have communications advantages that partially offset their numerical inferiority. Despite considerable functional specialization, members of the socioeconomic elite in most polities customarily have access to important political communication networks.

This is not true of people of lower socioeconomic strata. Throughout most of history they have been objects, not subjects, of politics. Their entry on the political stage is the drama of our times. The diffusion of democratic ideals has sanctioned their participation, but ideals have often been implanted in poorly prepared soil. Political competence may be lacking. Crude demands may exceed the material capacity of the polity; the revolution of rising expectations may give way to one of rising frustrations.

A crucial problem is leadership. How can lower strata secure capable leadership? Several universal patterns exist. One is clientelism, which relates individuals to a communications network by means of personal ties with one of its members. This is a widespread arrangement, found in feudal and industrial societies alike. Clientelism results in vertical communications channels that leave elites unchallenged; it nullifies the major weapon of the lower socioeconomic strata—their numbers. Political competition is restricted to the elite and may be irrelevant to the needs of their clients. Troublesome clients can be bought off, co-opted, or in some systems physically eliminated. Clientelism seldom results in effective communication of demands from those of low political competence; the sophisticated customarily receive preferential treatment. In general, horizontal channels are necessary for extensive and sustained efforts on behalf of lower strata.

Another pattern is the mass movement. Spontaneous mass movements are not unknown in political history. Lower socioeconomic strata have periodically communicated their demands through demonstrations, peaceful and otherwise, and even heroic manifestations of discipline and courage. Popular leaders have emerged from the masses, sometimes exhibiting considerable skill. More often, however, spontaneous mass movements burn themselves out in futile violence and rage, for leaders lack the requisite skills to direct these energies into meaningful sustained activity. Many peasant uprisings and proletarian movements share this failing, and the major distinction between prepolitical and political movements, to use Hobsbawm's categories, may well lie in the lack of communications viability of the former.[12]

Lower socioeconomic strata thus are faced with trying problems in acquiring adequate leadership, for individuals with the requisite political competence often have alternative career outlets. In the more class-conscious societies of Western Europe, trade union and Socialist leaders have often been quite able, as the talented European worker, at least in the past, found few outlets for his ambition outside of working-class organizations. Deficient in political competence and alternative communications networks, lower socioeconomic strata have had to rely heavily on specifically political organizations, especially parties and trade unions (which are almost everywhere more political than they are in the United States).

Leadership emerges easily among higher strata, but lower strata must *construct associations,* often bureaucratic organizations, to support stable, competent, and trustworthy leadership. As members of lower strata are particularly susceptible to demagoguery and other maladies of the mass society, bureaucratic organization is probably more important for them than for those of higher strata.[13]

12. Eric Hobsbawm, *Primitive Rebels: Studies in Archaic Forms of Social Movement in the 19th and 20th Centuries* (Manchester, Manchester University Press, 1959).

13. Max Weber noted this relationship between democracy and bureaucracy in political parties, but he wrongly attributed it to the desire for equality rather than the necessity to support a leadership ("Bureaucracy," in H. H. Gerth and C. Wright Mills, *From Max Weber* [New York, Oxford, 1958], pp. 211, 225).

The lower strata have sometimes been aided by pre-existing organizations. The Catholic Church has fostered an entire working-class subculture in several countries, and the role of Nonconformist Churches in the early years of the British Labor party is well known. In these instances, the maintenance of communications between social strata has been facilitated. In other European countries the churches acted too late, and communication broke down. Significantly, continental churches were more successful with workers and regions that lagged behind in industrialization, as in Flanders and the French Rhineland.

The emerging proletariat suffered repeated defeats until it painfully learned to convert numbers into influence through organization. Severed from existing networks, it seemingly had to displace the authoritative channels and create new ones. Marxism as an ideology justifies this outlook, and many of its basic tenets have taken deep roots within continental lower strata. Communism supplied two things these strata desperately needed: first, an explanation of the environment that could prevent the futile actions resulting from crude passionate demands (hence "scientific" socialism); and, second, an organizational structure to support political action.

Communism converted the Marxian analytical method into dogma proclaimed by Moscow and the party into an organizational weapon to achieve the goals posited by dogma.[14] As organizational theory suggests, the more strictly defined are the goals of an organization, the less significant is free communication within it. With basic policies not subject to wide debate, European Communist parties could act with a single-mindedness seldom matched by their democratic Socialist rivals. This often seemed a virtue. For the Communist method of organization, whether in a multi-party system or a Communist single-party system, permits and even requires widespread mobilization regardless of political competence and classic notions of partici-

14. In the words of Lenin: "The proletariat has no other weapon in the fight for power except organization." Quoted in Philip Selznick, *The Organizational Weapon* (New York, Free Press, 1960), p. 8.

patory democracy. Although it tends to eliminate goal conflict and the structural independence of constituent units that are so important to democracy, communism replaces them with strength, unity, and a sense of meaningful if largely vicarious participation on the level of the larger units. As this study has shown, substantial portions of those low on political competence perceive this as adequate from the democratic point of view. As levels of participation and education rise, this type of mobilization may be increasingly viewed as unsatisfactory by the individuals involved, as may be the case at present in some countries, including Italy. But the party itself can take steps to overcome many of the negative aspects of this type of mobilization by permitting freer internal debate and a more important role for the rank and file. If this process of internal "democratization" is carried out skillfully, a long time can elapse before the party loses the strengths of its former system and before the rank and file play a genuinely determining role within the party. Perhaps the Communist method is ultimately unsuited to units with widespread political competence. But once established it may decay slowly over a long period of time. Thus its long-range viability may be questionable, given the educational and other trends existing throughout the world today. However, the Communist system of organization is in jeopardy in only a few countries; in many others, the Communist system for mobilizing the politically incompetent is well-adapted to the human resources with which politicians must work.

The Italian Communist Party may thus be perceived by its supporters as being both effective and democratic. It is uncertain that the effectiveness of the PCI will be maintained once open internal debate is permitted, as seems to be beginning at least in Italy. Perhaps the rising level of political competence among lower strata will lead to a rejection of this form of party organization. It is of course also possible that the party will accommodate its structure to the changed socioeconomic environment. Regardless, in the historical period under discussion the PCI provided one model for resolving the problems of political competence and working-class politics; the model of the democratic Socialist Party is another.

PARTY DEMOCRACY

If the Communist system is well adapted to the characteristics of people of low political competence, there still remains the problem of maximizing the democratic potential of organizations. This means finding ways to maintain multiple autonomous channels of communication. Political competence, goal conflict, and structural bases all seem to be very important in their maintenance.

The first requisite for the existence of these channels is competent people to man them. Varying with the unit, an ample number of people with a sufficient level of political competence is required. This obvious fact merits more systematic attention than it has received. Unless those seeking a hearing form a significant portion of the total unit or possess some adequate substitute for numbers they are unlikely, for logistical reasons, to succeed. But not only must there be sufficient numbers; there must also be sufficient competence to communicate. As units and problems become more complex the level of competence required for meaningful communication rises. Competence is a relative thing, of course, but it is seldom distributed equally within units and between units, with dire consequences for democracy. Some units—parties, trade unions, and other organizations of the poor, for example—are often extremely deficient in competence. Sometimes skills are barely adequate to man the official channels. In this case, the unit literally may not be able to afford a second autonomous channel. This is probably the most important single impediment to democracy within working-class organizations. It also often applies to polities as well, as is evident from the experiences of many developing countries.

Other units, especially parties of notables, voluntary associations dominated by middle-class members, and rich Western democracies, may have a superabundance of political competence as operationalized in this study. These possess numerous informal communications networks and channels. As mentioned previously, it seems that as a general rule the lower the average level of competence within a unit the more important are the formal channels as a means of communicating with the larger unit. Industrialists and middle-class people in a democracy have many channels available to them for communicating demands. The poor, whether European industrial workers or American immigrants, often find the political party itself or its associated structures to be the sole or principal channel open to them. Classical liberalism and socialism thus both reflect some pragmatically important properties of communications networks, in that both implicitly recognize the class bias inherent in the liberal conception of the role of the state.

If the polity is considered the unit of analysis, then democracy within the polity under certain circumstances may not be facilitated by democracy within its subunits. For there are substantial groupings of people who presently lack the political competence to participate democratically. If they are to gain a hearing it will likely be through nondemocratic structures. To insist upon classical notions of democracy as participation might enhance the spread of democracy within the subunits of a polity but it is also certain to reduce the quantitative level of democracy, that is, the portion of the total population plugged into meaningful communications networks. Until the political incompetence of large portions of the population is reduced, democratic mobilization on the polity-wide level is incompatible with an insistence on democratic structures for all of the subunits of the polity. Such is the dilemma of contemporary democracy. It is a paradox the dimensions of which can in principle be expressed quantitatively. Under some circumstances, democratic participation is incompatible with total mobilization.

The level and unit of analysis problem enters again here also, for democracy is meaningless unless some choice between goals is available to the individual. But does this choice have to exist within every unit and subunit to which an individual belongs? [15] Undoubtedly, if the individual has no choice as to the unit to which he belongs, then this unit must be organized democratically if he is to participate democratically in the polity. This is one of the chief criticisms that can be made of American trade unions—that they are seldom truly voluntary associations. It is a point on which the situation of American and Italian workers differs greatly. But if an individual can choose among several organizations, then democracy in the polity would not seem to require that each of its subunits be democratically organized. In other words, the Communist Party of the Soviet Union does not contribute to democracy in the polity as it has been operationalized, but the Italian Communist Party may very well do so despite its system of organization. Indeed, it may mobilize segments of Italian society that would not be mobilized in any other fashion.

When the lower classes are a largely undifferentiated mass, as Marx conceived them and as often seems to be the case in developing societies, then having a single party represent them may not be as unreasonable as classic democrats are wont to argue. But development brings increasing differentiation and complexity along with a growing divergence, if not conflict, of interest within the lower classes. There is genuine goal conflict that a single party can resolve only with difficulty, and not at all if the legitimacy of goal conflict is denied. In this case, several parties representing the lower classes may facilitate the democratic mobilization of people of low political competence better than one democratic party, for this situation may give them a more realistic choice than would emerge from their formal participation in a seemingly democratic decision-making process. In this sense the Italian lower classes have more alternatives available to them in both the party and trade-union spheres than do Americans of comparable political competence. Whether they are more effectively and democratically mobilized is another question.

15. For the argument that it does, or at least that democracy is facilitated if it does, see Eckstein, *A Theory of Stable Democracy.*

Goal conflict within units thus seems to be essential for the existence of multiple autonomous communications channels within the unit. Without such conflict, it is difficult to organize the potential for internal opposition that exists within most organizations.

A final factor that greatly facilitates the existence of democracy within a unit is that of structural bases for opposition. Political pluralists have realized that democracy is greatly facilitated by the existence within a polity of structures independent of one another and of the state. Certainly the ability to maintain a separate structure is necessary to democracy within a unit. Thorough-going pluralism is perhaps not a necessary condition, but it is undoubtedly conducive to democracy. There are functional equivalents for traditional pluralism. People of great political competence and some minimum resources of time and money can create separate structures even in the absence of pre-existing structural discontinuities. And in the absence of political competence and goal conflict pluralism will not lead to democracy, a point evident in the absence of a relationship between pluralism and democracy in many polities.

But democracy is a matter of tendencies, and a given level of structural pluralism can compensate for a given deficiency in political competence or in goal conflict. If separate structures exist they can be utilized in politics even in the absence of the competence necessary for the establishment of specifically political structures. And if separate structures exist they tend to persist even if there is a minimum of significant goal conflict between them, as is often the case with political parties. All things being equal, therefore, in any particular unit internal democracy is facilitated by the existence of structural discontinuities that give it a pluralistic character. Any structural arrangement that reduces the capacity of unit elites to coerce secondary leaders and rank and file encourages the survival of internal opposition and hence democracy.

The autonomy of constituent units is one such arrangement. This is the insight of federalism, but the same dynamics work within other units, for if the subunits are independent then elites must bargain and convince, as they cannot command.

The same results may be achieved by the existence of related but independent structures based upon function or clientele. In the PSI the trade unions—associated with the party but not completely under its control—achieved the same results. And in many labor movements Communist or Socialist parties, or at least individuals loyal to Communist and Socialist principles, have provided the structural bases for internal opposition. This is an example of the democratic requirements of political competence, goal conflict, and structural bases being met by the same source. It is also an example of the advantages the Communist system of front organizations has over less professional forms of opposition, as the party structure implements competence, provides guidance on goals, and ensures a structural basis for opposition. It is a formidable organizational weapon, and even more imposing among people of low political competence. Its very success usually leads to the destruction of internal democracy, because the party claims for itself—and is usually technically able to implement its claim—a monopoly of competence, goal setting, and control of structure.

Making unions and other organizations "nonpolitical" is thus one way of frustrating democracy, as political differences, especially when they reflect party differences, are one way of sustaining an internal opposition. An emphasis on limited goals and functions, on consensus, and on expertise among leaders has the same effect. The implications for democracy of a politics of material abundance, consensus, and technocracy are rather discouraging.

DEMOCRACY IN THE POLITY

Although little firm evidence is available, one can speculate that the nature of the structural bases of opposition has a great deal to do with the quality of a polity's politics.[16] Some structural

16. For a thorough discussion of this topic see Dahl, ed., *Political Oppositions in Western Democracies.*

types of opposition have a built-in limitation as a means of mobilizing discontent. Regional, ethnic, linguistic, and religious structures may sometimes serve to develop competence and provide a structural basis for opposition without formulating alternative goals of a nature encouraging national integration. Often, for example, conflict over particular policies is replaced by conflict over the rules of the game. Rather than integrating opposition it may fragment it further. The result is often not democracy but warfare. Where these divisions do not coincide, or where there is a great deal of fragmentation, however, these types of differences may facilitate democracy. Encouraging the development of these nonpolitical structures as a basis for democracy is thus a dangerous game: it may facilitate opposition but make a thoroughgoing democratic mobilization more difficult to achieve.

There is much to be said for opposition structures based on political differences. From the viewpoint of democratic mobilization the encouragement of political differences, as, for example, economic and welfare policy and the like, is probably more desirable than other forms of division. For though religious, ideological, ethnic, linguistic, and regional differences all involve political differences, they also involve differences that are not political, or at least for which there is no simple political solution. In this case they are better left out of the political communications system, for they tend to overload what is already a heavily burdened network. Again, the advantages of political channels over nonpolitical ones are evident. He who makes use of a pre-existing nonpolitical network for political purposes brings into politics much that could better be left out.

On the other hand, the growing agreement on political matters in Western countries may mean that opposition will have to come from other areas of life. The very success of technocracy in achieving material well-being—which seems to be what interests masses if not elites—threatens to eliminate narrowly political opposition, converting it into a "how-to-do-it" or "I-can-do-it-better" debate. Perhaps the revitalization of democracy requires a more radical critique of goals than is likely to emerge from existing political structures. How such a critique will be made compatible with the realities of organizational dynamics is difficult to say.

The most important unknown in this respect is the impact of increased education. The upgrading of entire populations through education should greatly increase the portion of the population that is participant, politically competent, and ideologically sophisticated—in short, the part that can create and sustain democratic structures. On the other hand, the extent to which these qualities have the impact ascribed to them only in this present era and Western culture is unknown. There are indications that participation was much higher, at least in the United States, in earlier times when the population ranked lower than today on most indices conventionally associated with participation.[17] Education may not lead to an increase in the quality of participation; under some circumstances it may even increase the potential for manipulation. Certainly its impact is the great unknown in the future of democracy.

The theorist of democracy thus can suggest certain methods for increasing the democratic potential of organizations, including political parties. He can at least better understand what limits internal democracy in some types of organizations and why this is not always undesirable. He can understand why organizations that are themselves not democratic internally can contribute to democracy on the level of the polity. But situations change, and democrats can only win battles in a war that never ends. The nature of democracy in the epoch ahead may differ from that presented here. Michel's cruel game continues.

17. See Walter Dean Burnham, "The Changing Shape of the American Political Universe," *American Political Science Review*, 59 (1965), 7–28.

Appendix I

THE SAMPLE

The membership interviews are from a one-of-three sample of the membership lists of the psi in the sixteen sections in the commune of Arezzo. These lists were made available by the psi federation leadership, which also permitted the sending of letters signed by the federation secretary to the respondents requesting their cooperation in a "scientific study." Although party officials were cooperative and helpful throughout the study, this letter was their sole intervention with the membership, apart from reassuring several members who contacted the federation when approached by the interviewers.

There are periodic membership drives in the psi, but members are accepted at any time; the lists are thus not complete until the end of the year. The sample was drawn in February of 1963 from lists of all those who were members at the beginning of 1963, that is, who had bought a 1962 card. The original sample contained 370 names. The sample was reduced in the course of the interviewing when it was learned that 38 of the members should not have been included, for the following reasons: 2 were dead, 6 were away on military service, 10 worked outside the province though maintaining their residence and party affiliation there, 3 had moved permanently from the province, 2 claimed that they were not and never had been psi members, 8 were too sick or infirm to be interviewed (or to participate), and 7 were leaders and were transferred to the leadership census. The sample was thus reduced to 332, of whom 272, or 82 percent, were interviewed. Of the remainder, almost half refused to be interviewed, citing lack of time and "political reasons" in roughly equal proportions; almost one-third of the others (19) were unknown (it was claimed by the residents at the addresses given), while 16 could not be contacted after at least two call-backs. Most of these were undoubtedly polite refusals; appointments, which they did not keep, were made with

257

almost all of them. When it was certain that a name should not have been on the list, or that the interview could not be obtained, the name following that of the original respondent on the list was selected so as to maintain the balance among sections; an additional 29 interviews (10 percent of the total) were obtained with respondents selected in this fashion, bringing the total interviews to 301.

The interviews were administered in March and April of 1963 by students of the Faculty of Political Science of the University of Florence; most of the interviewers had participated in a seminar devoted to the planning of the research, and all were trained and supervised in the field by the author.

The leadership census consists of all members of the federation directing committee plus the secretaries of sections not included in that group, for a total of fifty-nine. All but one of these were interviewed, most by the author. The leader not interviewed did not live in the province and was not active in the party.

Appendix II

THE MEMBERS' INTERVIEW SCHEDULE

University of Florence
"C. Alfieri" Faculty of Political Science

No. of the Interview _____
Date _____
Section _____
Name of Interviewer _____
Length of Interview _____

FORM NO. I—MEMBERS

I would like to speak to you first about your family.

1. a. Is any other member of your family enrolled in the PSI?
   b. Would you say that your father is (was) *very interested, somewhat interested,* or *not interested* in politics?
      1. very   3. somewhat   5. not much
      7. not applicable   9. don't know
   (If applicable)
   c. What party does (did) your father support?
   d. And your mother?
   e. Are you married?   1. yes   3. no
   f. (If the wife is not a member of the PSI) What party does your wife prefer?

2. a. Do your parents consider themselves Catholic?
      1. yes   3. no
   b. Do they go to church?   1. yes   3. no
   c. Do you consider yourself Catholic?   1. yes   3. no
   d. How often do you go to church?
      1. one or two times a year   2. once a month
      3. every Sunday   4. never

    e. (If married) Does your wife consider herself a Catholic?
      1. yes   3. no

3. What is (was) your father's occupation? (PROBE)

4. a. (If married) Do you have any children?
  b. (If yes) How old are they?
  c. (If of working age) What kind of work do they do?
  d. (If of school age) Do they go to school?
  e. What grades are they in?
  f. How far in school do you expect them to go?
  g. How far would you like for them to go in school?

5. To what social class do you consider yourself as belonging?

Let's go now from your family to the Socialist Party.

6. a. When did you first become interested in the PSI?
  b. When did you join the PSI for the first time?
  c. Why did you join at that time?
  d. Did someone ask you to join the party?   1. yes   2. no
  e. Were you ever a member of other parties? Which? When?

7. a. In the last year have you attended a section meeting? (If
     yes) Which of the following do you consider closer to the
     part you played in the discussion?
     1. I listened only   2. I participated sometimes
     3. I often participated   4. I always participated
     7. I never participated
  b. In the last year how many times have you attended open
     executive meetings?
     (If yes) In this case also would you tell me which of the
     following is closer to the role you played in the discussion?
     1. I listened only   2. I participated sometimes
     3. I often participated   4. I always participated
     7. I never participated
  c. During the last year how many times have you attended
     CGIL rallies?
  d. During the last year in how many meetings or rallies spon-
     sored by the party have you taken part?

8. (IF THE RESPONDENT WAS A MEMBER OF THE PARTY AT THAT
  TIME)

a. Were you present at the precongressional assembly of 1961?
   1. yes   3. no
b. Did someone take you to the meeting?   1. yes   3. no
c. Did someone counsel you on how to vote at the meeting?
   1. yes   3. no

9. Which of the following have you done for the party?
   a. Have you asked someone to vote for the party?
      1. yes   3. no
   b. Have you asked someone to join the party?
      1. yes   3. no
   c. Have you distributed the party newspaper?
      1. yes   3. no
   d. Have you been a collector for the party?
      1. yes   3. no
   e. Other

10. Which of the following positions have you occupied in the
    party? When?
    Delegate to the provincial congress
    Member of the executive committee of the federation
    Member of the directing committee of the federation
    Secretary of the section
    Member of the directing committee of the section
    Other

11. a. Do you know what are the correnti of the PSI?
    b. Do you know which of these have the present majority on
       the national level?
    c. Do you know which has the majority in the federation?
    d. Do you know which has the majority in your section?

12. Do you think the existence of correnti in the PSI is a good thing
    or not? Why?

13. a. Do you know who the leaders of the correnti are on the
       national level?
    b. And in the federation?
    c. Do you know who the leaders of the correnti are in your
       section?

14. What is your corrente?

15. a. What do you think the difference is between the two correnti inside the party?
    b. Is there a difference between the national and local correnti in regard to these matters?

16. Do you think the existence of correnti weakens the party? Why?

17. Speaking in general what do you think of the present policies of the PSI? Do you consider yourself:
    1. very satisfied   2. satisfied   3. uncertain
    4. dissatisfied   5. very dissatisfied   9. don't know

18. What are the two things you would most like to see changed in the PSI?

19. Was there ever a time in which you were more interested in party activity than now? When? Why?

20. a. Could you tell me two things that particularly interest you in the life of the section?
    b. Could you tell me two things that are especially displeasing to you in the life of the section?

21. Think of someone whose opinion on party matters seems very important to you.
    a. Do you know him by reputation? (1)   do you know him by sight? (3)   is he a friend? (5)
    b. Does he have a position in the party? Which one?
    c. Does he work with you?   1. yes   3. no
    d. Does he discuss politics with you? How frequently?
       1. often   3. sometimes   5. rarely   7. never
    e. Is he of your corrente?   1. yes   3. no

22. When you discuss politics of the party with friends, which of the following best describes your role in the discussion? (SHOW CARD NO. 1)
    1. Usually I only listen
    2. I listen a lot but sometimes I express my own opinions
    3. I take part with others in the conversation
    4. I try to convince others
    5. I don't know
    6. I don't discuss political questions regarding the party

23. Think of all the friends that you met during the past week. What did you discuss with them?
    1. national problems
    2. communal problems
    3. PSI politics
    4. politics of the PSI federation of Arezzo
    5. problems of the local section

24. Now I want you to think of two of your closest friends. In order to distinguish between them, tell me their first names.

What is his occupation?	What is his occupation?
Is he a member of the PSI?	Is he a member of the PSI?
1. yes 3. no	1. yes 3. no
Member of your section?	Member of your section?
1. yes 3. no	1. yes 3. no
Member of your own corrente?	Member of your own corrente?
1. yes 3. no	1. yes 3. no

(IF NOT A MEMBER OF THE PSI)

Member of some other party?	Member of some other party?
Which one?	Which one?
What party does he favor?	What party does he favor?

25. You probably still have other friends who do not belong to your own party. Which parties do you think they favor?

PCI	PR
PSDI	MSI
DC	
PLI	Others

Now I would like to talk with you about your work.

26. a. What is your occupation?
       Could you tell me more about it?
    b. How many persons work in your factory (or office or store)?
    c. Have you always done this particular work?
       1. yes   3. no

263

(IF HE RESPONDS NEGATIVELY) What did you do before? When did you quit that work?

d. What was your first work immediately after the war?

27. Have you ever had any trouble because of being a member of the PSI? When?

28. a. Is there an NAS organized where you work? (PROBE)
    b. To what union do the members of the internal commission of your factory belong?
    c. To what party do they belong?
    d. Speaking of union activity, which are more active in your factory, Socialists or Communists?

29a. Now think of two people who work closely with you. In order to distinguish them tell me their first names.

Is he a member of the PSI?	Is he a member of the PSI?
1. yes 3. no	1. yes 3. no
Of your section?	Of your section?
1. yes 3. no	1. yes 3. no
Do you belong to the same corrente?	Do you belong to the same corrente?
1. yes 3. no	1. yes 3. no

(IF NOT A MEMBER OF THE PSI)

Is he a member of some other party? Which?	Is he a member of some other party? Which?

(IF NO)

Which party does he favor?	Which party does he favor?

29b. Do you discuss politics with them?
    1. often   3. sometimes   5. never

30. Now think of all the places where you see your colleagues outside of work. How much time do you spend with other members of the party?
    (DO NOT READ THE FOLLOWING LIST.)
    1. never   2. less than once a month
    3. one or two times a month   4. one or two times a week
    5. almost every day

31. Do you usually join the same group of people?

32. What do you think are the qualities necessary in a party leader?

Now I would like to ask you some questions about what you think of the life of the party.

33. In your opinion what do you have to do to become a leader of the party?

34. In general what do you think is better?
    1. have confidence in the persons that you elect
    3. have a way of controlling them   9. don't know
    Do you think that leaders of the PSI are different from the general type of leaders of other political parties?

35. Do you think that the rank and file have a *considerable influence, not much influence, no influence* on how the party conducts things?
    1. considerable influence   3. not much
    5. no influence   9. don't know

36. Do you think the rank and file ought to have *greater influence, less influence,* or the *same influence* as now?
    1. greater influence   3. same influence
    5. less influence   9. don't know

37. Now I would like to read some statements that persons we have interviewed have made and I would like to ask you whether you agree with them or not. I will read them one at a time and you just tell me whether you agree or not.
    a. The average member has   agree   disagree   don't know
       no influence at all on what
       the party decides. . . . . . . _____
    b. Sometimes politics seems
       so complicated that it is
       difficult to understand it. . . _____
    c. I don't think that public
       officials care very much
       about what people like me
       think. . . . . _____

  d. Voting is the only way for
     the rank and file member
     of the party to influence
     the policies of the party... _____

38. Now I am going to show you three ways of defining the con-
    cept of democracy. Which of these seems closer to your own
    conception of democracy? (SHOW THE THREE NO. 2 CARDS AND
    OBLIGE THE RESPONDENT TO CHOOSE ONE OF THE THREE DEFI-
    NITIONS.)
    1. A political party is democratic when the members are able
       to participate and influence the politics of the party.
    3. A political party is democratic when the members have the
       possibility of choosing among various leaders and various po-
       litical policies that are proposed.
    5. A political party is democratic when it represents the true
       interests of the most numerous and needy class of the popu-
       lation.

39. In your opinion what are the most important problems of Ital-
    ian public life today?

40. If you had to explain Italian political parties to someone that
    spent all of his life in another country, in a few words, what
    would you say?
    a. about the PCI
    b. about the DC
    c. about the PSI
    d. about the PSDI

41. a. Apart from the PSI, to what other organizations do you be-
       long?

	Member	Official	Frequency of attendance
Trade union. Which one?			
Cooperative			
Veteran's organizations			
Sports associations			
Professional associations			
Recreational associations			
Cultural associations			
Other			

    b. Do you hold an office in any of these? (WRITE IN THE BOX ABOVE UNDER "official.")

    c. How often do you attend the meetings of these organizations? (WRITE IN THE BOX ABOVE LABLED "frequency of attendance.")

        1. the major part of the meetings   3. half the meetings
        5. few meetings   7. none   9. don't know

42. Some people don't pay much attention to the electoral campaign. As for yourself, do you consider yourself as being *very interested, somewhat interested,* or *not very interested* in the present electoral campaign?

    1. very interested   3. somewhat interested
    5. not very interested

43. Now I will read you some sources from which you probably received information about politics.

    a. For each one of these sources tell me whether you receive a lot (1), some (2), little (3), or no (4) information.

    b. Would you tell me whether you consider these sources of information

        1. very impartial   2. impartial   3. not very impartial
        4. not at all impartial

	a	b
Radio broadcasts	___	___
Television broadcasts	___	___
Friends	___	___
Rallies	___	___
Newspapers	___	___
Party circulars	___	___
Party books	___	___
Party meetings	___	___

44. a. What newspapers do you read? How often?
    b. What magazines do you read? How frequently?
    c. Do you subscribe to any of these newspapers or magazines?

	Frequency	Subscription
Avanti!	___	___
Unità	___	___
La Nazione	___	___
Il Mattino	___	___

267

Il Giorno	_____	_____
Il Paese	_____	_____
Il Mondo nuovo	_____	_____
Mondo operaio	_____	_____
La Conquista	_____	_____
Il Mondo	_____	_____
L'Espresso	_____	_____
Other	_____	_____

1. always   2. often   3. sometimes   4. rarely

45. Which of the following do you or your family possess?

your own home   television
radio   refrigerator
record player   automobile
scooter   (ASK THE YEAR AND THE MAKE)

46. Do you think that your financial situation will improve if the Socialists enter the government after the next election?
    1. a lot   3. somewhat   5. little   6. not at all
    9. don't know

47. a. Nowadays people talk a lot about prosperity. As for you and your family, would you say that you are *satisfied* with your present financial situation, *more or less* satisfied, or *unsatisfied*?
    1. satisfied   3. more or less   5. not much
    6. not at all   9. don't know
    b. During the last few years has your financial situation
    1. gotten better   3. gotten worse
    5. remained the same   9. don't know

48. Parties often aid their members in various ways. Has your party ever helped you when you were in some kind of trouble, for example, in looking for a job? (PROBE)

49. How would you evaluate the following politicians?
    1. very favorable   2. favorable   3. indifferent
    4. unfavorable   5. most unfavorable   9. don't know

    Saragat
    Togliatti
    Nenni
    Moro
    Fanfani

50. Which of the following statements are true and which are false?
   a. Calabria has a special regional status.
   b. Twenty-five is the minimum age for being elected a deputy.
   c. There are seven countries in the European Common Market.
   d. The PSI abstained on the vote of confidence for the center-left government (Fanfani, 1962).
   e. AGIP is a private industry.
   f. In the past the PCI has taken part in the government.
   g. The Constitutional Court has yet to be established.
   h. Everyone who has reached the age of twenty-one can vote for the Chamber and for the Senate.

51. Now I will read several statements. Tell me if you are:
   1. in agreement   2. in agreement with some reserve
   3. uncertain   4. disapprove, but not completely
   5. disapprove completely

   (SHOW CARD NO. 3)

   a. The PSI must maintain its friendship with the PCI in local administrations regardless of what happens.
   b. The PSI must always maintain its friendship with the PCI in the trade unions.
   c. It is impossible to carry forward any effective social reforms with the participation of the DC in the government.
   d. With the center-left government the PSI runs the risk of losing its ideological identification and of becoming Social Democratic.
   e. Unification with the PSDI would strengthen the party.

52. a. Date of birth
   b. Commune and province of birth
   c. (IF AN IMMIGRANT) When did you come to the commune of Arezzo?
   d. What was the last class you went to in school?

(FOR THE INTERVIEWER)

Immediately after the interview rate the respondent on the following two scales:

Understanding/against/Incomprehension

/   /   /   /   /   /

U   I

Cooperation/against/Defensive attitude

/   /   /   /   /

C   DA

Index

Action Party: in Arezzo, 57; members in PSI, 61; mentioned, 200
Administration, Italian, 20–22
Adorno, Theodore, 235
Age and participation in local party, 198
Alienation, political, 38, 221
Almond, Gabriel: on political information, 36; on partisanship, 37; on political competence, 112; on motivations of Communist membership, 116
Analysis of variance, 211
Anarchism in Italy, 20
Apathy, political, 226
Area subdivisions (*nuclei territoriali*), 72
Arezzo commune, 52–56
Arezzo province, 52–56
Arrow Problem, 243
Assessori, 82
Authoritarian personality, 237
Authoritarianism, 238–40
Authority, ideal types of, 6–7
Autonomist faction in *1963*, 47–50. See also *particular subjects*
Autonomy, 240
Avanti!: Mussolini as editor, 41; under Autonomists, 49; readership of, 211; mentioned, 230

Basso, Lelio: as PSI secretary, 44; role in PSI in *1963*, 49; replaced as general secretary, 61

Belief systems: distinguished from ideology, 167–68; constraint in, 167–72; ideological sensitivity and constraint in, 169; education and constraint in, 169–71; factions and constraint in, 171–72; and party democracy, 215–19, 224–26
Books of party, impact of on participation, 209–11
Bureaucracy: and oligarchy, 3; and authority, 4; Italian national, 24–25
Bureaucratic organization and working-class leadership, 246
Burnham, Walter Dean, 255

Cabinet, Italian: role in nineteenth century, 20; under monarchy, 22; coalition basis, 23–24
Campanilismo, 19
Carristi, role in PSI in *1963*, 49
Case del Popolo (People's Centers) and PSI, 89
Catholic Action, civic committees of, and DC, 32
Catholic Church: role in modern Italy, 20; in age of Giolitti, 41; and political parties, 244; in France and Spain, 244; and working class, 247
Center-left government: PSI members' attitudes toward, 192; impact on PCI-PSI cooperation in